Winnebago Nation

Winnebago Nation

THE JAMES
RV B.
IN TWITCHELL
AMERICAN
CULTURE

Columbia University Press

New York

Columbia University Press
Publishers Since 1893
New York   Chichester, West Sussex
cup.columbia.edu
Copyright © 2014 James B. Twitchell
All rights reserved

Library of Congress Cataloging-in-Publication Data
Twitchell, James B., 1943-
Winnebago nation: the RV in American culture / James B. Twitchell.
p. cm.
Includes index.
ISBN 978-0-231-16778-9 (cloth: alk. paper)
1. Recreational vehicles—United States—History.   2. Mobile homes—United
States—History.   3. United States—Social life and customs.   I. Title.

TL298.T95 2014
303.48'32—dc23   2013029058

Columbia University Press books are printed on permanent and durable acid-
free paper.
This book is printed on paper with recycled content.
Printed in the United States of America

c 10 9 8 7 6 5 4 3 2 1

Cover & interior design by Martin N. Hinze.

References to websites (URLs) were accurate at the time of writing. Neither the
author nor Columbia University Press is responsible for URLs that may have
expired or changed since the manuscript was prepared.

For Stella, Vivian, and LD

You are your own master, the road is ahead; you eat as you please, cooking your own meals over an open fire; sleeping when you will under the stars, waking with the dawn; swim in a mountain lake when you will and always the road ahead. Thoreau at 29 cents a gallon. Time and space are at your beck and call, your freedom is complete. (editorial on car camping, *Motor Car*, June 1912)

Contents

Winnebago Nation

chapter one

THOREAU AT .29¢ $4.00 A GALLON

The Peculiar Place of the RV in American Culture

In the fall of 2008 I bought a small RV. In the literary and academic world I live in, this statement would be received in much the same way as would "I shop the blue-light special at K-Mart," "How do you like the diamond stud in my ear?" or "I own an Uzi." People who live near the ivory tower don't buy—or don't admit to buying—Winnebagos. After all, if you are looking for one object that typifies all that is wrong with gas-guzzling America, this is it. If you want to take a trip away from home, they reason, why take your house with you? At the prole extreme, the RV is a rusted-out deer camp on wheels; at the Richie Rich extreme, it's a black-windowed mobile McMansion. Either way, to most of my colleagues, having an RV is unnecessary—consumption gone haywire.

In my RV wanderings in the past few years, I've met only one other professor driving a motor bungalow, and he was a retired dean at a small school in South Carolina. He was traveling with his wife and mother-in-law in a rig just like mine—a 24-foot Winnebago View. We met in a parking lot in Wasilla, Alaska. I was amazed they could all fit into what could barely contain me and occasionally my wife and dog. I liked him a lot, but when I asked him his name, he smiled and said he'd prefer not to tell me. At first I thought he might be on the lam, but later I understood. Some info doesn't need to be bandied about the groves of academe.

Don't get me wrong. Sleeping in your car, or van, or truck is just fine—and if you want to write about it, so much the better. Just don't do it in an RV. Jack Kerouac made his cross-country jaunts in a brand-new step-down 1949 Hudson. John Steinbeck traveled with Charlie in a GMC truck outfitted with a slide-in camper unit. William Least Heat-Moon traveled the blue highways in a 1975 half-ton Econoline delivery van. But how many canonical writers ever took a trip in a rig made by Winnebago that had a bathroom, a 'fridge, an entire side that expands out, and an entertainment center with a remote-control wand and then had the temerity to rhapsodize about it? I can tell you. None.

Those bare-boned writers' rigs have all become iconic. Kerouac's Hudson is in the Beat Museum in San Francisco; the truck camper is down the coast at the Steinbeck Museum in Salinas; and Least Heat-Moon's Econoline van is out behind the Museum of Anthropology at the University of Missouri, seen "only by appointment." Go into the RV Hall of Fame Museum in Elkhart, Indiana, and you'll see RVs owned by cereal magnates and movie stars, beer brewers and baseball players, but not one owned by a writer, not even a Hollywood screen writer. When the Smithsonian Museum held a big retrospective "Commemorating 100 Years of the RV" in 2010, there wasn't a peep about any first-tier writer who owned an RV. The only big-shot scribbler I could even imagine owning one and being willing to admit it out loud would be the chain-smoking Ayn Rand.

I have wondered why this is. Why the midcult opprobrium? Why are RVs the thing readers of the *New York Times* love to hate? Just read some of the responses to the recent article "Just Me and My RV" (5/18/2012) and you'll get an earful. When the Anti-Christ comes, these letter writers suggest, this is what he'll be driving. Partly it's the category—*recreational* vehicle. No granola-eating traveler wants to see himself in a recreational vehicle. True, Supreme Court justice Clarence Thomas and his wife like to cruise around in their 40-foot Prevost conversion motorhome, but both Thomases are well known for not buying into liberal conventions. In fact, they knew exactly what they were doing when they allowed Steve Kroft and *60 Minutes* to film them in front of their monster rig (9/30/2007). They are not bothered that the size of their RV is about twice the size of Thoreau's cabin and that one of their favorite camping spots—the Walmart parking lot—is most definitely not Walden Pond. Their RV is a statement. In fact, the very word *motorhome* is uncomfortably close to *mobile home*, a term now used for those permanent communities that fester in almost every American town and are blights to the Bobos seeking paradise.

There is another reason that the anti-RV prejudice runs deep in the world that loves arugula. Although numerous television shows (notably on the Travel and Home & Garden channels) and a handful of glossy magazines (even *Architectural Digest*) foreground RVs, when I told my agent that I wanted to do a book on the culture of people who spend part of their lives in motorized nests, he looked aghast. It would be a hard sell, he said, because, "These people don't read, do they?" Perhaps he's right, I thought. There is the proverbial ton of books about how to buy or fix an RV, but only an ounce about what it's like to live in one and only a few grams on their history and culture.

One obvious reason for such neglect is that RVs are not part of city life, and publishers tend to be city people who ride around in taxis and zipcars. But here's just a whiff of how popular these things are outside metropolitan areas: There are right now about 8.5 million RVs *on* U.S. roads or slowly decaying *beside* U.S. roads. Of the people who own licensed vehicles, about one in twelve already owns an RV of some kind. If you're now in your fifties and own a car, chances are good that you have owned a recreational vehicle of some sort. Or, if not, you will. Almost 40 percent of the 60 million people over fifty will use an RV of some sort this year. Should you want the most up-to-date data on who owns what the Recreational Vehicle Industry Association (RVIA) is only too happy to supply it.

According to a 2005 University of Michigan study, owners use their RVs for twenty-six days each year and move around in them an average of 4,500 miles annually. Next time you're on the interstate, just note how many RVs either pass you at the speed of a greyhound or clog the truck lane at the speed of a tortoise. Then take a look at the drivers: They're most often men of a certain age—Geritol gypsies. Population trends favor long-term market growth: Every day, 11,000 Americans turn fifty. Although the industry is currently suffering the traumas of high oil prices, RVs are not going to disappear. In fact, they will be a major beneficiary of the truck and bus conversion to compressed natural gas and innovations in battery power.

The pull of RVs for the doddering male is powerful—so powerful, in fact, that in financial planners' lists of what *not to buy* (time-shares, speed boats, ski cabins in Vail . . .), the RV always makes the top ten. Ask the workingman of all social ranks what he wants in retirement (if not before) and you'll find RV high on the list. This speaks of more than just cultural ants-in-the-pants and a love of the internal combustion engine. It clearly reflects a desire to get the hell outta here, even at $4 a gallon.

The RV is worthy of study if only because it is that rare object in the American marketplace that is consumed at either extreme of the financial pecking order. What is a luxury object for some is a necessity for others. Much has been made recently about the Haves and Have-nots living in what is essentially two Americas. In *Coming Apart: The State of White America* (2013), the mildly notorious sociologist Charles Murray has called these two disparate lands Fishtown and Belmont. Residents of the former just get by; those living in the latter get by with ease. The so-called 1-percenters live in Belmont, the rest in Fishtown. His point is that the twain simply no longer meets in America. He needs to go to the Walmart parking lot at midnight.

Even more intriguing is that both Haves and Have-nots may even live in exactly the same structure—the large self-propelled RV, called the Class A rig. They just live in it at different times and for different reasons. Most of those huge, spangly behemoths that whiz past you on the highway are conversions of a commercial bus manufactured in Quebec by the Prevost Bus Company, now owned by Volvo. New, they cost millions. And those rusted-out hippie rigs that limp down the truck lane are often old school buses made in Georgia by the Blue Bird Bus Company. Used, they cost hundreds. One may be driven by the retired CEO and the other by an aging dropout, but the outlines of the thing itself are essentially the same. And it's been this way since the 1920s, when the Four Vagabonds (Henry Ford, Thomas Edison, Harvey Firestone, and John Burroughs) were on the road in their big caravans while the Tin Can Tourists were making their way up and down the eastern seaboard in their tricked-out Model Ts.

WE DIDN'T INVENT IT, WE PERFECTED IT

Although living in one's car is second nature to many Americans, it really started with the wheeled wagon. Here's the single-most important reason for the success of the RV: Humans do not want to sleep on the ground, no matter what the Boy Scouts say. Like chickens, we roost. And we also like to sleep covered up. Most primates camp out in trees or on cliffs for security. Only human beings and gorillas sleep on the ground, but when they do, they are not happy about it. Gorillas build nest platforms of sticks; we make beds of straw. Hence the allure of the hay wagon.

While the idea of camping out *for fun* starts with the English Romantic poets (Wordsworth, Coleridge, Southey) and Robert Baden-Powell, wealthy Victorians refashioned the decorated wagon as a moveable bedroom. On many country estates, spending the weekend in a garish "gypsy wagon" was considered tonic for those weary of city life. Plus the hunting wagon could be fitted out for overnight camping.

Once motors were added, the pastime in England was called *caravanning*, and the consuming class was no longer country gentlemen but workingmen from the town. The carping begins. Attach a small pop-up trailer to your Morris Minor and you're all set to infuriate readers of the pre-Murdoch London *Times*. So here's Andrew Martin, writing in the *New Statesman* in 2000, calling these RVs "a ludicrous and creepy fetish of the petit bourgeoisie" and wagering you wouldn't

Gypsy Encampment
Glenwood Road.

Figure 1.1: Proto-RV. Gypsy wagon, 1888 (Library of Congress).

find someone simultaneously possessing both a college degree and a caravan (6/17/2000). Yet today British commoners, like many of their American counterparts, spend more nights in the beds of these motor bungalows than they do at hotels and bed-and-breakfasts.

Though the Europeans may have started the love affair with sleeping in your caravan, née gypsy van, they were hampered by narrow roads and expensive fuel. But we Americans have loved it from the get-go, often for the exact reason that it so bothered the genteel Andrew Martin: RVing is so gleefully democratic. Here's just a bit of excitement from our own F. E. Brimmer, M.A. (owner of both a rig *and* a college degree) in his panegyric *Autocamping* (1923):

The autocamper and his family may go where they choose, may stop where and when they like, may ask odds of no man, because they are on the wide domain of the free and independent state of autocamping—the Roadside. You may be denied actual hiking over the hills and splashing in the streams, but they can't push you off that wide belt of highway running into every nook and corner of the country, and so you may camp and enjoy and exhilarate just about anywhere that fancy dictates.

Autocamping is something akin to Middle Age Feudalism, but with modern improvements. The feudal lord lived in his castle home, and on the manor about were produced absolutely everything that was necessary for his needs and his comforts. His willing serfs fled eagerly to the protection offered to them on the manor and cultivated the crops or did the tasks necessary to make the feudal fields free and independent of the rest of the world. There was the cobbler, the miller, the blacksmith, the priest, the jester or troubadour; there were the spinners and weavers, the soldiers and police men, and the skilled helpers of all kinds. The feudal manor was a little world in itself. Autocamping is just like that. The car or the trailer is Lord Auto-camper's castle. Hundreds of helpers supply him with necessities; from tents, and beds, and refrigerator baskets, and batteryless flash lamps to even touring phonographs, and fishing tackle, and hunting equipment, and the hundreds of other things that will aid in the pursuit of life in the outdoors, liberty along the highway, and the following of healthful happiness. These are the willing serving men of M'Lord Autocamper. And the whole wide world is his manor! The autocamper, equipped properly, is a petty feudal monarch in a horizon that is all his own. On his rubber-shod castle grounds, with all the *lareti et penates* of his home hearth carried with him, he may set up roadside housekeeping anywhere on God's green footstool, free and independent of the whole wide world. [17–19]

There are plenty of other reasons that auto camping became such a peculiarly American pastime. In addition to our often-discussed love affair with the internal combustion engine and man's primal unease with sleeping on the ground, here are a few: (1) our concept of vacation (especially in the summer for the kiddies) and mandatory retirement (for elders) provides the time; (2) pensions and social security provide the money; (3) interstate highways with only moderate grade changes provide big enough pathways; (4) relatively cheap fuel, especially diesel—even at $4 a gallon—provides the power; (5) the threat of terrorism makes at-home activity seem safer than foreign travel; (6) the ease of driving makes it fun—everything is power-assisted, and even the biggest RVs require no special driving license; (7) our national parks and relatively unpopulated sunbelt provide long-term destinations; and, of course, (8) developing technology provides a host of innovations like sophisticated suspension, cameras to the side and back, leveling jacks, retractable steps and awnings, sides that slide out to increase living space, redundant uses of propane and electricity, shiplike compression of living space, real-time satellite reception and mapping, and state-of-the-art sewage treatment.

And now here are two more reasons that tipped at least me over the RV edge. First, airplane travel has become exasperating. Getting there is not half the fun if you fly. And it has been no fun at all since the deregulation of the airline industry in the 1970s and the threats of terrorism beginning in the 1990s. Buying the online nonrefundable ticket, fighting traffic on the way to the airport, waiting in the dreary airport, being searched by sometimes surly people with big thumbs, waiting to board the plane, sitting in the middle seat for hours, waiting to take off, terrible food and squealing babies, waiting to land, waiting for the lost luggage, and then getting away from the airport is . . . well, everyone knows the drill.

Second, if you like to travel with your dog, the motel industry has done just about everything to thwart you. Few chains now even accept pets, and among these, you can't be sure that the individual motel will honor the franchise's pet policy. Not only that, but you have to pay higher and higher tariffs to get a room that cats, ferrets, and buffalo have (if my dog's nose is any judge) also frequented. It's almost as bad as taking your pet to the $40-a-night kennel. This is also a little embarrassing to admit, but as every RV owner who travels with a dog will tell you, dogs love RVs. After all, they have you living in their dog house.

OK, so RV travel is slow. In my opinion, you should never consider buying an RV if you want to go more than 200 miles a day and don't want to stop every hour or so for a nap and a walkabout. While it's not cheap, PKF Consulting did a comparison for the RV industry in 2008 showing that a family of four saves 27 to 61 percent on vacation costs by traveling in an RV (despite ownership costs and fuel costs), ultimately money is really beside the point. You either like it or you don't. I like fast food, slow travel, and sleeping in my own bed, an RV trifecta. For perfection, toss in the pooch and an occasional grandchild.

THE ANATOMY OF ALLURE

I think one reason the RV culture has been so underappreciated by students of popular culture is that the experience inside the box is so hard to get hold of. In many ways, it seems the opposite of the sedentary, bookish life. But it's not. You are inside a little world made cunningly, but you are moving around in it while it moves around. I agree with those who say it should not be called camping. Auto camping is passé. But what to call it? *Glamping* has been suggested by someone with a tin ear. Before the vehicles became self-propelled, it was called *trailering*. The English still use *caravanning*. In a Special Report on Camping 2011, the futurist Marian Salzman characterizes the general kind of activity as *soft rugged*, but that term doesn't capture the aspect of RVs that is both outdoor/indoor and stable/moving. *Winnebagoing* seems too much on the take. Maybe the RV experience is too variable for a precise term.

When traveling in an RV, you're surrounded by all your things—it's your space—and it's moving, but in a sense you're not. Talk to anyone who has spent time in an RV and you'll hear how important *home* is, but now it's your home in many unpredictable locales. The usual comparison to RV travel is the boat. Maybe it should be called *land cruising*. I have a friend who "did the Loop" in a trawler—the loop being the waterway that comes up the Hudson, cuts across to the Great Lakes, then down the Mississippi, across the Gulf, around Florida, and then up the Inland Waterway—as I was driving up to Alaska and back. We were both struck by the similarities. Not only were the deferred dreams similar, but the objects were too. In fact, there are obvious overlaps—shore power, on-board generators/batteries/water, sewage disposal, and the endless grousing about the high price of fuel. Not for nothing has Airstream,

Inc. introduced a new line of high-end rigs designed by Italian yacht designer Mauro Micheli with the humble nameplate *Land Yacht*.

The biggest similarity, of course, is the occasional bout of cabin fever. To enjoy life aboard either conveyance you have to like small spaces. When my wife is in the View, I sleep in a bed over the front seats in a space eerily similar to submariners' cubbyholes. If I suddenly sit up, my head meets the roof. This is not an experience for the claustrophobic. And once the dog is taken aboard, the space is so small that we have to make the beep-beep noise of large trucks going in reverse whenever one of us is moving around. The dog's morning shake sets the whole rig in motion. Communal life in a small RV is the Visa card tagline made real: The other person *is everywhere you want to be.*

Although boat/RV size is similar, the range of variations is vastly different. Boats always need tying up and fixing into safe space; the water is always the same (dangerous and often deep); and they can float away. The captain has to pay attention. The RV is much tamer. Plus, the RV goal is to wander around and not put down anchor, to float, yes, but not for long. To me, boats are just too adventurous. RVs are boats with training wheels.

I sometimes think that the RV seems a particularly American boat in that it allows us to float in our imagined past. Like Huck, we are drifting down the river, except our stream is made of cement and it usually flows east–west. Tie up when you want. I don't think it's happenstance that per capita there are far more RV owners in the West than in the East. The spirit that set easterners casting off to the west has not been quenched in their western descendants.

And, like so much else that is American, the craft is powered by the internal combustion engine. Every RV owner I've met is mildly delusional about what he's up to when he turns the key. It's all about pushing off and pulling in, moving out and settling down, and then up and moving again. I admit it—the stop-and-start process is highly informed by imagined history, and I have found RV owners singularly interested in the American obsession with movement. Perhaps our history really is all about aimless migration. RV owners think the yearning to head out defines this country, and maybe they're right. Think the Pilgrims,

THE ROAD YACHT

FOR FAMILY WEEKENDS • VACATIONS • SEMI-PERMANENT LIVING

The "road yacht" touring car with living accommodations for five persons. Below: luncheon from the "galley" is spread for the auto's driver

The vehicle, which looks like a large metal bug on wheels, is the latest in touring luxury. Speed of forty-five miles an hour may be easily attained. An electric "galley," completely fitted lavatory, two sleeping cabins, book shelves, writing tables, and a radio complete the equipment of this automotive innovation, which accommodates five persons.

"Road Yacht"

$985

A Complete Home

Note compactness of bathroom unit which combines tub and shower, lavatory and roomy towel cabinet

SEE & BUY AT THE 1928 AUTO SHOWS • DEALERSHIPS ARE OPEN

Figure 1.2: In a 1928 ad for a rig that was never manufactured, the RV is a road boat. The intended audience was bi-continental. (Note the right-hand drive but the price in dollars.)

Roger Williams, Natty Bumppo, the pioneers, Davy Crockett, mountain men, fur traders. Rig makers exploit this yearning to connect with the imagined past. Consider their brand names: Heritage, Voyager, Searcher, Ameriscape, Outfitter, Free Spirit, Independence, Surveyor, Trail Blazer,

Prairie Schooner, Frontier, Montana, Flagstaff, Out Back. . . .

How ironic that the people piloting these exhaust-belching homes should see themselves as part of a primitive landscape, but so it is. In their own ways, they are part of one of the more powerful myths of modern life—the return to simpler times. It's a kind of perverse romanticism that makes the act of putting the machine into the garden seem acceptable. That they are not driving *to* Walden Pond but rather driving *in* Walden Pond seems not the least paradoxical.

I'm not sure what to make of this, but just as most Civil War re-enactors like to be Confederates, most RVers I have known like to imagine themselves as Native Americans. Every January in Quartzsite, Arizona, a group of people who live in these metal houses come together and assume the roles of members of various tribes. The gathering is simply called the Pow-Wow. Again, consider the RV brand names: Superchief, Bigfoot, Sundance, Big Horn, Chinook, Seneca, Cherokee, Brave, Lakota, Grey Hawk, Grey Wolf. . . .

Figure 1.3: Covered wagon trailer, 1930s (RV/MH Hall of Fame and Museum).

(A note in passing: Some scholars have claimed that it was the appearance of Europeans that caused many Indian tribes—the Comanche being the exception—to become nomadic. In this theory, the Spanish introduced horses to Native Americans, and the abundance of wild horses abandoned in the Southwest provided the means for tribes to move around. Although we were taught in school that Native Americans were nomadic, usually following buffalo, it now seems that many were perfectly content to stay put for long periods. We know from excavating ancient dumping grounds that they didn't want to move. The coming of the white man was what really made them get up and go, and the white man's horse made it possible. Such an irony that RVers now imitate the activity that we essentially forced on many Native Americans and consider themselves to be living like Indians.)

Of course the RVer is also liable to identify with the other side of this encounter. Instead of a tepee, the RV is a covered wagon; instead of Indian blankets, there's cowboy art on the wall. Ads for RVs often show cowboy scenes going on outside the windows. One of the first companies to mass-produce overnight campers was the Covered Wagon Company in the 1920s. When RVers go to Pow-Wows, they often circle the wagons just like the pioneers did. In fact, sometimes you can pass a Walmart parking lot at night and see them there: noses in, tails out. Truth be told, the covered wagon of yore was more U-haul truck than RV. You put your stuff into the Conestoga wagon and then walked beside it. The pioneers slept in the wagons, however, no matter what you may see in the movies. They didn't like sleeping on the ground either.

But history matters less than our notions of it, and the typical RVer likes the idea of being part of the age of western exploration. In the late nineteenth century, when the American pace of movement dramatically slowed, the prairie schooner got parked out behind the farmhouse where the rusting recreational vehicle now resides. After the Civil War, *Go west, young man* became a yearning we learned to repress with *Stay put, get a job.* Factories and mass production meant workers had to settle down. And, as Fredrick Jackson Turner famously argued, once the frontier disappeared, there was nowhere left to go. No more West left except in the imagination.

WHAT MEN WANT

Wanderlust still remains, however, deep in the American Spirit (another RV brand name). I can't tell you the number of times that I've pulled up to a country store or rest stop and had someone, almost always male, come up and ask me where I've been and where I'm going. Invariably, they want to take a look inside. I always oblige. After all, for years I did it to others. John Steinbeck saw this too. Males of all ages would come up to *Rocinante*, as he named his RV, after Don Quixote's nag, and ask for a peek:

> I saw in their eyes something I was to see over and over in every part of the nation—a burning desire to go, to move, to get under way, anyplace, away from Here. They spoke quietly of how they wanted to go someday, to move about, free and unanchored, not toward something but away from something. I saw this look and heard this yearning everywhere in every state I visited. Nearly every American hungers to move. [*Travels with Charlie*, 10]

Not to edit the master, but when Steinbeck says *American* I think he means to add *male*. I don't know of any empirical research on this subject, but I suspect that had Pavlov done an experiment on how various males respond to certain words, he would have found that the combination of two words—*road trip*—triggers secretions in the American wander gland. The RV industry is built on this tension between staying put and getting going. While there is something unsettling about aimless wandering, especially in midlife, it is still acceptable on either side of maturation. In this, as with so much, adolescents and retirees share much. First be footloose, then put down roots, then pull them up. You may want to become a gypsy in your youth, but then you learn to fear gypsies in midlife, only to become that gypsy in retirement.

Among Americans in the last phase of this cycle, something quite extraordinary is currently occurring. In nomadic cultures when the older members become too weak to move, they are dropped behind to become sedentary, at least for awhile. In our culture, the real nomads are the elderly who have hit the road, essentially acting out the gypsy life of youth. Meanwhile, the young hitchhiker has pretty much disappeared. The real romantic dreamers in our culture are the sixty-year-olds who sell house, car, and furniture; buy the rig; slap "I'm spending my children's inheritance" on the RV bumper; and take off.

These "full-timers" are the cultural heirs of Whitman, Emerson, Thoreau, et al.—except that they are not heading out to Fruitlands, Amana, or Oneida but to Quartzsite, Burning Man, and Slab City. The bohemian life has become the style of Gramps, not Junior.

Look at the hobo in American culture: The so-called *full-timer* is an object of both envy and scorn. Go into any RV park and you'll hear the inhabitants joyfully self-describe as hobos and road junkies. And the hobo affliction is called hitch itch, road fever. "Hobo" is even a brand of RV, as are Gypsy, Hitchhiker, Mallard, Escaper, Scamper, Free Spirit, Fun Runner, Nomad, and, my favorite, the very popular Bounder (clearly named by someone who had no idea what the word meant in Victorian times).

In the modern world, the adolescent and the retiree are the most susceptible to the allure of rambling. Remember "The Wanderer," Dion's song from the 1960s? The song is ranked about halfway up *Rolling Stone* magazine's list of the five hundred greatest songs of all time. The singer is a teenage bounder with a tattoo of Rosie on his chest who enjoys the company of many girls (Flo, Mary, Janie . . .), but whenever he finds himself falling for some girl, he "hops right into that car of mine and rides around the world." To appreciate the midlife complexity of the song, listen to the Bruce Springsteen version where the end of the throwaway line, "I roam from town to town and go through life without a care, I'm as happy as a clown with my two fists of iron, but I'm going nowhere," is drenched in melancholy, even self-pity. "Going nowhere" is the penalty of wandering in midlife but the mixed promise of retirement. Needless to say, the song is now a favorite among seniors, included on numerous mixes developed for RVers. Doubly needless to say is that the Wanderer is yet another brand name of an RV.

THE ANTHROPOLOGY OF MOVEMENT

Anthropologists have recently been paying attention to this aspect of RV life. Nomads are a hot topic. In the vanguard of new interpretations of wandering are Dorothy and David Counts, a husband-and-wife team of anthropologists from central Canada. Although they spent most of their careers studying how elderly people get along in the villages of Papua, New Guinea, they came to realize that they had a population right at home that was at least as compelling—people who live full-time on wheels. As they looked closer, the Counts found hundreds of thousands, maybe more than a million (neither Canadian nor US Census Bureaus count them) of these "full-timers." Most of them move through the American Southwest.

Like the European gypsies, these nomads have their own inside lingo, rituals, songs, clubs, nicknames, watering holes, and even places for medical care (across the Mexican border). Surprisingly, they are not just elderly but often middle-aged. Many are single. What holds them all together is not the traditional bonds of family, religion, bloodline, or job life. Rather, their glue is a common sensation—restlessness—and a common object: the recreational vehicle.

The Counts first presented their research to the 95th Annual Meeting of the American Anthropological Association and were so encouraged that they wrote it up in monograph form as *Over the Next Hill: An Ethnology of RVing Seniors in North America* (1996, rpt. 2001). This little book has been repeatedly republished and is, in fact, not only a favorite of those who study nomads but of the nomads themselves. I often saw it for sale in RV campgrounds. It seems they do read, after all.

Over the Next Hill opened up a corner of modern life, a corner of which the Census Bureau had no accurate understanding, and with good reason. These people literally live off the grid: They don't fill out forms; they don't pay much in the way of taxes; and they really aren't visible unless you see a cluster of them in a campsite. These full-timers are people who are not working a lot in order to travel a little, but who are traveling a lot in order to work less. Home is where they park it. They are modern gypsies. And they may also be harbingers of how more people will live.

We know a good deal about these full-timers not only because of the Counts' questionnaires and interviews but because these people themselves often chronicle their movement. Thanks to the blogosphere you can read what they are doing, where they are, and, most interesting, how they are feeling about it. If you ever wanted to see the vaunted social network at work, don't just look to the texting kids; have a look at their finger-tapping grandparents too.

As this transformation from the sedentary to the nomadic is occurring, social science is doing what it does best: providing after-the-fact explanation. Not to put too fine a point on it, but some anthropologists now suggest that earlier views of nomadic culture as being less advanced than sedentary culture need to be rethought. In academic jargon, stability may have been unfairly *privileged* against mobility, city life against country life, citizen against gypsy.

The singular development of modern times is that for the first time we can be a productive member of society and not go to work in an office. You can work right where you are. Machines that once had to be surrounded by workers are now liberating workers. Thanks to new ways of interacting via the Internet, the necessity of settling down near the office, the plant, the classroom is no more. *Working at a distance* is the new catchphrase. Innovators like Timothy Ferris (*The 4-Hour Workweek: Escape 9–5, Live Anywhere, and Join the New Rich*), Chris Guillebeau (*The $100 Startup: Reinvent the Way You Make a Living*), and Chad Mureta (*App Empire: Make Money, Have a Life, and Let Technology Work for You*) are showing how easy it is not just to "work at home" but to make that home transportable. And Jaimie Hall Bruzenak, who spent eight years working full-time on the road in the 1990s, has shown how easy it is to make the RV a mobile office (*Support Your RV Lifestyle! An Insider's Guide to Working on the Road*). Maybe the RV, object of scorn, will come to be seen as an object of liberation.

The RV industry, ever-responsive to the need to escape, has been less sensitive to this new use. Some RVs are losing their dreary nestiness and picking up a bit of the workspace motif. There are now models with fully stocked electronic offices where the mirrored Naugahyde sofa pit used to be. Under solar panels, satellite dish antennae, wi-fi, and smart phones, the mobile electronic office is here, puttering behind you on the interstate. Perhaps new brand names will appear to express this shift: the Cubicle, the Corner Office, the Phone-it-in, the Twitter, and the one I am currently using, the Tax Deduction.

THE IMPACT OF THE RV ON THE CONCEPT OF TRAVEL

As the concept of *nomadic* is being transformed, so is the notion of travel and how to write about it. Although there are thousands of blogs electronically streaming from RVs, most of them are the predictable "where I am, how I got here, now look at my pics." Sometimes it's all about the rig. For instance, numerous websites are dedicated to the chatter from owners of the same brand. And there are sites for people on the same road, like the Alaska Highway, Route 66, or parts of Mexico.

Sometimes it's a commercial blog, as with GoRVing by Brad Herzog. Herzog is a travel writer (*Turn Left at the Trojan Horse: A Would-be Hero's American Odyssey*; *Small World: A Microcosmic Journey*; and *States of Mind*) who has been loaned a rig by Winnebago in exchange for saying occasional nice things about the product. But no matter that he is slightly on the take, Herzog tries to tell you what it's like to move around in a bubble on wheels, especially with a handful of kids (blog.gorving.com). He's writing for families. Then again, sometimes it's a quasi-commercial site like Nick Russell's www.gypsyjournalrv.com. Nick is a past owner and publisher of several western newspapers who now makes his living writing for full-timers. His website, blog, books, and pamphlets are so chockablock with tips, reviews, musings, recommendations, and observations that you wonder how he ever gets his fingers off the keyboard and onto the steering wheel. And sometimes it's a blog written for the pure joy of it like rv-a-gogo, composed by two young women from New Orleans who putter around in a big rig and provide a biweekly stream of observations of their life on wheels (rvagogo.blogspot.com). Not only is the writing fresh and personal, it's from the point of view of a couple who are having to deal with the problems of a Class A motorhome. The accordion stairs don't work, they bump into trees, there are problems with the slide-out, they have questions about the engine, they have to balance the damn thing, a pesky stress crack appears in the fiberglass, the dog needs a walk. The subjects that Brad, Nick, and the other men silently tough out, these women talk about solving. And they do it with good humor, self-deprecating wit, a good appetite, and some great pictures.

In a sense, the snapshot view from the moving house is redefining what travel and travel writing means. It's no longer about going from point to point. Years ago, when travel was a profit center of the publishing world and there were no other competing media, the writer described where he was along The Route—in detail. Destination was king. No more. The modern traveler is often a gadabout tourist, and the writing reflects this.

Whereas generations ago, writers railed against the *tourist* as opposed to the *traveler* (Hilaire Belloc's, "We wander for distraction, but we travel for fulfillment," Thomas Fuller's "A fool wanders; a wise man travels"), the modern gypsy/hobo in the RV wants precisely that distraction. In a sense, modern travel writing itself has become a kind of subversion of the traditional as the writer often sends up the idea of destination as not just unnecessary but something that gets in the way. If destination is important, stay away from the RV. As Nick Russell says, the RVer writes his itinerary in Jell-O.

Before his untimely death, Bruce Chatwin was working on a defense of this new kind of travel-as-puttering called "The Anatomy of Restlessness." Although this essay was the trying-out of a longer work, you can see where he was going. His thesis, as he develops it in draft essays collected in his posthumously published *Anatomy of Restlessness: Selected Writings 1969–1989* (1997), is that we've got it all wrong with settling down. Movement is the natural, stability the fluke. We were made to dawdle, daydream, drive around.

Typically, Chatwin goes a step farther by claiming that this movement is what all religions preach. Don't they tell us something about seek and ye shall find? And what does seeking entail? Make of it what you will, in almost every religion there is a crucial period of what looks to be aimless wandering for the prophet. Buddha seems aimless in the Punjab, Christ and Mohammed wander in the desert. Almost every religious leader goes through a refractory period in midlife that seems pointless to others. "Nobody," Mohammed said, "becomes a prophet who was not first a shepherd," and shepherds, as we know, follow, do not lead, flocks. The hadj and the pilgrimage are to Chatwin just secondhand renditions of these earlier migrations, and these earlier migrations result from something eternal at the core: the deep yearning to move, to be nomadic, to be in flux.

I certainly don't mean to make too much of Chatwin's thesis other than to say that restlessness is a mode of natural learning, the counterpoint to the contemplative state of the medieval monk who never leaves his cell. Chatwin's point: Why did we ever think that contemplation was silent and still? Why do we need such quiet to meditate? The principle of life is breath, it is ambling, it is motion. Could it be that as some of us came to favor the sedentary life we also started to rejigger the holy into states of quiescence, to make the monk replace the shepherd, to make reading the book replace roaming the pasture, to make contemplating the navel preferable to turning the key and pressing the accelerator?

There are many paths to the palace of wisdom. Restlessness in and of itself (at least for a while) may be one to consider. It is, after all, the nature of adolescence, and adolescence is the time most of us learn by movement, by hands-on experience. Why try to tamp down this learning? What great explorer didn't have a florid case of *wanderlust*. Why "settle down" when there is still road ahead? Why try to constrain the "balm of motion" when it seems at the heart of human life? Maybe *getting outta here* without knowing where you'll be tomorrow is worth considering as an epistemology. The Germans have a word for it—*fernweh*—literally, an ache for distant places. Maybe the dowdy recreational vehicle can be a vehicle of discovery, a cure for farsickness, a Huck Finn raft of escape for the middle-aged. But that doesn't have to be decided by us. Perhaps, just as the cigar is sometimes simply a cigar, the RV is sometimes just a cool way to get out of the house and see some new stuff—even at $4 a gallon.

Chapter Two

AT HOME ON THE ROAD

A Fleeting History of the American Dream in RVs

Strange to say, but the *recreational* vehicle has been with us for a lot longer than most people think. In fact, when the Ford Model T's appeared at the beginning of the last century, the first thing many owners did was to go out and sleep in them. You simply lifted the car doors off their pin hinges and pitched a tent over the frame. You could spend the night in your front yard, and many people did.

As Warren Belasco has argued in his ground-breaking book *Americans on the Road: From Autocamp to Motel, 1910–1945* (1977), we usually think that *destination* travel was a primary goal of car culture, but that was not the case. The railroad took care of destinations. It had a fixed route, down the rails, no wandering around. This machine mandated

Figure 2.1: Car camping ads.

March 24, *Outdoor Life* ad for a "real spring bed," not just a mattress that allows you to save hotel costs.

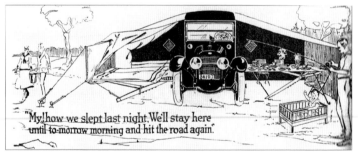

1917 ad for J.H. Whittmann Mfg. Co. of Kansas City, which rolled up the tent on the running board (*RVs & Campers, 1900–2000. An Illustrated History*, p. 17).

(Opposite Page) The best of both worlds: touring or camping. The bed, as it was to be in the Monaco Treks of the late 1970s, was lowered from the roof—very savvy use of space (*RVs & Campers, 1900–2000: An Illustrated History*, p. 42).

SLEEP IN YOUR CAR

Are you going camping or touring?
Stop worrying about a tent—its high
cost and the trouble handling it. Snap
your fingers at the grasping hotel man.
You can forget both if you take a Foldaway Bed along and *sleep in your car.*

Easily installed in a few minutes' time
—comfortable—when not in use folds
up into shape and size of golf bag,
weighs only 13 to 14 lbs.—low in price.
Models for practically all cars—closed
or touring, including Fords, Chevrolet,
Essex Coach, etc. Sold on "money
back" guarantee if you are not satis-
fied. Write us for details.

Outers Equipment Company
329 Wrigley Bldg.   Chicago, Ill.

A 1924 ad for a bed system that could be used inside or outside your car—either way far from the "grasping hotel man" (*RVs & Campers, 1900–2000: An Illustrated History*, p. 38).

THE BLAKE PULLMAN LIMOUSINE
Camp Comfort DE-LUX

Patents Pending

The *perfect* touring car.
Exteriorly the construc-
tion and appearance is
that of the standard
limousine; no extra parts
are visible, yet when
touring, it is a business,
pleasure and camping car.
All of these features are
so practical and simple a
child can operate them.

Contains full sized bed, tent 10x12, tables, chairs, two-burner
stove, sink and running water. Bed and tent concealed in top of
car, lowered by a lever from the driver's seat; tables and chairs on
running board concealed; stove, sink under hood. Can be installed
in any car.

FRANK R. BLAKE, 78 Grove St., Factory: Portsmouth, N. H. **BANGOR, MAINE**

RED HEAD BRAND
AUTO BED

Sleep in your car The RED HEAD BRAND Auto Bed is dandy to sleep in! Up or down in three minutes. Fits any sedan or touring car Weighs 30 lbs. Folds to package size of a golf bag.

Many other useful articles in our "Auto Campers' Guide." Be sure to write for a copy.

ALWARD-ANDERSON-SOUTHARD CO.
Incorporated 1916
921 West Chicago Ave., Chicago, U.S.A.

Indeed a "dandy to sleep in! Up and down in three minutes," 1925 (*RVs & Campers, 1900–2000: An Illustrated History*, p. 42).

The Jim-Harry Auto Camp Bed

is the latest, most compact, most convenient Camp Bed (pat. pending). It's a one piece bed, which includes a warm, comfortable mattress pad—folds 6 by 7 by 44½ in. Shipping weight 44 lbs. Will fit into any touring or sedan car, in the tent or home. Write for circular. Price $18.00. Sold only by

The Johnson Auto Top Shop
207 N. Victoria Avenue
Pueblo, Colo.

For $18 you have an "auto camp bed," or at least a mattress (*RVs & Campers, 1900–2000: An Illustrated History*, p. 42).

not just stops but overnight stays in its own hotels, and it literally set the clock of modern life. Only with the railroad did such matters as timetables, pocket watches, and even time zones come into common use. Cars, however, needed roads, and roads needed durable pavement. Car travel needed time too, but time for breakdowns.

Say what you want about how important the rails were in opening up the American West, the one thing rail travel was was uncomfortable. It antagonized many travelers, especially women. The hotels, owned and controlled by oligopolies, catered primarily to a new kind of traveler: the drummer, the male salesman. He was raw, often impolite, and noisome. And the people who served these travelers—a new class of clerks, bellhops, chamber maids—were often also off-putting, eagerly stretching forth open palms to receive a new form of payment, the tip.

So *auto camping*, which let you putter around, was refreshing. And auto camping was female-friendly. In fact, an overlooked aspect of this new form of travel was that many women felt safe sleeping in cars. We usually celebrate the men who crossed the country in their cars, most especially the 1903 cross-country trip of Colonel Horatio Nelson Jackson in his gleaming cherry-red Winton touring car. We forget that a few years later many women did the same.

The most famous of these young women was Emily Post, the future doyenne of respectable behavior. In 1916, against the advice of many— including her banker, who wagered she'd never make it ("They'll never get there! Unless I am mistaken, they'll be on a Pullman inside of ten days!")—Emily essentially RVed across the country. True, she had lots of help along the way, but no chauffeur and no servants. She wrote about being an "auto gypsy" in *By Motor to the Golden Gate*

At last when the vividness of colors begins to soften into vapory purples, deepening again to indigo, you gather a little brushwood and for the mere companionable cheerfulness make a campfire to eat your supper by. You probably heat a can of soup, roast potatoes, and finally, having nothing else to cook or heat for the present, hit upon the brilliant thought of boiling water, while the fire burns, for next morning's coffee. At least this is what we did, and poured it into a thermos to keep hot. Also we climbed back into the car. Personally

I have an abject terror of snakes, though there was very likely none within a hundred miles of us. For nothing on earth would I make myself a bed on the open ground. Also the seats of our car—there was at least one satisfactory thing about it—are only four or five inches from the floor, and sitting in it is like sitting in an upholstered steamer chair with the footrest up— a perfectly comfortable position to go to sleep in. So that bundled up in fur coats with steamer blankets over us we were just as snug as the proverbial bugs in a rug. For my own part, though, the night was too beautiful out under that starhung sky willingly to shut my eyes and blot it out. My former fears of prowling Indians, strange animals, spooks, spirits—or perhaps just vast empty blackness—had vanished completely, and instead there was merely the consciousness of an experience too beautiful to waste a moment of. I could not bear to go to sleep. The very air was too delicious in its sparkling purity to want to stop consciously breathing it. Overhead was the wide inverted bowl of purple blue made of an immensity of blues overlaid with blues that went through and through forever, studded with its myriad blinking lamps lit suddenly all together, and so close I felt that I could almost reach them with my hand. [181]

Emily was hardly alone. We've forgotten that the Great American Road Trip, now seen exclusively as a rite of passage for young males, once involved young women as well. Before Jack Kerouac and the Beach Boys made cruising around in your automobile a guy thing, young women were often at the wheel. Even families chose to traverse the continent by automobile, taking an exciting month-long voyage in an open touring car instead of the three-and-a-half-day trip in a stifling Pullman car. Their well-publicized endeavors inspired the Good Roads movement and ultimately the construction of the Lincoln Highway, later Route 66, and still later the north–south Dixie Highway.

The railroads fought the Good Roads movement every step of the way. Although the railroads opposed national funding for transcontinental highways, they could not subdue Americans' passion for "going out for a drive." The upgrading of horse paths in the early twentieth century was for the joy of auto camping, of just going over to the next town to see what was there. As roadways got better, the average maximum mileage went from 125 miles a day in 1916, to 170 in 1920, to 200 in 1925, to 240 in 1928, to 300 in 1931, to 400 in 1936.

You could camp almost anywhere. In fact, as Emily Post explained, farming folk liked the idea of other people overnighting on their land. And remember that until the mid-1930s, these early RVers were a decidedly upper-class clientele, people who were easy to befriend and who cleaned up after themselves. In fact, this popular bit of homespun doggerel was spoken by a farmer observing auto campers passing by:

> There are hermit souls that live withdrawn
> In the place of their self-content;
> There are souls like stars, that dwell apart,
> In a fellowless firmament;
> There are pioneer souls that blaze the paths
> Where highways never ran—
> But let me live by the side of the road
> And be a friend to man.
>
> *The House by the Side of the Road*

Two other factors helped make auto camping popular, both having to do with the rise of newspapers and a new kind of viral knowledge—the *news*. First was the widespread panic caused in 1915, when Kaiser Wilhelm II sent his U-20 attack submarine to sink the very image of oceanic safety, the *Lusitania* More than 1,200 passengers died when the *Lusitania* went down. The effect on travel at sea was much like that of 9/11 on air travel: No one wanted to travel to Europe by ship.

The second factor in the rise of American tourism was impact of modern public relations. Railroads and the cities they served paid newspapers and magazines to run "See America First" campaigns. Just look at the ads in the *National Geographic* before World War I and you'll see images of snow-capped mountains, serene deserts, welcoming Indians, Old Faithful, and especially the Panama-Pacific International Exposition in San Francisco (which drew 13 million visitors in 1915 just after the *Lusitania* went down), all brought your way by the Union Pacific, Southern Pacific, and Santa Fe railroads.

Moreover, the car companies encouraged customer tinkering. Use your car to go vacationing. It's safe. You stop when and where you want. As we will see in the next chapter, the amusing exploits of the so-called Vagabonds (Henry Ford, Thomas Edison, Harvey Firestone, and the poet/naturalist John Burroughs) not only made front-page stories but taught consumers how to turn their newfangled automobiles into RVs. *Automobility* could be as exciting as an ocean voyage, and a lot safer. It was every bit as safe as traveling by rail, much more fun, and you didn't have to tip the porter and the housemaid.

A TAXONOMY OF RVS

Thus was born the car-as-traveling-companion. Not only did it get named, like the horse it replaced, but the Tin Lizzie (Lizzie was also a common name for Irish household help), aka Flivver (etymology unknown, but any cheap car), soon seemed to take on a life of its own. Because the biology of RV evolution has proven so extensive, I'll try to provide a brief taxonomy.

As Paul Ingrassia has recently shown in *Engines of Change: A History of the American Dream in Fifteen Cars* (2012), the battle for self-definition via cars is brutally Darwinian. Recall the Great Tail-Fin Wars of the late 1950s; the Prius–Hummer smackdowns of the first years of this century; how the drab little Ford Falcon moth became the Mustang butterfly; or even how Hitler's people's car, the VW, became the counterculture's car of choice. The struggle for RV dominance may not be as bloody or as colorful as car culture, but it's close and equally revelatory. In my family tree I'm leaving out a lot of minor mutations, and I admit to including personal favorites, but I hope this will give the gist of how dynamic (and unappreciated) this aspect of American wheel culture has been.

In the Kingdom of Houses on Wheels, which has the gypsy wagon as the Ur-Campwagon and the Conestoga wagon as the unique American continuation, two bloodlines descend. On the left are the motorized RVs, and on the right are the nonmotorized versions (aka the trailer). They cross-pollinate from time to time, producing new

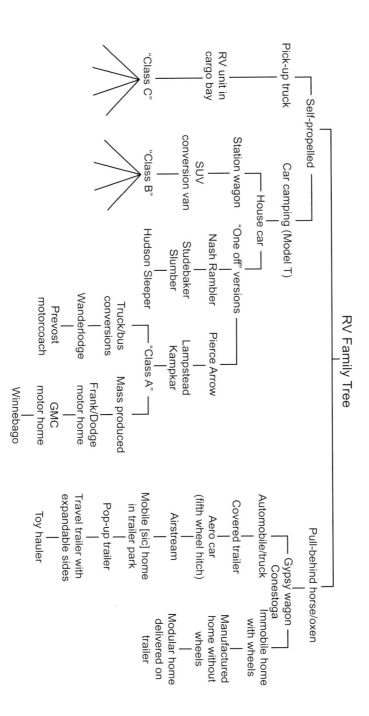

Figure 2.2: My prejudicial taxonomy of RVs (Susan G. Duser).

hybrids. And sometimes they get mixed up with other phyla, like trucks and station wagons. In addition, many new orders and species get subsumed and redirected, some lasting only a few years. This process is ongoing: Think conversion van, minivan, SUV.... In fact, until the 1960s, most of the RV branches were really short stubs, what the English engineers call "one-off" concoctions—rigs that were made only once. So forewarned, my drawing of the blood lines is an admittedly prejudicial family tree of *auto camping*:

On the right side of the graph are the objects that have to be pulled. For instance, the gypsy wagon begat the tent trailer, which begat the platform trailer, which begat the pop-up trailer, which finally got covered in Masonite and aluminum and resulted in the inaptly named *mobile home*. But no matter what it's called, this is the world of the towed-behind, the trailer, the world sealed in a can with no power of its own. I'm not really concerned about these trailers, other than that from time to time a development occurs like the monocoque construction of Wally Byam's Airstream, which evolved into the fiberglass molds of the RV, or the dropping of the trailer into the cargo bay of the pickup truck, which became the basis of the Class C RV.

As we know too well, this line of RV evolution comes to a dead end. The 50-foot-plus faux trailer is really the *immobile* home that, when clustered, ends up in the mobile home park, better called the *immobile* home park. About fifty years ago, the immobile-home industry said enough of this subterfuge and started calling them what they really were: prefab houses, or, better yet, manufactured homes. Once the double-wide appeared, the jig was up. So this side of the evolutionary path has run aground, literally.

Our anxiety about this strain, however—the so-called *trailer life* and *trailerites* (as the occupants were called)—was intense. As Roger White, curator of the transportation wing of the Smithsonian Museum notes in his *At Home on the Highway* (which followed the 1985 museum's show on the same subject), critics of living in your vehicle have been around for a while. They were (and still can be) nasty. Remember that the word *mob*, a recent coinage, comes from *mobile vulgus* (vulgarians on the move). That trailerites can move around is not comforting. Gypsies may be alluring to some; they unsettle many others.

So in the 1940s, the economist Roger W. Babson, famous for forecasting the crash of 1929, claimed that soon half the population would be creeping around in trailers. A little later the midcult fussbudget Gilbert Seldes trumpeted, "We are facing a movement of population beside which even the Crusades will seem like Sunday school picnics." And Lewis Mumford, the famous urbanist, denounced the house trailer as a toxic expedient that destroyed family and community ties. In a way, these critics had (and have) a point: When the RV gets anchored in the ground, it can become blight. And, worse, from the point of view of the neighbors, it's hard to tax. Trailerites take advantage of services like schools and police/fire protection while essentially getting a free pass on taxes because they are supposedly just "passing through" (quotes from Roger B. White, "At Home on the Highway," *American Heritage* 37, no. 1 [1985]).

The other side of the taxonomy, the self-propelled camper, will also come in for criticism, but not until the end of the twentieth century. And that's because the people who first owned them were not the mobile workers but those who owned the factories where the mobile workers worked. Those who owned the first *house cars*, as they were known, were the Haves, not the Have-nots; the Man, not the Mob; the residents of Belmont, not Fishtown. If you brewed beer, milled breakfast cereal, made movies, flew airplanes, or, especially, built cars or buses, you might well own a one-of-a-kind house car.

RV LIKE A HOUSE, PART 1

Should you ever wonder where that monster McMansion bus with the psychedelic paint job that comes whizzing past you on the interstate comes from, the 1910 Pierce Arrow Touring Landau started the love affair with RVs that may have tempered but has not diminished. This rig has it all: on-board potty (under the seat), hot and cold running water, a rear seat that morphs into a bed, a separated chauffeur's seat, and, as you can see, plenty of rooftop and rear-end storage. The matching bespoke luggage comes with the RV. Historians of the house car point to this as the beginning and, in a sense, the apogee of auto camping. Unveiled at

Figure 2.3: Pierce Arrow Touring Landau was the Prevost conversion of its time, 1910–13 (Division of Work & Industry, National Museum of American History, Smithsonian Institution).

Madison Square Garden, only three were made: one for the president of Pierce Arrow, another for C. W. Post of breakfast-cereal fame, and a third for some lucky unknown master of the universe from Buffalo. Post paid $8,250 for his at a time when the Model T cost $950. If you want a sense of how this line of RV heritage has mutated, realize that this rig would today be considered a pee-wee Class B RV.

A decade later, W. K. Kellogg refused to be outdone by C. W. Post. He wanted what would be called today a Class A rig, a really big 'un. So Kellogg had a house car built from a White Motor truck. He modeled his rig after a Pullman railroad car, complete with mahogany paneling, leather upholstery, adjustable armchairs, upper and lower berths, a battery-operated radio, shower, electric kitchen, and even a rudimentary ice crusher. It weighed almost 4 tons. He humbly called it the *Ark*.

It was only a matter of time before this competitive interest in automotive one-upmanship created another strain of motorized vehicle: the mass-produced gentleman's house car that you could accessorize, the so-called *kampkar*. So out in St Louis, George Steedman, who had built a car with the wondrous name of the Road Cruiser Wampus, joined up with Arthur Lambert, a scion of the Lambert Pharmaceutical Company (producer of Listerine), and maker of his own Camping Car, to produce the Lampsteed Kampkar. During the Prohibition era the company was purchased by Anheuser-Busch, which turned its attention from making beer wagons to making RVs. This vehicle was converted from what looks to be a Ford sedan into an elegant safari wagon complete with beds, expandable dining room, and a nifty veranda. A 1923 advertisement makes the case:

> Go Anywhere Over Your Own Railway System, In Your Own Private Car and On Your Own Schedule.
>
> All set for breakfast! Notice the convenient arrangements of beds, gasoline cooking outfit, table dishes, ice box, and sun shade. In five minutes two persons can make up the beds, put away the dishes and cooking utensils, and drive off across the country in the Kampkar.

The only drawback was that it took two people about three hours to unfold all the water- and vapor-proof canvas. The kampkar may have been intended "For Vacationists—For Campers—For Outdoor Hon-

Figure 2.4: Zaglemeyer Kampkar, 1921 (Al Hesselbart collection at the RV/MH Hall of Fame and Museum).

eymoon Tours," but getting it ready for the night might mean the end of the marriage.

Like home radio, home brew, and the telephone, these camp cars became the rage for men with money. So Henry B. Joy, president of the Packard Motor Car Company, had a wood-and-canvas house car built by his shop in 1915 and furnished with cots, an alcohol stove, and cooking utensils just like home. Meanwhile T. Coleman du Pont, the Delaware industrialist, owned a similar vehicle that he used to inspect his roadways in Delaware. What these camp cars all have in common is a wonderful exuberance, a Rube Goldberg delight in the mechanical, a joy of the car as origami. How else to explain a phone to speak with the chauffeur?

The kampkar's advertising notwithstanding, the early RV is analogous not only to the private Pullman railcar, as Roger White argues in *Home on the Road: The Motor Home in America* (2001), but to the public Victorian parlor. These vehicles did not move around a lot, but they certainly did invite inspection. In fact, they were even nicknamed "knockers" because curious passersby often rapped on their doors, hoping to take a peek inside. The parlor condition still exists today. I have never met an owner of a big rig who was not willing, nay excited, to show you the private quarters of his RV (just take your shoes off before entering). And what's remarkable in the history of these behemoths is how quickly their owners and makers adapt whatever new innovation has appeared in American parlors. House cars are not to get away from home as much as to take home-sweet-home away from home. In a sense, they were mobile dollhouses for adults, albeit rich adults.

RV LIKE A GYPSY WAGON

Occasionally one of these one-off vehicles leaves home base and really heads out into the Great Beyond. The most famous of all the early motor homes was the Gypsy Van owned and operated by the Conklin family of Long Island. In 1915, Ronald R. Conklin, president of the New York Motor Bus Company, decided to convert one of his buses into an English manse. It was huge: upstairs/downstairs/observation deck, sofas, beds,

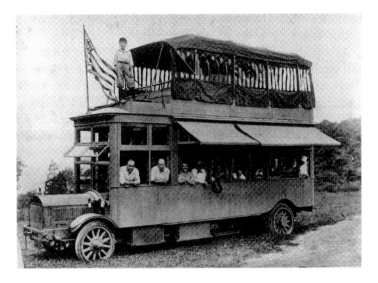

Figure 2.5: Superior Truck, aka "Gypsy Van," owned by the Conklins of Huntington, NY, 1915 (Huntington Historical Society).

full kitchen with a special range on the manifold so cooking could occur while driving. The top deck proved especially important. It was supposed to be for dancing and musical interludes, but it provided livable space when crossing sandy plains. The Gypsy Van had nine forward gears and three reverse—all used. Not only did the family go most of the way to San Francisco (they put it on a railcar for part of the journey), but they (or many of them—when at full complement there were six, staff of two) made their way back home. Much as Emily Post would later do with *By Motor to the Golden Gate*, Mary Conklin kept the country informed with her newspaper dispatches from the road.

RV LIKE AN AIRPLANE

Although the trailer is now the step-brother of the self-propelled RV, this was not always the case. For decades the trailer was king and the house car was the eccentric prince. The economies of mass production were applied to the construction of trailers simply because that was where the

Figure 2.6: Aero car ad (The Glenn H. Curtiss Museum Hammondsport, NY).

The
CURTISS AEROCAR
for 1938

money was to be made. The one-off bespoke house cars were interesting, to be sure, but they were individual playthings, not real profit centers. So whereas motorized bungalows were rare, trailers were everywhere. And, as we know, the critics were not far behind.

Because trailers were relatively simple to manufacture, they came from all over the country: Upstate New York, around the Great Lakes, and southern California. One of the most famous manufacturers was outside Detroit. It called its trailers *covered wagons*, which at least showed that these people knew what their market was all about. At the height of the Depression, the Covered Wagon Company was selling about fifty units a day. Let the rich have their overnight cars sitting in the garage; the rank and file would have something far more practical on the road, their own prairie schooners.

This was the context that aircraft engineer Glenn Curtiss understood. His goal in the 1930s was to bridge the gap, to make money on both sides of the market by building a trailer worthy of a house car. He would build a trailer for the rich, make a Fishtown object worthy of Belmont, make those critics of trailering eat their critical words. And he would do it not by aping the private railroad car or the yacht, but by imitating what he knew best—the airplane. He called his creation the Aerocar.

Curtiss made his trailer just like the fuselage of an airplane and then he made the towing vehicle to fit it. The final product was long and sleek with art deco lines that flowed from the nose prow of the cab to a single rear axle in the tail. The skeleton was made of thin oak struts connected by crossed nickel-steel truss wires. These wires had turn-buckles that were used to "tune" them to maximum tension, thus giving rigidity to the structure. The Aerocar lived up to its name: It looked like it was about to become airborne. Buy it and you would become a land-based Lindbergh (who, incidentally, had his own trailer, though, alas, not an Aerocar).

Curtiss's enduring innovation was how he linked both vehicles. He connected the trailer to the car not by attaching it to the chassis or to the bumper but to what he called the *fifth wheel*. His joint was an airplane tire bolted into the trunk or rumble seat of the pull car. The joint itself was not new – big horse-drawn wagons had used it – but Curtiss then set the trailer tongue onto the horizontal tire so that it could swivel around on the rubber sidewall. He then adjusted the air pressure in the tire to get the proper balance and so lessen vibration. Essentially, the trailer rode on a tire donut that cushioned the bumps. Although he called the hitch the "Glenn Curtiss Aero Coupler," it commonly became known as the *fifth-wheel hitch*. A version of it is still used when a trailer is connected to a coupler located in the cargo bay of a pickup truck.

Curtiss contended that when the rigs were properly joined, the aerodynamics of the 2,100-pound Aerocar actually made it go faster. Passengers could catch the views from fixed armchairs in the lounge or stretch out on the rear-facing divan in the prow and listen to a built-in Philco radio. A table snapped into place so that passengers might play cards or sit down to a meal created in the galley, with its two-burner gasoline stove, icebox, and sink. Curtiss thought of everything. His chemical toilet had its own private compartment, something other house cars usually solved with a bedpan. He even included a privacy curtain that turned the galley into a shower stall with water running out through a drain in the floor. Of course there was the hard-wire phone connection to the chauffeur so you wouldn't have to open a window and yell out directions.

Although the Aerocar never really caught on (Curtiss died in 1930 and the Depression descended), the aerodynamics were not lost on other designers. Almost all the great designers of manufactured objects (Norman Bel Geddes, Walter Dorwin Teague, Henry Dreyfuss, Raymond Loewy, Buckminster Fuller) were impressed by the elegance of his design and borrowed from it. Commercial interests finally also saw the potential for harnessing its curb appeal. The Aerocar was eye candy. Hotels used versions as airport shuttles; businesses used them to display wares. Cities Service modified one into a rolling movie theater , and a competitor, Pure Oil, used one as a sound truck to attract customers to its gas stations. Grolier Encyclopedia Company outfitted theirs as a tasteful mobile reading room. General Electric had one to showcase their household products. The Aerocar was especially traffic-stopping when outfitted as a hearse.

The RV industry never really harvested the visual excitement of the Aerocar. True, a few RVs like the Ultra Van, the Flxible Clipper, the Dodge/Travco Motor Home, and the GMC Motorhome picked up on its svelte lines. But for reasons known only to them and their cost accountants, RV designers aped the railroad boxcar more often than the airline fuselage. Only German RVs really tip the hat to the concept of streamlining. Alas, most big Class A rigs have the barely rounded edges of city buses. This same deficiency of taste is still evident on the inside of most RVs. As my wife says, most big RVs today look like they're designed by middle-aged midwestern men who are dreaming of French whorehouses.

RV NEIGHBORHOOD, THE TRAILER PARK

So why did the trailer take off in the early twentieth century and the self-propelled RV sputter? As with so many networks, success depends on *heft*. It depends not on a service but on the creation of a community of other users who are sharing the service. If only a few people are using telephones, the industry can't survive. The Internet search engines depend on having thousands of people logging on. Crossing the *tipping point*, as Malcolm Gladwell showed, is crucial with many objects. So too with the self-propelled recreational vehicle. As opposed to the car and the trailer, which simply needs service stations and a place to pull over,

Figure 2.7: Life in public campgrounds, 1930s (Al Hesselbart collection at the RV/MH Hall of Fame and Museum).

RVs need places to hook up, to recharge their electric systems, and to drain their septic tanks. They need space to linger.

Ironically, as Warren Belasco has shown in *Americans on the Road*, the horse and buggy provided the answer. For generations, horse travel required public stables where one would change horses and even find overnight accommodations. Many early gas stations simply shared the horse stable. And many of the 15 million or so campers who were tenting and trailering between 1908 and 1930 also spent the night at the stable/station.

These stations were often located downtown. Over time, merchants realized that they had a captive audience, so why not make the accommodations comfy and encourage long stays? By 1922, the *New York Times* estimated there were some eight thousand free campgrounds, many inside towns, with some providing potable water, sewage, and even showers. The campers did indeed spend money, about a dollar a person per night. One free autocamp in Denver boasted eight hundred camp lots with a clubhouse that featured a restaurant, ballroom dancing, running water, showers, and much more. Another in Desoto Park in Tampa, Florida, essentially created a wintertime city, with all the services provided gratis by the town.

Ironically, it was these *public* campgrounds that caused such trouble during the Depression. Attracted by the largesse offered by the campgrounds, a new type of camper—the male hobo—began arriving. Travelers with a jingle in their pockets were replaced by drifters with nothing to jingle. Women were no longer safe there. One of the reasons so many Hollywood movies of the mid-1930s featured hobo parks was because almost every town had one. These parks soon became public battlegrounds between downtown Babbitts and the itinerant freeloaders. The merchants who had lobbied to open them now often pressured the police to close them down.

Commercial parks developed to take up the slack. Again, they were often downtown, but now they were fenced and policed. Riffraff were kept out. Soon the parks started providing tent platforms and even bunks inside for bad weather. Women felt safe. In fact, women often ran these camps. (Most downtown hotels were still owned by railroad interests and run by men.) There were playgrounds for the kids, no reservations, no clerks, no tipping, free parking. Some private campgrounds were so popular that they limited the time of stay. A usual overnight charge was fifty cents.

To convey a sense of jollity, these private campgrounds often had humorous names like U-Smile Kamp, Kamp Kozy Kabins, U Wanna Kum Back. Oddly enough, these areas were often called Kampgrounds, with a *K* to go along with the cutesy names like Kampkar. This kuteness kontinues. The current franchise operation called KOA, or Kampgrounds of America, is a vestige from this time of kabins, kampers, and kottages. Over time these beside-the-highway commercial parks became less concerned with tent and trailer camping and more focused on the kabins, that were finally linked together to become the modern mo-tel (another cute coinage: *mo*-tor + ho-*tel* = motel).

Bit by bit, the infrastructure was taking shape that would make the mass-produced motorized RV possible. The roadways were in place, having been paved with concrete or a new mixture of small stones and a tar binder called Macadam. This durable road crust repelled water and was strong enough to support trucks and buses. The places to spend the night were no longer farmers' fields or the railroad hotels but in-town campgrounds. By 1926, the American Automobile Association (founded in 1902 to lobby for durable roads) estimated there were 12 million campers in 3 million cars on the road.

It is at the junction of car, roads, and campgrounds that one of the most transformative events happens, an event that fires a new piston of capitalism: *public relations.* Hard perhaps to believe, but convincing people they needed a car and teaching them how to use it were real problems for Detroit. Just as tobacco growers had to teach people to smoke, car makers had to teach people to drive around. Proclaiming "See America First" was easy; showing how to do it was a bit more complex.

Here, in the early 1920s, is where the so-called Vagabonds—Thomas A. Edison, Henry Ford, Harvey Firestone, John Burroughs inter *alia*—played such a crucial role. Realizing that they had plenty of product to sell but an audience that needed to learn how to use it, the car builders hit the road. It was a PR spectacle worthy of Edward Bernays and the fledgling ad men of Madison Avenue. Show these people—the Detroit titans—actually car camping—the country vagabonds. Edison, Ford, and Firestone made the stuff. John Burroughs was a noted naturalist who often criticized this stuff. If they could travel together in harmony, why not you?

So the Vagabonds took to the road with their photographers and scribes in tow, and, as we will see in the next chapter, they literally showed their customers how to car-camp, what to see, where to go, how to behave, and how to enjoy a lot of hearty camaraderie in the process. They even invited such stay-at-homes as President Warren Harding to join them. There they were on the front pages of almost every American newspaper (except the ones that hated Ford), chopping wood, unfolding tents, smoking cigars, tree climbing, and back-slapping. To be sure, they were car-camping with a bit more sophisticated equipment than the ordinary Joe (a Lincoln truck was outfitted as a chuck wagon followed, and each titan had a retinue of helpers), but they were going places *you* could go.

The Vagabonds were even lobbying the feds to create what would become the National Park Service so that people would have places to take their cars. It is ironic that today much is made of keeping motorized rigs out of places like Yellowstone when in fact such places were initially established for exactly such camping. Ditto many of the state parks, which even today have large sections dedicated not just to hikers but to car campers. In the original plans, however, cars were to be parked outside the parks. But once it became clear that people would pay to get inside, the toll booths appeared and the paving of paradise began.

But the RV for the masses still didn't take hold. One reason was that Ford stopped making the open car in the late 1920s, which meant that tent sales and conversion kits declined. The truth was that no one had figured out how to car-camp successfully in an enclosed car. By the time of the Depression, auto camping was starting to resemble scenes from the 1940 movie version of Steinbeck's *Grapes of Wrath*.

THE UNSUNG RV, THE STATION WAGON

That's not to say that house cars and car camping disappeared, only that they moved off the main highways. The rich still had their estate cars—gypsy wagons decked out in finery—but they drove them pri-

Figure 2.8: Advertising image of Nash Rambler fold-down seats, 1950s.

vately. And house cars were certainly appearing in the imaginations of boys. In 1929, Victor Appleton's *Tom Swift and His House on Wheels* was being scooped up by underage drivers with no immediate prospect of ownership. But the general revival of both interest and production would have to wait until after the war, when the wheels would get put back on Detroit's imagination.

And it was in the late 1940s that Detroit fooled around with the car. Designers took the top off, souped up the engine, and even tried to make it a sleeper by providing a fold-down front seat. Cars like the Nash Rambler, the Studebaker Slumber Coupe, and the Hudson Sleeper Kit showed that there was a market for sleeping in your car. But it was a tight squeeze.

Meanwhile, trailer sales were soaring. Why should the major auto-makers lose market share to these trailer makers? Why not find a form that would let people sleep in their cars that did not entail the complexity of fold-down front seats or the need to tow something behind? Why not just build a car with a compartment in the back that could be fitted out for sleeping at night and then during the day be returned to normal seats? Why not stretch the sedan into a wagon?

And, in the 1950s, this is exactly what happened. While we usually think that the new form of the *station wagon* developed as a function of suburban family life—for schlepping the kids around—this was not entirely the case. The automakers thought they could have it both ways: a car to buy after your second child was born and a car that could also function as a house car. A second family car was unheard of in the pre-war culture. The rise of the Do-It-Yourself Craze added impetus to the trend. With a station wagon you could go down to the lumber yard and load up. The second car was a work car. Both mom and dad were sold.

So the *station wagon* entered car culture to do almost what it said: Drive guests (or hubby) and their baggage to the *station*. At first no one knew what to call these things. However, since the predecessor was the *depot hack* of the 1850s, a horse-drawn carriage that picked up passengers at train stations, the *station wagon* name made some sense. And that's also why early station wagons often had those faux wooden sides, a vestige of earlier construction and use.

As with so many objects, the real innovators were not designers but consumers. After World War II, the serendipitous confluence of suburban life, DIY household projects, and the rage for overnight camping finally made these things part of family life. Like Formica, the bread toaster, the dial telephone, and the black-and-white television set, the station wagon soon became standard equipment for the Good Life.

Consumers fiddled and tinkered. As early as 1949, the *New York Times* was publishing first-person dispatches on how owners were adapting the object to their needs. In "Camping in a Car: Station Wagon Becomes Portable Home When Equipped with Bed and Stove," freelancer Walter Sosnoski reported on his trip to the Canadian Maritimes. He sounds almost gleeful to be free of the very motel/hotel culture the car has created.

> Regardless of the type of accommodations that were available, at no time on our trip did we feel that we were limited in our choice of stopping places. One of [t]he great advantages of camping in a car

is mobility. If we did not like the looks of a place, we simply drove on. We were not held to a rigid travel schedule because of advance reservations, and this freedom to do as we pleased made our entire vacation an easy-going adventure. [12/11/1949:24]

What the Model T initially wrought for auto camping, the Ford station wagon *almost* perfected. About 29,000 station wagons were sold in 1946. A decade later, that number had exploded to 707,200. Of all the producers, Ford was the most eager to lend a hand, hoping to direct this market to its brands. The company even published a series of books and pamphlets with names like *The Ford Guide to Outdoor Living on Wheels*, *The Ford Treasury of Station Wagon Living* (two volumes), and *The Newest Adventures in Station Wagon Living*. These

Figure 2.9: "Wherever the wagon stops, you're home" Ford and station wagon living, from *Ford Treasury of Station Wagon Living* (a scanned reproduction of the magazine by Franklin Mering, 2010, p. 17).

books were essentially Cub Scout handbooks for the wagon masters and consisted, to a considerable extent, of submissions from owners. They were writing apps for the machine. The company cheerily reminded their customers that the "wagon is really a school bus . . . the wagon is a workhouse for the do-it-yourself suburbanite . . . the wagon is a bedroom . . . the wagon is a kitchen . . . the wagon is a traveling nursery . . . the wagon is a rolling recreation device . . . the wagon is an entire mobile home." Take your pick because even the company wasn't sure what they were making.

With the savvy of computer companies to come, Ford created the Station Wagon Living Program, through which the company acted as clearinghouse for all these suggestions for camping. In *The Newest Adventures in Station Wagon Living*, the company reported:

> During the past five years, in its Station Wagon Living Program, the Ford Motor Company has encouraged the growth of a hundred small industries, all of them inspired by the generous dimensions of the station wagon. Backyard inventors are producing kitchens that slide out of the rear of the wagon, car-top tents, doubledeck bunks, shelters that enclose the opened tailgate, lightweight collapsible chairs, tables, cabanas, lounges, baby cribs and playpens that can be stowed in the wagon and hauled, cabin and camp. [1959:3]

You name it. If it was in your split-level ranch house, you could put it in your campmobile: plug-in coffeemakers, portable generators, foldaway beds, and transistor radios.

In 1958, Ford even collaborated with the Reynolds Metal Company to produce a concept vehicle from a standard-issue Country Sedan wagon. And they did it with the new miracle metal that was once more precious than gold: aluminum. The two companies piled on almost a half ton of shiny accessories, including a boat, a tent, a shower with hot and cold water, and a gleaming kitchen. All of it could be activated by the new open-sesame product—the push button. The energy source was the wagon's humble 12-volt battery. In retrospect, you can see where this all was going: Here was the mass-produced RV in embryo.

Figure 2.10: Author on Ford station wagon during camping trip in New York, 1954.

But it didn't work, at least not yet. The station wagon just wasn't big enough to handle all these extra tasks. I know. In 1954, I went with my dad up to Messina, New York, in a Ford Ranch Wagon to watch the construction of the St. Lawrence Seaway. Dad and I slept in the back, cooked over a Coleman stove, and ate our dinner inside because all it did outside was rain. We got stuck in the mud, and a farmer had to pull us out. There simply wasn't enough room. Maybe we should have had the folding canvas tarp and the mud package with tire chains.

By the 1970s, the station wagon was running out of gas. In true Darwinian fashion, new organisms had appeared that were more adaptive and spritely. Soccer mom got the minivan, and weekend dad got the monstrously misnomered SUV. Station wagon production peaked in 1965 at 968,771, then started its slow atrophy. Meanwhile, the camper had migrated to more efficient forms. On one hand, the Germans introduced a nifty variation on the gypsy wagon—the Westfalia—one of the many permutations of their Type 2 VWs. And on the other hand, the construction trades patronized a new truck form, the pickup, and soon trailer makers devised a box unit that could be lifted up and slid into its cargo bay called the *chassis-mounted camper*. In RV lingo, the Westfalia

Figure 2.11: Author with daughter and VW Westfalia camping in Oklahoma, 1973.

evolved into the Class C RV (an expanded version of which becomes the motor home proper, the Class A, which, in turn, evolved from bus conversions), and the slide-in became the Class B, mutating still further to form the cab-over single body sometimes called the B+. In both cases, you can see how the bones and cartilage of the old standby—the depot hack made station wagon (made Chevy Cameo, made Ford Styleside, made Dodge Sweepside, made Chevy El Camino, made Falcon Ranchero, and so on) were changing until, finally, in the mid-twentieth century, the new beast was slouching towards the Midwest to be born.

RV LIKE A HOUSE, PART 2

To find the modern RV you have to leave the manicured lawns of the suburban station-wagonites and head off into the high grass of the American Midwest. For here, after World War II, came the fertile confluence of two distinctively American traditions: backyard mechanics and deer hunting. Many of the advances in house cars came as servicemen who had learned to bend metal making airplanes and submarines had a real motivation to make a camper car that would provide not the *comforts* of home but all the *aspects* of home. In other words, they wanted a way to drive into the woods, spend the night, be warm, cook, go hunting, clean up (but not much), and then get out.

Many of the early RVs of the late 1940s looked just like what they were: deer camps on wheels. Often they were converted school busses, sometimes converted trucks, and only occasionally from-the-ground-up creations. You won't see them on the floor of the RV museums, in Hollywood, or on the glossy pages of devotee appreciations (like *Mobile Mansions: Taking Home Sweet Home on the Road* or *Home Away from Home: The World of Camper Vans and Motorhomes*). Nor would you have seen any of them in the famous New York World's Fair of 1939–40, where the RV was famously neglected. If you want to see them, take a hike through the woods of the upper Midwest and northern New England. They're still there. These rusted-out hulks sit in mute testament to the ancient urge to go into the woods, drink some mead, shoot at an animal, and not sleep on the ground. Now vegetable life grows up from the ground, curling around the wheels, fenders, engines, bunks, tables, and cupboards of men who are sleeping deep under the ground.

These two traditions of "getting away" and "being at home" came together when, in 1953, Ray Frank, a trailer maker north of Detroit, decided to try to combine the man cave with something his wife would also like. His plan was to take a truck chassis and essentially put all the stuff from inside his trailer on top of it. Like many others who were circling the self-propelled house car, he was essentially going to motorize his version of the house. When he didn't know what to call it, his wife suggested the term *motorhome*. His early cohorts often had better names than products: the Victour coach, the Graf Zipalong, the Howard Safari, the Sani-Cruiser, the Live-N-Roam Cruiser, the Ultra, the Traveliner, but Frank had the breakthrough idea.

While his competitors had to build everything anew for each RV, he went downstate to Dodge to buy the frames, lots of them. He also asked for a little start-up money and a little expertise. Dodge Motors had never dealt with an individual who wanted to buy 100 skeleton units, so they sent him to one of their dealers to cut the deal. The company was curious about what he was up to and so provided him with some

Figure 2.12: Frank/Dodge motorhome before (late 1950s) and after (1963) application of the French curve (Al Hesselbart collection at the RV/MH Hall of Fame and Museum and Dodge ad).

engineering advice. In 1960, he made six Frank Motorhomes; the next year he made 180. Wisely, he changed the name to Dodge Motorhomes, and wisely, Dodge didn't object. In fact, they were thrilled.

These early units were boxy, just what you'd expect from someone whose expertise was in making trailers and hunting deer. After all, he was just putting his trailer on top of these truck frames out behind his barn. In a bit of RV-apocrypha, Ray had a highschool–aged son, Ron, who was taking classes in mechanical engineering. Ron had a French curve drafting tool, and supposedly he put the curved template on all the right angles of his dad's motor home and turned what looked like a toolbox into a breadloaf. As Glenn Curtiss had done with the Aerocar, he streamlined it.

His dad adopted this new curvaceous look using fiberglass forms fitted over a steel frame, and the Dodge Motorhome zoomed into pop-cult, powered by a Chrysler 318 "polysphere" engine. Everything about this rig said *moderne*. It was as if the Conestoga had been mated with a Super Chief locomotive and then decorated by Betty Crocker. The rigs could be bought at car dealers in 21- and 27-foot models. By the late 1960s, the Dodge Motorhome outnumbered all other self-propelled RVs combined. Frank and his son sold out to a local conglomerate named Travco, which added things like air conditioners, generators, and even a composting toilet with a wondrous name, the Destroilet. But, at the heart of it all, the Franks' genius remained: They had put the deer camp on wheels *and* made it attractive to women.

When, in 2004, *Playboy* magazine was searching for the most impor-tant fifty "inventions that changed the world," they included the Franks' motorhome. As well they should have because here indeed is the playboy mansion for the man who reads *Playboy* in the deer camp. Let Hugh Hefner have his gothic stone pile in Chicago and his black 747 Boeing; loyal readers of the magazine can have this nifty getaway. So the Frank Motorhome joined *Playboy*'s other *vade meca* for men like the Big Mac, Pampers, and breast augmentation for women.

The other car companies were not asleep at the ignition. They, too, could see what was happening. Just as the cart and engine had been compressed into the automobile, now auto and house were being compressed into the self-propelled mobile home. So this was what the station wagon would finally become—the motorhome. The *moho* was going to be the next big thing from Detroit.

The car makers were not alone: Bus companies were eager to jump on this bandwagon. Blue Bird of Ft. Valley, Georgia, built what would become the Wanderlodge, which made it onto the pages of 1964 *House Beautiful*. Heavy equipment makers like Clark Company tried out their Cortez line of RVs, which was rhapsodized over by reporter Kathleen Mudge in numerous magazine articles. Plus every week on the *CBS Evening News*, there was Charles Kuralt puttering around the county in a monster RV. Even Hertz and Avis started to rent big rigs just like they were cars.

The Big Three had the edge. After all, not only did they have all the hardware and the metal-bending and assembly expertise, they had the dealer network already in place. Plus, they had the clout to advertise it. So Ford, which had already seen the potential market for auto camping with the station wagon, started producing the Condor, an inauspicious name as its namesake would soon appear on the endangered species list.

Figure 2.13: GMC motorhome 1973–78 (RV/MH Hall of Fame and Museum)

General Motors, which had introduced some mutations of their Chevy truck line, decided the business was going to be so huge that they would completely engineer a rig from the ground up.

GM was blessed as they entered the fray. Not only were gas prices low and the interstate system exploding, but the company had come to own the concept of countrywide travel—"See America First" had become "See the USA in your Chevrolet." With an RV in its product line, GM would have a stable of cars that led inexorably up from Chevy to Caddy and then jump the tracks to the ultimate: living in your GM vehicle. The term—let alone the concept—*gas guzzler* was still unimaginable.

The highlight of Detroit's entry into the RV market was the GMC Motorhome. It came at a time—the 1970s—when American automobiles were at their zenith and nobody was having a better time than GM. When they called this thing the GMC Motorhome, the bean counters knew they were at the end of the rainbow. To update the famous misquote, What's good for GM is not just good for America; it is America. The object still exudes the confidence of an industry that could put anything on wheels, including your split-level house.

First, of course, the object itself was an eyeful. It was as if Ron Frank had given his French curve a French curve. The GMC Motorhome still turns heads: Its form is nearly perfect. It's the self-propelled Airstream trailer with wraparound windows. The front-wheel drive (the same drivetrain as the famous Tornado) makes the interior space easy to enter. Since there's no driveshaft to cover, it's all one floor. The rear suspension is like a bus, making the ride as comfy as a sofa. Even the dual rear wheels had special tires for even better ride and control. Much of the exterior used the same molded fiberglass as the Chevrolet Corvette.

The GMC Motorhome said good-bye to the man cave and howdy to unabashed public display. This was an object dedicated to being looked at, looked in, looked around, and looked from. Looking out from the swiveling driver's seat through the curved windshield is like seeing the world in VistaVision. The company made it in 23-foot and 26-foot models—short for a motorhome but just right for someone a bit intimidated by driving something really big. The size was kept compact because there were no permanent sleeping areas. Everything popped out, like Russian nesting dolls. The beds were converted from seating areas, tables folded down from walls, passenger seats became divans.

The panjandrums in Detroit thought of everything. For instance, to provide for hot water while traveling, marine water heaters were used, which incorporated engine heat. Power for the refrigerator was provided by a standard automobile wet cell made into a house battery so it could be used for overnight use without recharging. Body panels could easily be removed and replaced, and, best yet, GMAC would do all the financing. Even Barbie, of Ken & Barbie, had one.

Then lightning struck! Overnight the oil embargo and energy crises of the 1970s started making Detroit dreams a nightmare. Goodbye CinemaScope, hello slide projector. To economize, the company dropped the 455 cubic inch engine for the 403. Whoops, too late. The GMC Motorhome, born of such optimism, died a melancholy death in November 1977, gasping for gas.

The plug was pulled with little fanfare. After all, the motorhome was never a high-volume vehicle, and it was rumored never to have been profitable. Besides, another love affair was heating up, one that would prove to be more passionate: the pickup truck. GM simply switched the assembly lines to the production of light trucks, relieved, no doubt, that they could produce about one hundred light trucks for every motorhome. GM had poured oodles of money and talent into its RV, but nothing relieves regret like gushing profits.

Although only thirteen thousand motorhomes were made, about eight to nine thousand are still on the road. No Edsel owner is more loyal. The company may have cast them aside, but a cottage industry now exists to supply the faithful with parts and service. Of all the owner groups, the GMC Motorhome International is the most long-suffering and patient. They are also the largest vintage group in the Family Motor Coach Association. *Die Hard* is not only a battery and a movie franchise, it's a GMC Motorhome owner.

Detroit's love affair with the motorhome was platonic. There was no second generation. To the sales guys, the RV customer was usually deep-pocketed and eager. But to the car guys, the RV was not really what

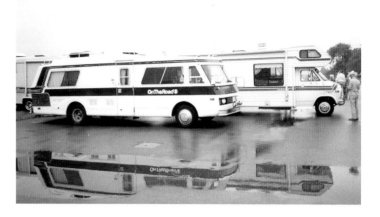

Figure 2.14: Kuralt's RV, 1994 (Al Hesselbart collection at RV/MH Hall of Fame and Museum).

they wanted to make. Where's the sex appeal in a house on wheels? No one in the RV world cared about o–60; no one cared about torque and thrust; campers didn't rhapsodize over pistons, they wanted couches; there was no planned obsolescence in an object with replaceable panels, no tail fins. The concern of the GMC Motorhome buyer was for more Naugahyde, the nifty on-board generator, the atrium entryway, and the fact that they might tow a *small* car, maybe one from Japan.

Although Detroit forsook the RV, the middle-aged male did not. The escape vehicle still had miles left on it. Symptomatic of this abiding interest was that long after Detroit had pulled the plug, Charles Kuralt was still puttering across the TV screen. Starting in 1967 he captured the romance of life on the road, wearing out a Travco, two Cortezes, a Revcon, and an FMC. He covered more than a million miles over twenty-five years. Note that they were from small Midwestern specialty shops. Don't note that almost every night on the road he and the CBS crew slept in motels.

Even before the Big Three left the scene, the successful builders of these things were often small and nimble producers who bought the frames, engines, and drivetrains from Detroit and then assembled them elsewhere. Many of these companies ended up in northern Indiana around Elkhart. Why? Two reasons: The state of Michigan taxed all vehicles made inside its borders, but it did not tax the component parts. So a company that was going to be in the RV business and was going to take advantage of proximity to assembly materials, as well as to the know-how of production, would simply set up shop just over the border.

And, second, the real distinguishing selling point of RVs has always been the interior. An RV cliché: The man *wants*, the woman *buys*. And the craftsmanship of the cabinets and kitchen space is crucial. The Mennonites had, and still have, a passion for fine woodwork, and they still do much of the interior fabrication. So should you ever wonder how Elkhart, Indiana, became the headquarters of all things RV, just look at a map of Mennonite communities.

Of these early satellite assemblers, none has been more important than the eponymic Winnebago. It was an incredibly nimble company that could quickly innovate, just like the Elkhart colleagues. But it paid

Figure 2.15: Winnebago D-22, 1967 (RV/MH Hall of Fame and Museum).

attention not to Detroit but to Tokyo, where a new kind of production process was unfolding—just-in-time delivery of parts that were soon often made by the company itself.

The genius behind Winnebago was John Hansen, a civic-minded undertaker in Forest City, Iowa, who also sold cars and tractors. He cared deeply for his neighbors. In the early 1950s he undertook a buy-out of a local trailer fabricator to help save jobs. Over time he moved production from trailers to RVs. Like Henry Ford, he was forever tinkering with both manufacturing and marketing. By the late 1960s, Hansen was savvy enough to do two things that neither the big boys nor the small boys were willing to do. First, he covered the skeleton of his rigs with Thermo-Panels, sidewalls that were interchangeable and cheap. And second, by using assembly-line techniques, he was able to sell his rigs for about half the competition's price.

What Detroit wrought, Hansen mastered: mass production. He even named his original models—the Winnebago D-19 and D-22—after the assembly line. Sales of these distinctive "Eyebrow" Winnebagos (so called because they have a sleeping bunk over the split-front windshield) allowed him to control about 70 percent of the market by 1961. A decade later the corporate name, like Kleenex or Scotch tape, had become generic: Winnebago = RV.

Hansen knew that if the house on wheels was essentially just a house on wheels, sooner or later price would become central. Once a product becomes truly interchangeable, low price, not quality, wins. The D-22 became the Model T became Levittown. With dogged persistence, Hansen gradually integrated all his components. He made not just all his own Thermo-Panels, but all his carpets, cabinets, and even mattresses. He was soon producing "America's first family of motor homes," five models from 16 to 27 feet long that sold for as little as $5,000 and upward of $25,000. Additionally, just as the Japanese had different nameplates inside the same company (Acura is made by Honda; Infinity, by Nissan; Lexus, by Toyota), he started a parallel brand inside Winnebago—Itasca—which essentially made the same rigs with different price points.

If you were going to buy a RV in 1970 you would at least have to look at Winnebago/Itasca, and, if you were price sensitive, you would have to consider them seriously. In that year, Winnebago claimed that its D-22 model outsold—by itself—the entire production of any other brand of motorhome. By November 1970, a writer in *Trailer Life* quipped, "If you fall down in a motorhome park, chances are you'll be hit by a Winnebago."

Although Winnebago's glory days have now passed (there is a handful of large suppliers in various conditions of financial health), the general format of the industry has been settled. At the top of the RV taxonomy are big rigs called Class As, divided into *pushers* and *pullers*, depending on what engine is used—gasoline or diesel. Smaller and less expensive are the so-called Class Bs, van conversions that represent the time-worn compromise between soccer mom's bus and dad's idea of a getaway camper. In a sense, the modern SUV is part of this phylum. And then there are Class C motorhomes, which are scaled-down Class As. These are essentially boxes on wheels with an in-house outhouse.

More than a vehicle, the RV, in all its paradoxical glory, is a most innovative and uniquely American contribution to the history of housing. It belongs with the skyscraper and the ranch house. As the Big Three automakers learned, mass-producing these things was a risky business. Every fifteen years or so, like clockwork, the bottom falls out. True, the halcyon days may be over. But as long as the components are in place (the male yearning for escape, the female willingness to set up housekeeping in a new nest, the bankers' eagerness to provide financing, and the tax man's deduction for interest paid on a second home), these "unfixed abodes" will continue to be built and continue to reflect what it means to be *at home on the road.*

Chapter Three

WHEEL ESCAPE Consumption Communities on the Road

Although it looks as if the RVer is *heading out* (and indeed the advertising touts this from the early "We All Have a Little Gypsy Blood" to a current "Gone RVing" and "Find Your Away"), in truth, he's often just turning around and settling down. Following the lead of Thoreau, who spent mornings musing on the solitary life and afternoons mooching on friends, RVers often become more social after announcing their independence. More often than not, once they get free of all their old stuff, they become enthralled to new stuff.

Do you ever wonder where all those rigs are going as they either zoom past you on the interstate or hold you up at a stoplight? Often their destination is a meeting of people just like themselves. If you follow them after they pull out to explore a new world, you may soon see them pull into a highly predictable world, rather like their old one. Not only are some of these roadside worlds worth a second look, but they're also part of a fascinating subculture that says much about modern life. In the next two chapters I'm going to explore some of these communities, such as Lazydays RV Park in Tampa, the largest RV dealership in the world; the generic RV park and some variations created by an organization called Escapees; an RV flash-city in Arizona called Quartzsite; and a RV dump-city across the border in California called the Slabs.

I'm going to take seriously a conjecture put forward a generation ago by Buckminster Fuller and now echoed by climatologists and futurologists that the nomadic life may well become the life of the future. We may end up in cities on wheels that move around as food and climate dictate. The peripatetic life may well become a survival pattern. Social scientists even have a name for these new communities, *unsettlements*, and a new name for their inhabitants, *leisure nomads*.

INGROUPS FOR OUTLIERS

First, the obvious: Many RVers—I daresay most—are members of *consumption communities*. They don't think of themselves this way, and certainly this is not what we usually think of as *community*, but it is. In many ways an RV *affiliation group* is both more modern and more ancient than what most of us think of as community. Many RVers are like modern Bedouins, on the move together. They are loosely joined when they travel but in tight when they are camped. Although there has been much recent hand-wringing about the loss of stable community (think Robert Putnam's *Bowling Alone*, Eric Klinenberg's *Going Solo*, or Sherry Turkel's *Alone Together*), often groups are simply being spun around new centers. No longer are religion, education, family history, or job the primary magnets for affiliation; more often it is some material object, some brand, or even some piece of hardware.

I first became aware of this at a urinal in a washroom at a KOA campground in Van Horn, New Mexico, when a guy about my age came in and immediately began describing his afternoon dealing with the base plate on his busted Blue Ox tow bar. I was a little put off. We'd never met before. But he behaved as if I knew exactly what he was talking about and he was trusting me not for advice but for understanding. It was as if I was in the teachers' lounge back at work and a colleague started talking about some departmental problem. He was convinced I could sympathize with him even though we'd never seen each other before. I wanted privacy, but I was also aware that he and I were part of some fraternity. That's why he felt he could talk to me while I was taking a pee.

I was away from home. I too was on the road in a machine I didn't fully understand. I wanted to help him. I felt anxious, like a teenager. Kids are sensitive to such simple things as their choice of blue jeans or baseball caps. Their parents are no different. Their dads may come together over sports teams or affiliation with certain bottlers of beer. He said he saw that I also had a Winnebago. It was out front. I'd never thought of this RV as what marketers call a *badge good*, but I was learning different. Think of the behavior of Apple computer owners. They talk to each other like family, even taking pleasure in the pains of their Microsoft cousins. Think of the relationship between Hells Angels and Harley Davidson. In the

Figure 3.1: Yearly Grand National Rally in Forest City, Iowa (Winnebago Corp, 2010/2012).

modern world we often find community in branded objects, community in consumption, social bonds in commercial brands.

RV owners are no different. Large national groups exist, like the Good Sam Club or the Family Motor Coach Association, that are essentially umbrella organizations, like AARP or AAA. They don't generate much affinity beyond what comes with putting decals on different objects. More intense, though, are the RV ownership groups. Almost every brand of RV has an affinity group that not only has an active website and support network, but also holds rallies throughout the year. These rallies are literal consumption communities, complete with ranks and orders. You can't get into the group without buying the product. Savvy manufacturers don't just deny membership to those who have never owned their product; they make it known that if you ever switch brands, you're out of the group. It's like they have seen the movie *Mean Girls* too many times. The affiliation process is powerful because it benefits both manufacturer and consumer. For people who have broken bonds by literally taking off from an old life, these new bonds are especially powerful.

A few years ago I attended a summertime rally of the Newmar Kountry Klub in Essex Junction, Vermont, and the centrifugal forces became clear. Newmar is owned by Mennonites in Indiana and makes top-of-the-line motorhomes. The club is made up of both owners of rigs and the company owners. I had a long conversation with a couple who were living in a large Newmar coach. The man said he really wanted to buy another brand, but his wife was so upset that she would have to say good-bye to her old friends that he re-upped and bought another. The company spends almost as much time coddling members as it does making the object. The company, he confided in me, even helped pay for the rally.

Then I had a pleasant conversation with Mahlon Miller, the bishop of the Mennonite group that owns the company. He's also the CEO of Newmar. He is a very smart engineer who invented the apparatus that allows the slide-out to operate. He is a profoundly religious man. He didn't patent the invention because it belonged to God. We sat outside his coach, a huge monster of a rig, a 2012 King Aire LE Diesel Pusher. All outfitted, it costs more than a million. He was wearing suspenders and had one of those little half-beards on his cherubic face. I mentioned how similar the consumers of the product were to the religious group that made it: They were both passionate about a thing. He said, yes, both groups cared deeply about each other and about the thing.

I couldn't get it out of my head that that the people who do the hand labor were all men who wore these beards, sometimes came to work in horse-drawn carriages, and don't care much for all the electronic stuff inside the RV. But they shared with the consumers a deep sense of pride of affiliation. When the Kountry Klub holds a rally, Bishop Miller and many of the Mennonite workers get in the company RVs and travel there. Sometimes they hire professional drivers because they don't want to operate certain kinds of machines. They do this to help their consumers with troubles they may be having with the motorhomes. The workers, the bishop told me, take it personally.

Months later I spent a day at their manufacturing plant in Nappanee, Indiana. The bishop/CEO has gotten special dispensation from the denomination for these workers to use air-driven power tools. But there is no assembly line, which presumably would be too mechanical. So the massive rigs are pushed around on jets of compressed air. Various groups of workers do such things as install the stainless-steel appliances, the granite countertops, the hardwood floors, the flat-screen TVs, and the psychedelic paint job. No one says a word.

Often, after buying a Newmar product, people come to visit this manufacturing plant. Or they go there to get their rig serviced. It's like a pilgrimage. At the plant you notice there are two parking lots, two lounges, and two tours, one for owners, the other for visitors. When the company is working on your rig, it's not called by the brand name, such as the Dutch Star or the Mountain Aire. It's called by your surname.

This understanding of the central irony—that people who are heading out really want company—was not the initial brainstorm of Mahlon Miller; it was the insight of Wally Byam, producer of the Airstream trailers and serious student of human nature. In the 1930s, he organized the first Wally Byam Caravan Club to replace what supposedly was being left behind—community. The bold numbers painted across the back of an Airstream refer to club membership. Wally had number 1.

So by virtue of the brand of RV I own, I am a member of the Skinny Winnie club, have a website to which I can go to chat or ask questions, and can attend a handful of rallies restricted to those who own the same object. I go to these rallies. I'm embarrassed that they are such fun. And then there are dedicated listservs for people traveling to the same area in the same rigs. The one for Alaska fills up my in-box all summer and fall. I've been there; it's fun to explore it again vicariously. It's like I'm back in the KOA restroom and someone comes in with a question—only this time I might know what to say.

Pick any brand of RV and there is a members-only community. So big motorhomes like Marathon have a group called *Prides*, RV owners of the unfortunately named Bounder have *Bounders of America* and *Bounders United*, and so on down the line. The affiliation is intense, far more than for any other object for adults that I've seen in the American marketplace, short of a Harley. Birds of a feather do indeed flock together. And these birds often fly really close. As Bishop Miller inadvertently showed me, it's close to religious.

A few years ago in Fairbanks, Alaska, I stayed at the Riverview RV Park. Most of the clientele was fairly ordinary, like me. But about a quarter of the park was filled with Beavers, a RV brand now out of business, made by a top-of-the line company called Monaco, now part of the truck company Navistar. In its heyday, the Beaver was the envy of all other Class A owners. You can see this mild hauteur in the names of Beaver models: Marquis, Patriot Thunder, Contessa, Monterey.

Here the Beaver owners were, about twenty-five of them, halfway through a seventy-five-day trip through Alaska. Most were *full-timers* from the Midwest, retired from either the armed forces (hence, I think, Patriot Thunder) or small businesses. Some had been farmers, some were from the professions. They all agreed that it was a sad day when the company had gone bust during the recession. They had been left high and dry. But they had each other.

Many of the owners displayed little toy beavers on their dashes and had beaver flags that they flew when parked to announce their affiliation. I admit my first thought when I saw their yard art of fluttering flags of earnest beavers was that I had happened on the International Order of Friendly Sons of the Raccoons, the fraternity attended by Jackie Gleason and Art Carney on *The Honeymooners*. It was hard not to laugh out loud.

The Beaver owners were all about my age, mostly retired, and wore impressive name badges that looked as if they were designed for the French Foreign Legion or a Masonic Lodge. Yet they all seemed to know each other. The name tags displayed their ranks, like Commander, North Dakota Unit. They were all—well, almost all—eager to show off their coaches. Now, remember, these rigs are no longer being built. The Beaverites are on an island floating away from the mainland. And so, in a way, they have to lash up together if only because when something breaks, they can help each other get it fixed. In fact, one member of the group had really broken down and was still in Tok, Alaska, waiting for a part. Fellow Beavers were all in cell phone contact, concerned about his welfare.

A hunk of iron and plastic is keeping them organized. Although they don't mention this as important, the Beavers all know exactly what model each member owns, i.e., Marquis, Patriot Thunder, Contessa, Monterey. They know this hierarchy because it provides them place. When I asked a few Monterey owners if they wanted a Marquis, they said no, they really didn't. They were happy where they were, but they all knew who owned the top-of-the-line model and were eager for me to have a look at that rig.

In fact, they arranged it. The most elegant Marquis (which in palmier days retailed for about $800,000) was owned by a retired owner of beauty salons from one of the Dakotas. The inside was pretty fancy, with mirrors on the ceiling and a giant drop-down television set. In fact, it looked like it was on loan from a Las Vegas casino. When I told the owners what I was driving, they smiled. They owned a View too. They used their View for weekends. This was not said down the nose, but they were not members of the Skinny-Winnies. In no way were any of the Beaver owners snobby about their consumption. They were proud and not the least embarrassed about hanging out all their club paraphernalia and wearing those grandiose nametags.

I'm not the only one to have noticed this intense community among free spirits and to have been slightly perplexed by it. Doreen Orion, a psychiatrist in Boulder, Colorado, has also encountered it. At the beginning of the twenty-first century, her husband, also a psychiatrist, decided he wanted to hit the road. He bought a big, expensive bus conversion from Vanture, which specializes in one-of-a-kind buses. In her *Queen of the Road: The True Tale of 47 States, 22,000 Miles, 200 Shoes, 1 Poodle, a Husband and a Bus with a Will of Its Own* (2008), she tells what it's like to go from being office-bound to bus-bound for a year. She was also struck by the "yard art" that seems omnipresent in RV settlements and was initially a little put off by it:

> Throughout our travels thus far, we'd scoffed at rigs, RVs and buses alike, for sporting various kitsch, from oh-too-cutesy stuffed animals clinging to the ladder in the back, to lawn gnomes perched precariously on the steps, to custom wooden signs in the windshield announcing the owner's name and hometown, usually with some little logo signifying a favorite pastime, like a fishing pole, golf club, or bowling pin. Once, in a weak moment, undoubtedly after some disaster that reinforced how alone and vulnerable I felt, I made the mistake of wondering aloud if, as a token of our solidarity with other motor-homers, we should get one, too. But Tim

[her husband] said no, since depicting my favorite pastimes would entail a logo of a bed and a credit card and result in our imminent arrest for solicitation.

We had promised ourselves, therefore, that we would never stoop to such tacky displays, but then . . . in the midst of all the good cheer, even recalling our many catastrophes, we could not help but appreciate everything the bus thing had given us. We were at the one-third mark in our year, and although the time we had left seemed to stretch endlessly before us, we also understood that was not really an accurate perception. The thought of resuming our former lives in eight months' time saddened us. So, then and there, we made a vow to us and to our bus: The next time we stayed in our rig for Christmas, we'd mend our ways with our own bus bling. And more, we'd remember these days in our mobile home and with each other, and try to keep the spirit of the bus thing alive, even when stationary. We realized that despite our prejudices due to our educations, our professions, and yes, even our wardrobes, we truly were RV people—and proud of it. [163–65]

Over the year, Doreen comes to love the footloose life, especially when it ties up. What is unique about the RV community is that most of the participants have asked for unification of some sort, and they asked for it in the name of, ironically, separation. These people share a love of escape, a passion for the nomadic, a flair for the gypsy life. That's why the wheels are on their houses. Their sense of community is most obvious around the object itself but also generated around their interests in *taking off* and *tying down*.

I've never seen such clubby people elsewhere. So, for instance, in my particular subset there are Winnebago-Itasca Travelers (WIT) clubs known as the 365 Club (for six-month to full-time RVers), with subsidiary clubs like the NETWIT club (computer users), MILWIT (military), WIT LEO (retired or active law enforcement officers), WIT Singers, WIT Alleycats (bowlers), and WIT Duffers (golfers). There are also scores of local clubs with names like Iowa Cornbelt Campers,

Vegas Rollers, and Inland Empire Explorers that go off weekend camping together. There is a National African American RVers Association and a club known as Yehudim Al Galgalim (Jews on Wheels).

There are many groups for single owners (Loners on Wheels, Retired Singles, RVing Women), as well as groups for home-schooling families (Families on the Road). Rainbow RV is the largest gay and lesbian RV and tent camping membership club in North America with some seven thousand members and a string of RV parks well worth visiting. They do not discriminate against heteros. There are groups for handicapped (Handicapped Travel Club), collectors of vintage Wanderlodges (Vintage Birds), devotees of rigs from the 1930s (a revival of the Tin Can Tourists), and, well, you get the point: These people get it both ways, community for people who claim not to want it.

Later on I'll have a look at the *Escapees Club*, which provides the legal apparatus and living space around the country for more than a hundred thousand of these full-timers. It even offers an assisted-living site with a nursing home in Livingston, Texas. You park your rig, and a nurse comes in daily to make sure you are taking your medicine. Something a bit less comprehensive and more mixed-in with selling these objects is to be found outside of Tampa, Florida. If there is a home base for this paradoxical RV culture, it is here: the Lazydays RV Campground on Lazydays Boulevard. Their motto tells the story: "If you love RV-ing, this is home."

LAZYDAYS: HOME FOR PEOPLE LEAVING HOME

Ask a serious RV-er about Lazydays and chances are you'll get an earful. True, the business of Lazydays is selling these things, and, true, it sells more of them than anywhere else in the world—about 6,500 units a year—but what makes it noteworthy is that the campground has Mecca status. Lazydays is visited by more than three hundred thousand people a year. You go here if you believe, or if you want to believe. That it's near Disney's Magic Kingdom is no coincidence.

Here's what you find on its 124 acres: a 300-space RV lot for campers; a Hampton Inn and Suites for those spending the night waiting for their rig to be serviced (those who are not motel-willing can also stay in their RV right in the service bay); its own Camping World outlet selling accessories for the "lifestyle" that was the highest-grossing store per square foot in the entire franchise; and their own Flying J service station to fill the RVs full of fuel. Lazydays even has its own side of an interstate exit: number 10 on Interstate 4. Lazydays also has a western branch outside Tucson.

The place in Tampa is so huge that it provides a fleet of 170 golf carts to help you get around. Interestingly, all the for-sale rigs are open so you can just stroll around peering in hundreds of units without feeling the warm breath of a salesman on your neck. They also serve 250,000 complimentary meals a year. That's right, free food. All you do is get in line, and you can have breakfast or lunch on the house. There are eighty-five *transfer sites* where you drive your old rig in head-first and then they drive your new *coach* (as they invariably call it) in butt-first beside it so you can transfer your stuff from one wheeled cabin to the other. Under the awning of your new and old rigs, you effortlessly change your life. Simple as that.

When you read about the most popular destinations in and around central Florida (Disney World, Busch Gardens, SeaWorld. Universal Studios . . .), you'll find Lazydays on the list. People don't go there just to buy. They go to *feel* something. Not to put too fine a point on it, but it's clear the customers at Lazydays want to feel family, a family free of soggy diapers and snotty noses. They don't come here with a family. They come just as their family is starting to ebb away. They come to find new family.

This place has been carefully crafted to reflect and support the ideals of *heading out*. It's all about new life. The customers at Lazydays look a little anxious, as well they should. After all, many are here because they either want to change rigs (homes) or have a rig (home) repaired. Or just to check out the possibilities for a different home and a different life.

The allure of an ideal, albeit imagined, family is seen as you drive up through the bosky dell to the main house. The *home base of RV life*, as they call it, is patterned on George Washington's Mount Vernon, complete with pillars done in gold paint. As you pass through the main doors, a greeter meets you, just like in church or at Walmart. Past the greeter on your right is an entire wall of golden plaques called the Wall of Honor. At first sight, you might think that these are awards Lazydays has received from its suppliers, from the RV industry, or maybe from the local Chamber of Commerce. But look again.

The wall, framed in mahogany, is made up of small golden nameplates. Only about half of them carry a name. The rest are blank. Over the top is inscribed *Family and Friends*. It's here, at the wall, that I meet David Castaneda, who was going to give me the Cook's tour. His business card said: Chief Learning Officer/Vice President/Director/Manager of Corporate Education at Lazydays RV Center, Inc.

No matter what his card says, David is a salesman, a very friendly and sincere guy in his forties, and he starts the tour by asking me to guess what the names represent. I can't do it. It doesn't have to do with service to the country—there are no military titles. And it doesn't have to do with some commercial connection to the organization. No, he says, it has to do with family and what makes a family. After I confess that I still can't figure it out, he explains.

You get your name on a plate on the wall by getting a friend to come to Lazydays and buy a rig. If you get four people to buy, you get a bigger plate, a still larger one for seven people, and if you get ten sales, you become a lifetime member. Your name never disappears. You've become more than a friend; you've become family, and you stay on the wall forever.

Weird shades of the Vietnam Veterans Memorial Wall in Washington, D.C., I think, but what I say is that this seems a bit like Amway or something cooked up by Bernie Madoff. Dave returns a shocked *no*. There is no reward for these referrals, no future discount, just the satisfaction of moving deeper into the bosom of family. So if it's not like a Ponzi scheme, I suggest, maybe it's like a university or a hospital where you find a "memorial opportunity" by contributing money? You get naming rights. Yes, David says, that's closer. But you find your place not by contributing money but by building the family. Remember, he says, only a third of the people coming through the front door have walked in off the street. They're the ones who need to be sold. Two thirds are already members of the family. They have already bought. They just haven't picked up the new life (and put down the deposit).

How could I not be skeptical? But David was absolutely sincere. Yes, these people want the object, the recreational vehicle, but they come here, as opposed to other places where they'll get a better price, because they want what they have lost, namely, a sense of community, of belonging, family. The man who first put all this together in the 1970s was H. G. Wallace, along with his two sons, Don and Ron. Ron died tragically, and Don really took over. Ron's death crushed the family, said David, yet it proved important. H. G. was depressed. The business kept the family together. That's when H. G. realized what it was that he was truly selling. He became a student of Wally Byam.

H. G. and Don already knew they had a problem selling this product. Would people come to Florida to buy a home away from home? Wouldn't they rather trust their local dealer? Plus, just as General Motors was selling the same kind of cars as Ford and Chrysler, the Wallaces were selling the same kind of RVs as their competitors. Lazydays' Class A RVs were just the same as their competitors'. Their Bounders and Intruders were the same. So H. G. decided to quit competing on the basis of price and to start selling the experience. And the experience the product offered was a way to get away from and still be with family.

And how did he learn this? David asks rhetorically. From going next door to Disney World. What the Wallaces saw was essentially a series of carnival rides configured to represent a family narrative. Walt Disney told different stories (Peter Pan, Donald Duck, Mickey Mouse, Chip 'n Dale, Lil Bad Wolf, Scamp, Bucky Bug, Grandma Duck, Brer Rabbit, Winnie the Pooh et al.) inside the overarching myths of Main Street, Adventureland, Frontierland, Fantasyland, and Mickey's Toontown. He then inserted the appropriate county-fair ride.

The Wallaces looked at the Disney MO and saw their future: they had to create RV Land. And that is exactly what Lazydays does. The key to their inclusive operation is the sense of exclusivity it imparts. Living in an RV may make you an outlier, but here you belong, you're a member. You can really see this, Dave tells me, in the club structure at Lazydays. Club structure? I roll my eyes in disbelief. Yes, he says, as we get on the electric golf wagon to visit the two classes of clubs. There is the *Bay Club* for the owners of regular rigs like mine, rigs that were in for service or staying in the RV park. In Charles Murray's terms, this is *Fishtown*. And then there was the *Crown Club* for the big motorhomes, the really expensive ones. For Murray, this is *Belmont*. But over in the parking lot the rigs are parked side by side regardless of size. The clubs are a distinction, not a difference.

The Bay Club was just what you'd expect: a swimming pool, a tennis court, and a free *USA Today* at your RV door each morning. But the Crown Club was nestled in the trees, in what was appropriately called *the hill section* that I had driven through to get to the Mount Vernon HQ. The Crown clubhouse looked from the outside like a warehouse with a frothy façade. Inside, however, it looked just like an airplane rewards club, as well it should because that is exactly what it mimics. As you pass through the front door, you are met by a greeter who swipes the membership card that allows you access to the downstairs facilities (pool, dining room) or to climb the stairs and enter the bar. Downstairs you get dinner free (for breakfast and lunch you have to go over and eat with the general public in the main building). At the bar the drinks are free—the first three drinks, David says, arching an eyebrow. The bar opens at 4:00 p.m.

Now, Dave tells me with a smile, the card that allows you access is programmed for three years if you bought a big rig new. It's good for only two years if you bought a used version. The club proved so successful that when it was time to re-up, the members used to come in and ask how much for another year. They liked getting together for dinner and drinks. Now the kicker, David smiles. You can't buy a membership. You gain access only by either purchasing another new rig or a used one. Then you get either the three- or two-year extension. And does this work? Do people really buy from Lazydays to get into the club? Dave tells me there are a number of customers who have extended their memberships until 2020 by buying and trading in so many vans. Remember, he says, these people know each other. Lazydays giveth, Lazydays withholdeth.

I'm overcome again at the irony that what initially links these people is the yearning for separation, for getting away from a known life. They want the cabin in the woods, the home on wheels. Roll on outta here.

Figure 3.2: Lazydays map with brown-roofed clubhouses on right side (Lazydays. "If you love RVing . . . this is home").

But then roll on back. They are self-proclaimed individualists who want to be left alone so they can get together.

I suggest that maybe the men like the trip out and the women like the trip back. But Dave, who is also chief of sales training, tells me the women want something else, and the salespeople (called *consultants*, he reminds me) need to know what gets the wives to go along with the program. It's not complicated. They too want to have back what they've lost. They want to regain control, control of a space they find themselves losing, control of the nurturance. They want to *tend to things*.

Dave explains with an example. Many RVs have awnings. The men don't seem to care about these public extenders of personal space. The awnings are often complicated to open and get stuck. But women like them. Women like to sit out in front of their RV as if they are on the porch of an old house in a remembered neighborhood. There is even a model with a massive extendable veranda that literally comes sliding out from the side. It's a 43-foot motorhome called simply Veranda. It may not have sold well, as the men pass it by, but the women are interested.

Where you really see this yearning to recoup a lost life, Dave says, is in the kitchen design. RV kitchens are carefully constructed to reproduce the former province of the wife. And this is why all innovations in the kitchen space are so cautiously introduced. Take the convection oven. Lazydays consultants noticed that women would balk at certain kitchen configurations, and the salespeople couldn't figure out why. Over time they learned that the women knew how to work the microwave but not the convection oven. "So," Dave says, "we added it to the curriculum." "The curriculum?" I snort. Dave pulls out the schedule for classes and there it is: convection cooking. And what are the other courses at Lazydays U? How to check your tires; how to trouble-shoot your air conditioner; how to hook up properly; how to operate your onboard generator; how to store your RV; and, especially popular, how to use the Internet to keep connected while moving. By far the most popular course is how to drive the damn thing. Women take the course (both classroom and road test) and then report to hubby what they've learned. No courses in how to negotiate for the lowest price on an RV, however.

David and I say our good-byes back at the Wall of Honor. We've been together most of the morning. While I must say I was a little put off at first by Dave's candor, which I misinterpreted as cynicism, I came to realize it wasn't. Lazydays wasn't hiding anything. They had just learned how to do it, how to extend the sensation of being in your comfy cabin at Walden Pond to a slightly larger context—a lakeside community of RVers. This place was a kind of assisted-living community for people who like the idea of independence and want a sense of being part of a family. In many ways, it was adolescence all over again. I'm a big boy; now read me a bedtime story. Lazydays tells the story.

After Dave left me, I wandered around the sales office—whoops!— *consultants'* office. It was hokey. The sales cubicles had pictures of American scenic vistas on the glass walls and were separated by make-believe street signs: Welcome Way, Good Times Blvd, Vacation Highway, Adventure Way, Destination Highway, Freedom Highway, Journey Highway, Discovery Lane, Scenic Court, Leisure Court, and the like.

Over the avenues of offices, this large sign: *We have an RV for everyone's dream . . . Describe yours.*

THE VAGABONDS: BELMONT HITS THE ROAD

As I saw in the Lazydays club structure and as we saw in the development of the actual RVs in the beginning of the last century, there is a pronounced split in this consumption community. There are hoity-toity consumers right alongside hoi polloi. Shiny deluxe models are parked next to rusted-out junkers. In marketing jargon, there are "high touch points" and "low touch points" both in the same market. Just as the Crown Club separates itself from the Bay Club, so did the Lamsteed Kampkar separate itself from the Model T tent expansion, and so too does the Prevost conversion bus separate itself from the converted school bus. But they all share the same road and the same campgrounds.

But that's not what is really special. What's singularly American is that in this consumption community the extremes coexist by desire, not necessity. In fact, extremes want to be together. That's one of the powerful attractions of RVing: The Haves recognize themselves in the Have-Nots and the Have-Nots (at least the ones I've talked to) often feel good about the Haves. After all, they are having the same experience at a fraction of the price.

Go into almost any RV park, whether it's private or part of the national parks, and you see an aspect of American Exceptionalism that commentators often claim is fast disappearing. No class warfare. Richie Rich is parked next to Hobo Hank. Whatever else it is, this is a culture where people can buy different versions of the same product and essentially share the same experience. They do not just coexist—they intermingle. If there's separation, it's based on mutual agreement, not on net worth, school tie, or place in the pew. The RV experience is one of the few melting-pot events that has not evaporated over time.

You can really see this in the two RV communities that moved around in the early twentieth century: the rich Vagabonds and the ratty Tin Can Tourists. For the first time, Belmont and Fishtown went car camping. The so-called Vagabonds were self-consciously aping the behavior of the English aristocracy, who went out in their gypsy wagons to mingle with nature and the common folk. Only these American make-believe nomads tricked out their gypsy wagons with rubber tires, internal combustion engines, and a retinue of spare parts and retainers. Meanwhile, the Tin Can Tourists were traveling on many of the same roads, not to revel in weekend frolic but to migrate out of the cold down to the sunny South. And the Canners were motoring together not from a desire to have their pictures taken but because they needed each other for support. No matter, both groups car-camped through the 1920s, enjoying a new kind of recreational lifestyle—the bonhomie of living on wheels, the pleasures of home away from home. Make of this what you will, both groups came primarily out of the American Midwest.

No one knows exactly who coined the term *Vagabonds* or *The Four Vagabonds*, but the idea of camping jaunts for the rich and famous seems to have originated in the trips into the Everglades made by Henry Ford and Thomas Edison. They spent winters together in Ft. Myers, Florida, building Newport "cottages" next to each other, and puttered around together in Ford products sampling Edison's inventions. In 1915 they were both on the West Coast, and this time they added Harvey Firestone, who supplied tires to Ford. Ford suggested making a yearly event of these "gypsy jaunts," and all agreed. And they decided to include John Burroughs, the naturalist. It was an inspired choice. That he didn't fit the mold of the captains of industry was just the point: He was along for a change in subject matter. And so Ford later included visits by the likes of Professor R. J. De Loach, an expert in botany, as well as the noted naturalist Luther Burbank. *Going camping* meant appreciating nature, not talking shop, and these scholars added a bit of self-improvement.

Ford was clearly the ringleader, and he was acutely aware of his hard-charging reputation and his need to ameliorate it. He wanted to go into politics, and these trips were a kind of early barnstorming and image burnishing. Not by happenstance did he invite President Harding, then very popular, to join the party. The president did, along with a retinue of forty. Point made: Ford was a confidant of the powerful, a man who could be trusted, a man you could buy a car from and . . . vote for.

The trips, and there were about six of them, were all public, very public. Ford saw to that by activating his PR staff. Although Firestone was shy and Edison was deaf, Ford knew that showing these elderly men (he himself was in his fifties) in the company of a well-known lover of nature was just what was needed to show the softer side of the automobile industry. The "boys" were concerned about the finer things. And indeed they were. Often they discussed high-cult literature and even parsed poems in the evening around a campfire. But when it was time to hit the hay, they didn't sleep on the ground. They headed for their cots inside screened tents lit by electric lights powered by Edison's portable generators.

Ford, his later gaffes with the unions notwithstanding, was a master of image building. He was well aware of the Chautauqua movement in which adult education was combined with getting outdoors. In a time in which many Americans worked a six-day week, laboring ten or more hours each day (thanks in no small part to his demands), here was a way to uplift culture, sell product, and reposition himself as a man of the people. To tenement dwellers who believed that the only people who camped in tents were either soldiers or those suffering hard times, auto camping could be connected to self-improvement. Going *outdoors* was a necessary tonic, a return to roots, an exercise in the remembered past. And that it was being done in a machine made by Ford—well, that irony was not foregrounded.

So in three-piece suits, subdued ties, and their ever-present starched collars, the Vagabonds motored into such places as the Great Smokies, the Maryland watershed, the Vermont mountains and across to New Hampshire, the West Virginia forest, all in a caravan of two Packards, two Model Ts, and two Ford trucks. In the spirit of "just us cowhands," Ford brilliantly fashioned a "chuck wagon"—an early example of a sport-utility vehicle—by adapting a roadster that he ran repeatedly through the assembly line for updates. When complete (and you can see it in the Ford museum in Dearborn), it had a kitchen and pantry, a large gasoline stove fed by the car's gas tank, an icebox, and a rear panel that folded down into a table that seated twenty. It also had a gong to call the cowhands to chow. The caravan was moved around by a staff of seven: tent strikers, cooks, bottle washers, and chauffeurs. Occasionally, both Edison and Ford brought along their male personal secretaries. When their wives accompanied them, the crowd was swelled by wardrobe keepers and attendants.

Figure 3.3: 1921 Henry Ford chopping wood for the Vagabonds while being photographed (Library of Congress). (For video, see: http://www.youtube.com/watch?v=C0zKDIs_bWs&feature=relmfu.)

Ford saw to it that they were followed by a pack of scribes and photographers, eager to record their every move. The Vagabonds had high-jumping contests and tree-chopping contests—all front-page material. But the overarching story line fashioned by Ford was that the titans were just folks, and that they loved camping. Every day they would stop at local companies or at farms and chat with the workers. They would offer advice and lend a hand. The press didn't miss a moment of it.

So, for instance, at a garage in Connellsville, Pennsylvania, the caravan had to stop to repair one of the Packards. The town mechanic said that the radiator fan couldn't be fixed. Order a new one. Ford politely borrowed the man's tools and did the job while Edison entertained the crowd by discussing how much energy could be generated if a dam was placed across their flowing river. Scribble, scribble, scribble went the pens. Click, click, click went the cameras. Next-day headlines: *Henry Ford Demonstrates He's Not Afraid of Work: Repairs His Damaged Car.*

Gallons of ink were spilled on such stories under such titles as "Millions of Dollars Worth of Brains Off on a Vacation" and "Genius Sleeps under Stars." And clearly apocryphal tales entered folklore, always emphasizing that these men were just folks out driving their cars through nature. Here's one of the most famous: The Vagabonds are in the Appalachians and need a new tire for one of the Ford Model Ts. They find another crotchety mechanic. Ford introduces himself as the man who made the car, then Firestone comes forward and says he made the tires, and Edison interjects that he invented the light bulb in the garage. The mechanic turns to John Burroughs, who had a bushy white beard, and says, "Yeah, and I suppose he's Santa Claus." Same joke, different year: This time the mechanic turns to Warren Harding and says, "Yeah, and I suppose you're the president of the United States."

Here's another: One time the "boys" came upon a motorist whose car had conked out along a back road. "Maybe I can help," the ever-polite Henry Ford offers. Needless to add, he quickly diagnoses and fixes the problem. When the grateful fellow insists on paying, Ford demurs, "I've got enough money to last me a couple lifetimes." The motorist observes, "You can't be doing that well—you're driving a Ford." Readers loved it, Detroit loved it, and so did the captains of industry.

(An interesting sidebar to the history of outdoor living is the role Ford played in the development of outdoor cooking. Since he needed vast quantities of lumber to make the frames for his cars, he bought a number of sawmills in upstate Michigan. As a byproduct, these mills produced vast quantities of scrap wood and sawdust that was going to waste. Ford hated waste. So he started a process to compress and char these tailings into hard black pills known as charcoal briquettes. He later packaged them and began selling the Ford Charcoal Picnic Kit in his auto showrooms. Later he added the Ford Camping Grill. Barbecuing as we know it today was born and put on the Ford assembly line. In 1951, the Ford Motor Company finally sold the briquette plant to the husband of Henry's first cousin and occasional vagabond, E. G. Kingsford, the same name you'll see on bags of charcoal briquettes in supermarkets from coast to coast. But it was Henry Ford who had the insight and wherewithal to introduce the product.)

The Vagabonds took their last trip in 1924. Burroughs had died, and Ford's presidential aspirations were ebbing. Alas, some of his more peculiar views on nationalism, unions, and Jews were becoming too well known. He who had done his damnedest to ring the bell now claimed that the trips were just too brassy. True, the jaunts had become a formidable undertaking with the wives and servants in tow. Worse, Harvey Firestone Jr. had started taking along his horses. As much as Ford loved getting back to nature, the whole point was to get away from the damned horse. Ford called it quits.

The impact of the Vagabonds was immense. If these men could have such a good time out in the woods in their automobiles, so could the rest of us. The Vagabonds' influence on the Good Roads movement and on lobbying for public camp lands was profound. Much of the impetus for creating the state and national parks came from the cherished belief that getting outdoors was salutary and necessary for the well-being of the common man. Also, inside the Ford Motor Company, Henry's well-publicized car camping led to the early experiments with the station wagon as family RV and even to the development of the short-lived Condor. Getting a house on wheels was indeed one of the company's early projections for their industry. It didn't work out quite as they expected, but you can see how all the Ford products and publications about camping in the 1950s like *The Ford Guide to Outdoor Living on Wheels* came directly from the boss's vagabonding activities in the 1920s.

LIVING IN (AND OUT OF) A CAN: THE TIN CAN TOURISTS

The nesting impulse that Lazydays features today has been a central part of auto camping from the get-go. Fly away solo, then flock together. In fact, just 50 miles southwest of "the place RVers call home" is indeed where early RVers landed a century ago. Like the Vagabonds, this early gaggle of RVers self-consciously drew attention to themselves as proud outcasts from the humdrum travel of their peers. No railroads and overpriced hotels for them—they chose the open road. But unlike the

Vagabonds, these folks used their cars to sleep in, to travel together, and to generate community.

They called themselves *Tin Can Tourists*, and, in 1919, they even received an official Florida state charter. As well they should, for they did much to publicize the Dixie Highway, that central north/south highway that functioned as a migratory route for Midwestern snowbirds. The Canners colonized Polk County, and, to a considerable degree, they made modern Florida.

The *tin can* of their sobriquet did not come from their cars, namely, the Tin Lizzie of Ford, but rather from the object they proudly soldered on their radiator cap: a tin can. The image replaced the nameplate of the car with an announcement of rugged independence and a new affiliation. While the empty tin can might symbolize garbage for us, for them it was just the opposite. It was an emblem of a community dedicated to modernity on wheels.

The tin can came from eating a new kind of packaged food—food that had been created for this kind of travel under vastly different circumstances. The ability to preserve food in a galvanized can had become possible thanks to the exigencies of the Civil War. Soldiers can't march on an empty stomach, and being able to ship preserved foods allowed the long supply chains of the North. The problem was often how to open the can, and that was solved by the invention of the hand can opener in the 1870s. Prior to that, the can had to be bayoneted open. By the 1920s, the galvanized can and the hand opener allowed for the appearance of such luxury items as canned meat and even canned vegetables.

So the adoption of the can as an ID image by these car campers announced not just their self-sufficiency but also their hipness. They were living "off the grid" as it were, not slaves to small-town hotels but able to support themselves and each other. Each camper carried a large assortment of canned goods. They stashed cans under, over, and alongside the seats; behind the cushions; and on the floor. Along with the car, the can said one thing: We cannot be stopped; it's our declaration of independence.

But the trip down the Dixie Highway was fraught with stoppage. Rigs were always breaking down, and flat tires were a daily occurrence.

A kindly Henry Ford was not standing by to lend a hand and have a few pictures taken. So brandishing the tin can on the tip of the radiator also telegraphed, Let's help each other out. Since car jacks could be difficult to operate and the vehicles were relatively light, the Tin Can Tourists might stop four or five times in a travel day to literally lift up the rigs of compatriots as tires were changed.

The Canners transformed a liability into a rallying point. They were carefree (after all, they were escaping the northern chill), but they were also concerned about each other. You see this throughout their efforts to generate community. They valued friendliness among campers, decent behavior, wholesome entertainment, and elaborate induction ceremonies for new members. Like modern RVers, they didn't have much in common other than their "gypsy feet" and their mobile homes in the street. So they became clubby. An inductee needed to learn by heart the awkward "Tin Can Ode" (to the tune of "Battle Cry of Freedom"):

The Tin Can forever Hurrah! Boys Hurrah!
Up with the Tin Can, Down with the foe.
We will rally round the campfire, We'll rally once again.
Shouting the auto camper forever, We will always be faithful.
We will always be true. We will stand by the canner, our duty we will do.
And we will rally around the campfire as we go passing through
Shouting the auto camper forever.

And they sang a more manageable hymn with a similar tin-ear libretto: "The More We Get Together" (to the tune of "Have You Ever Seen a Lassie?"):

The more we get together
Together, together
The more we get together
The happier we will be.
For your friends are my friends
And my friends are your friends

Figure 3.4: Tin Canners convene in Gainesville, FL in 1922 (Al Hesselbart collection at RV/MH Hall of Fame and Museum on top, and below is a photograph of a Curt Teich postcard from State Archives of Florida, *Florida Memory*.)

The more we get together
The happier we will be.

The Tin Canners loved mumbo jumbo of all kinds. It united them; it was cement. As with the modern-day RV clubs, they had their own secret handshake (a sawing motion), a secret sign (a *C* made with thumb and forefinger), nicknames (*soupbone* for the old timers), little emblems (a metal ID tag on license plate—diamond-shaped with TCT imprinted), and endless rallies. The main business of the Winter Convention was to decide when and where the Summer Convention was to be held, and vice versa.

It doesn't take a sociologist to see that what is going on in these ceremonies among people unmoored and at risk is much the same as what happens at RV rallies like the one I saw in Fairbanks, Alaska. The Beavers were concerned about generating community and protecting each other from the hazards of a life unmoored. Ditto Tin Canners.

In this context it might be noted that the Tin Canners also took their religion seriously. Sunday service was mandatory. Although at home they affiliated with different denominations (Lutheran was common, as was Presbyterian), when they were encamped they went to an ecumenical service. They needed a day to clean up the campsite and meet together, and Sunday was it. Billy Graham recalls in his autobiography, *Just As I Am* (2007), that he began his ministry preaching at a Tin Can Trailer Park:

> On Sundays I often preached on streets of Tampa, sometimes as many as five or six times a day. But in those days, the greatest ministry that God opened up to me was the trailer parks. One of them, the largest (or close to it) in the country was known as the Tin Can Trailer Park. Two ladies there had gotten the concession to hold religious services on Sunday nights, but they had no preacher; they asked me if I would come. The crowds ran anywhere from 200 to 1,000. They would take up a collection, which I think the ladies kept and used for some worthy project, and they would give me $5.00—a tremendous help to my meager budget. . . . From that night in 1938 on, my purpose and objectives in life were set. I knew that I would be a preacher of the Gospel. [53]

As might be expected, the Florida locals at first welcomed the Canners with open arms and outstretched palms. After all, here was a seasonal tourist who didn't depend on the town for schooling or services. As the transient populations grew, however, the townsfolk had second thoughts. Downtown merchants soon had a saying that the Tin Canners arrived with two things: a twenty-dollar bill and a T-shirt, and they never changed either.

So although they started in Tampa, the Canners were eased over to Arcadia, where they built a self-contained park. In the early 1930s, some thirty thousand to one hundred thousand Canners would appear over the season. It was just too much for the local infrastructure, especially because of problems with potable water and sewage. So the Canners were wooed by Sarasota, which also came to the conclusion that the Canners were spooking the other snowbirds. So Sarasota, too, tried to edge them out. A contrite Tampa offered the Canners a five-year deal to return, but only if they would stay far from downtown. A special municipal park was built to contain them, but by the beginning of World War II, the bloom was off the rose.

As was happening elsewhere, the self-sufficient and responsible nomad population was supporting a less desirable population in their midst. When the Tin Canners pulled out in the spring to head back up the Dixie Highway, these vagrants stayed behind. Hobo parks, Hoovervilles, shantytowns were the legacy of the Canners along the Dixie Highway. The era of the municipal trailer park was over. Membership plummeted.

The Canners then divided into different subgroups and went to different places around the state. Although Polk County was still their favorite (in large part because of the good roads), as the state opened up—thanks, ironically, to the hated railroad—they moved south. Bits and pieces of the original group even purchased lands across the state so they could control their campgrounds.

In a nifty conjunction of snowbird migration routes, smack in the middle of Gold Coast Florida, right between Palm Beach and Boca Raton, was one of their camps, called Briny Breezes. This place, which accommodated its first Tin Canners in 1921, is still owned by some of the descendants of the original residents. To protect itself back in the 1930s, Briny Breezes set itself up as both a corporation and a town. The town/park still owns 600 feet of ocean frontage and more than 1,000 feet of Intercoastal Waterway. Turnabout being fair play, in 2007 the owners of 488 mobile homes almost sold out to a developer for $510 million. If you do the math that means that lots of Canner descendants could be driving huge Class A RVs with flashy paint jobs and heated floors. The deal fell through: The Briny citizenry was not convinced that the money was worth it.

Briny notwithstanding, almost as rapidly as the tide had come in for the Tin Can Tourists, it started to go out. The *consumption* part of this consumption community was disappearing. Vagrants made the host communities understandably anxious, and the Depression made travel expensive. In addition, as cars became more sophisticated and especially as tires became tubeless and manufactured from carbonized rubber, the recurring annoyance of changing tires became less a concern. The invention of the easy-to-use platform jack meant that a single person could do the job. Roads improved too, thanks to the passage of the Good Roads program, which paved many major highways, especially A1A. As the need to travel in a caravan lessened, so did membership in the Tin Can Tourists.

In many ways, Florida itself caused the disappearance of the Tin Canners. As the state opened up on the Atlantic side as a result of Henry Flagler's Florida East Coast Railway and as DDT put a quietus on the mosquito, the general migration poured southward toward Miami. No longer a playground for the wealthy, the eastern seaboard was open for business. An estimated 2.5 million tourists came to Florida in 1925, and they came in cars. Florida's landscape would soon add gas stations, car dealers, diners, and new *mo*tor ho*tels* where guests could park at their door and sleep in cool conditioned air.

Florida's land boom, in part spurred on by the Canners' yearly migrations, soon led to not just hoards of vacationers but also land speculators. The Tin Can Tourists were pushed aside by the oncoming throngs. Towns that had once set aside land for them to camp on now asked them to go elsewhere. The welcome mat was pulled away.

In the RV revival of the 1970s, the Tin Can Tourists reconstituted themselves, and they now putter around the state in vintage rigs, re-creating the sense of magical community of a century ago. I have visited them when they come to Florida. They now sometimes camp out at Cedar Key on the Gulf, due west of my Gainesville home, and because their housecars are forever breaking down, they have a great sense of camaraderie. They, like those groups of Bounders, Beavers, Kountry Kampers, Skinny-Winnies, Georgie Boys, and all the other affiliation groups, show what goes on just below the surface of *heading out*. In a sense, they have circled back a century later, creating a stable community among those who claim separateness.

Whatever that paradox of nomadic settlement is, it's deep in the American experience, whether it be in the circuitous migrations of the settlers, the gypsy re-creations of the Vagabonds in the 1920s, the wayfaring Tin Canners, the commercial narrative of Lazydays, or, as we will now see, in the sometimes bizarre settlements in the RV culture of today. Pull up stakes, put them back down. Go away, come back. Take off, land. When the wagons get circled, an often intense culture gets created. Then it's wagons-ho and they pull apart. It's to look closer at that peripatetic, systolic culture, especially in the American Southwest, that we now shift our focus. Is there something in the open air of big spaces that produces intense community in tight confines? Is there something in the compression of high and low, of Belmont and Fishtown, that produces that piston stroke of the American experience? Is the RV experience a condensation of the wider culture?

Chapter Four

PARK IT From Kampgrounds of America to the Slabs

As RV owners have transformed Thoreau's 10- by 15-foot cabin, they have also transformed his Walden Pond. I'm going to take a quick look at a few of those ponds: the standard RV park (of which there are some eight thousand), the state or national park (of which there are thousands), the KOA brand (of which there are about five hundred), the theme-park version (a few hundred), the football/NASCAR special-event camping (hundreds), and then the ever-present parking lot of Walmart (too many to count). In these places, Belmont and Fishtown coexist; spangled million-dollar conversion buses park side by side with rusted pickup-truck campers.

There are other, more fascinating ponds, some of them even more distinctively (and peculiarly) American. Many of these are in the American Southwest, a region fertile for nomadic innovation. If you're going to hit the open road, sooner or later you'll end up in the quadrant of states surrounding Arizona. If you want *open*, here it is. And so it's here that we find such bizarre RV-topias as Quartzsite, Arizona, and Slab City, California.

STOP RIGHT WHERE YOU ARE: YOU'RE HOME

Let's face it: the standard RV park is a rather dreary place. Driving on the interstate, you'll see those signs announcing which motels, fast-food restaurants, and gas stations are at the upcoming exit. The first of these signs reads *Camping*, but it's anything but conventional camping. What it really is is a place for RVs of all kinds to park. It may call itself a campground, but it's almost never for camping on the ground. It's for parking your wheeled living room.

In these RV parks you'll usually have a choice: a pull-through lot for big living rooms and a back-in for smaller ones. You have a choice of power supply too: 50 amps for big ones from Belmont and 30 amps for smaller ones from Fishtown. And then there's sewage treatment of some kind, either a dump station where you do your business on leaving the park or a hookup at your lot. Relative to what you get, it's pricey. Most parks charge around thirty dollars a night, but all kinds of discounts are available if you join organizations like the Good Sam Club, Camp Club USA, or AARP.

You drive in and chances are there's a shabby office, a surprisingly clean washroom, an often broken laundromat, a usually scummy swimming pool, and then a farmyard of little graveled or paved plots that were once level but now are undulating. On the side of the lots is a metal pedestal stuck in the ground that carries power and television hookup, and a faucet for water. Nearby often is a portal in the ground for attaching the sewer pipe from your rig. Almost always there's a sign announcing wi-fi but no mention that it's intermittent or that it covers only half the park. Worse, it's often operated by a company called Tengo Internet, which delivers low-fi, cold-spots, high prices.

And then there are rules, always rules, often delivered on little maps that show where your pedestal for the night (or week or month or year) will be. These rules speak volumes about the free spirits who head for these little splashes of gravel. Here's a typical version, copied verbatim:

BONITA LAKES RV PARK RULES

It is the intent of the BONITA LAKES RV PARK to maintain a clean, friendly, peaceful, enjoyable atmosphere for all of our guest and visitors, so please observe the following:

1. Please keep your space clean of all trash and cigarette butts. (the gravel, grass nor concrete pad are ashtrays) The cleanliness of your space is your responsibility.
2. There will be no clotheslines or clothes racks.
3. Each RV is to be clean and self-supported, not blocked up or propped up.
4. All dogs must be on leashes at all times. They can be walked any (outdoor) place in the park but must be cleaned up after. Please if they poop, you scoop. It's not nice to step in it.
5. There is no heavy mechanical work to be done in the park.
6. From 10:00 pm to 8:00 am, is considered to be quiet time, but please no loud music or noise at any time. Please be considerate of your neighbors.
7. All overnight guests are to be registered in the office. You are responsible for the actions of your children and guests, therefore any damages to the park or property will be charged to the renter. The park management is not responsible for accidents or theft on your space. Insurance of your RV is totally your responsibility.
8. The speed limit in the RV Park is 5 mph for the safety of all. Motorcycles & ATVs are to be ridden to and from your space only.
9. Children Driving or Riding Golf carts or ATVs MUST ALWAYS BE ACCOMPANIED BY A PARENT OR GUARDIAN. (18 years of age or older)
10. Recreational vehicles can be removed from the park for failure to abide by the rules. Young children playing out of your space should be supervised by an adult at all times.

11. Please no littering outside of your space as well. Please place all trash, bottles, cans, cigarette butts, food wrappers etc. in trash receptacles. We are striving to keep this park as clean and litter free as possible. Please help us keep it that way.

12. No smoking or pet washing in the bath house. This is strictly prohibited. (Please be considerate of your neighbors.)

13. There are no lifeguards at the swimming pool on duty. Swim at your own risk.

You don't have to be an English teacher to read between these lines to get a sense of the spirit of Bonita Springs (a real park in Meridian, Mississippi). Here are a few more I've enjoyed parsing:

No guests or extra vehicles allowed without permission
Barbeque grills must have legs
No leaving hair in the sinks
No metal detectors allowed
No Frisbees or Ball Games of Any Kind
All rights granted to registered guests in our park are through a revocable license which may be revoked at any time
Under no circumstances should you consider yourself a tenant with a lease
Do not spit anywhere including into this trash can
Flush when you are done doing your business

If you judge a culture by the content of its laws, then you might conclude that the campground is a pretty authoritarian state. And, in a way, it is. Although I've rarely seen any of these rules enforced, they do remind you of the Fishtown nature of the experience. You have to face it: Many of the folks parked near you are there not for recreation but out of exigency.

I would say that about a third of the rigs in a standard RV park are there as residents, not guests, a fact that understandably excites various zoning agencies. Retirees and other habitués are in their rigs for long periods, and although they may move around, their yard art and rig decoration suggest that they have put down roots. When you see the quaint little wooden signs reading "Buddy and Melissa" that give the name of the park as their address, you know you're in the company of long-timers. The same is true when you see a rig draped in Christmas lights in July.

The quality of the campground makes almost no difference to the transient. Pull into a seedy motel and you'll have a dreadful night, what with ratty furniture, poor plumbing, saggy beds, and maybe a wall-pounding, caterwauling neighbor. But pull into the usually seedy RV park and you're unaffected. You have the same furniture, plumbing, and bedding you had the night before.

All that matters is that the electricity is properly grounded, and that can be easily checked with a polarity tester. Small and inexpensive, the tester displays two green or amber lights when plugged into a properly wired outlet. The water pressure can also be checked with a pressure regulator that you insert into your water supply line to detect abnormally high pressure. Of course the fact that such equipment is needed by the camper says something about the relationship between guest and host. And this is not to mention sewage treatment, other than to say it's best never to drink the water at an RV park for reasons discussed shortly.

In years of RV travel and thousands of miles, I have balked only once at entering a "campground," and that was just south of Jena, Louisiana. It wasn't just the Confederate flags that put me off; it was that the rigs, many converted school buses, were mostly stuck in the mud, and their inhabitants were clearly not eager—perhaps not even able—to leave.

I would like to be a proprietor of an RV campground. It looks like my kind of job. Just stand around, don't enforce the rules, and chat up the visitors while taking their money. And, indeed, I'm not alone. Most of the proprietors who run these places are along in years, and most seem happy to be on the job. As opposed to motel personnel, who have to stay awake all night, the campground staff calls it quits at twilight and often leaves the checking-in process to the camper. So the camper pulls in, fills out a form, scouts around for an unoccupied site, and then "hooks up." All of this is done in the dark, which provides entertainment for the locals. Payment on exit. I've queried a number of attendants, and they say that scofflaws who skip out before paying in the morning are few.

In many campgrounds (especially the state parks), the day-to-day work is done by "work campers." These people are usually retirees who exchange free lodging for doing the chores necessary to keep the place in business. They clean it up and fix it up, stay for a few months, and then move on to another campground. Work campers have their own websites and plan their lives by where they want to go next. You recognize them because their rig is invariably parked near the entry to the park and they'll have a little sign out front saying: Bucky and Melissa, Hosts.

Although there is no ideal time to discuss this subject, perhaps this is the place to say a word about a subject all RVers, especially Bucky and Melissa, find compelling: septic. It is indeed the dirty little secret of the RV life because how to unload the poop has been a problem since the Lampsteed Kampkar. And how to "treat" it is a bane of the campground host.

A generation ago, RV engineers divided wastewater into two separate compartments, literally. There is a *gray-water* tank that holds the shower and sink water, and there's the dreaded *black-water* tank that holds the other stuff. An interior gauge, often malfunctioning, shows the levels. In the earliest rigs, a chamber pot sufficed, but over time these onboard containers were added along with gauges telling how much the tank was holding. The gray water was usually just dumped on the side of the road, and you can still legally do this in many states.

Not so with the black water. And it's the black-water gauge that usually gets fouled. Septic sludge sloshing around in the tank invariably starts to cake on the sensor. One of the most popular aftermarket devices is a spray device installed in the tank and hooked up to an external hose that essentially whirls water along the sides of the tank to wash the cake off. Most RV owners will tell you how they have made peace with the "idiot lights" falsely warning of sewage Armageddon.

Campgrounds usually provide two ways of emptying black water: a private sewer connection near your rig into which you insert a plastic tube that you carry with you, or a public one where you do the same thing, but in full view of folks who are waiting their turn. You can tell the greenhorns at the dump station because they are always looking slightly guilty as they flush in public what was generated in private. They are often wearing the recommended elbow-high blue plastic gloves like something out of a sci-fi movie. You can tell from their faces what they are thinking: gastroenteritis, hepatitis, typhoid, intestinal parasites. Plus, for obvious reasons, the black tank gets emptied before the gray one, so they have a look of concentration. Did they open the valves in proper sequence? Veterans, however, tend to casually do their business with a *sangfroid* gained from months of opening the valves in public.

When this job is done and the tanks emptied, you have to get the accordion plastic pipe back into the rig. You have to "milk the hose" back into its compressed state so you can store it in a special compartment (along with those gloves). You raise the hose at the coach end and walk it toward the sewer inlet. You keep raising the hose as you walk, thereby "milking" it dry. Even a properly sloped flexible sewer hose may have residual fluid and waste particles still inside. These particles will become an odor generator over time, so it is imperative to completely remove as much moisture as possible. A lot of spraying goes on. Needless to say, this whole operation is done by the male while the female waits patiently in the rig.

These indignities are not for more permanent residents of RV parks. You often see their plastic sewage lines resting on what looks to be a little centipede of plastic supports holding the pipe at a gradual pitch. The key to the success of this system, however, is only flushing your tanks when full, because if you leave your valve open for too long you'll have all the odors flowing backward up through the toilet and into your living space. In some parks you'll see portable holding tanks called *blue boys*, which are filled and then carted to the dump station rather than moving the whole rig.

The dumping process is something that all RVers, be they from Fishtown or Belmont, experience, and therefore it is a common subject of male conversation. The Belmonters may have a superfancy sewer pipe that automatically extends, cleans itself, and then retracts back into the bus. But it still has to be attached to the sewer coupling—a potentially nasty transaction. Should you ever attend a movie about this lifestyle, especially if it intends to be funny, such as *RV: The Movie* with Robin Williams or *Meet the Parents* with Robert De Niro, you will see that the waste-management issue and the coupling event is a central concern. Everyone has a story to tell. Here's mine.

On our first long RV trip across the American South, I was just getting the hang of the process, how to attach the accordion pipe to the rig, how to drain black before gray, how to unfasten the pipe, and then how to clean, and repack it. The pipe that comes with the rig as standard issue is invariably cheesy, with a flimsy plastic bayonet coupling. Why the industry doesn't mandate high-quality fittings to avoid trauma at the connections is a standing mystery. Maybe it's an initiation ceremony of some sort.

My wife and I were in a beautiful Georgia state park built around the sacred burial grounds of the Kolomoki Indians. The dump station was in full view at the top of a hill running down to a little pond. Leaning under the rig, I turned the plastic pipe into the opening on the underside. Thinking it was fastened tightly, I put the other end of the pipe in the drain hole for waste and then opened the black-water valve. You can hear the sound of sewage swirling into this pipe as it leaves your world and goes around the corners into the hole. Instead I heard a splashing sound and saw to my horror that the pipe had come apart at the attaching joint. The accordion pipe had come loose from the rig and gallons of raw human sewage were spilling out all over the roadway and now slowly flowing down toward the pristine pond. For reasons known only to God, I didn't panic but quickly closed the valve.

I don't like to use the phrase *beyond words* but I must. It was not just that this was sewage, but it was *my* sewage, something intensely private and personal. And it was flowing down a public roadway in full view. I couldn't yell out to my wife, who was inside the rig doing the morning Sudoku. I mean, what would I say? Shit happens? All I could do was to open the freshwater tank in the rig and send as much water down the hill as I could, hoping it would at least dilute the sewage, my shame. There was a hose and well water in the pump-out station that is used to clean up whatever small mess you may have made, and I sent this water cascading down the hill as well. I do recall trying to remember if the nice ranger we had met the previous day was wearing a sidearm.

KOA: THE BRANDED EXPERIENCE

Here's rule number 1 from marketing: When you have a product that is interchangeable, like gasoline or water or meat patties, you can compete on price and lose your shirt or you can compete on branding and perhaps make a bundle. Exxon, Evian, and McDonalds have been successful because they have branded their products—economists call them *fungibles*—with a nifty story so you think that they are better than Texaco, tap water, and Wendy's. While there may indeed be some small content difference, the real difference is in the story line and how consumers feel about the story. As they say on Madison Avenue, you smoke the brand, not the cigarette; drive the nameplate, not the car; drink the advertising, not the beer.

The run-of-the-mill RV park is in many ways a fungible product. After all, it's just a supposedly level pad providing access to water, TV, electricity, septic, and not much else. The locale changes, but the product—the level space you are renting—remains essentially the same. So it was only a matter of time before someone tried to brand the generic campground with a narrative, tried to separate one park from another on the basis of story line and, if it worked, make some serious money. In a way, it has worked. In another way, it hasn't.

The company that tried this storytelling is called Kampground of America—KOA. Essentially, this is a collection of almost five hundred parks that have employees dressed in yellow shirts, a company store with lots of KOA merchandise, a clean pool and playground for the kiddies, an operating laundromat, and some Kamping Kabins for mostly motorcyclists. Almost everything that can be is spelled with a *K*. Except for the KOA Value Card, which has a magnetic strip on the back.

This card is the brainchild of the current CEO, Jim Rogers, and is crucial to the KOA brand. Mr. Rogers, who came from the gambling industry, knows that gambling is an almost perfect example of a fungible industry. The odds are fixed by the state. You are no more likely to win at the Bellagio than at the Flamingo, but the goal of the casino is to convince you of the opposite. When you check into a Vegas hotel, you get a plastic card with the same magnetic strip. The card records all your betting wins and losses and hence provides a snapshot of the depth of your gullibility. If you are betting a lot, the card announces "bargains" in the casino when you insert the card into the electronic slot machine.

So, too, when you check in, the KOA card tells the company how often you go camping, what kind of RV you have, what you buy at the store; it then gives you discounted prices on future trips. If you are a newbie, the card even tells the KOA manager to go to your rig and wish you happy trails. And it tells about veteran travelers, where they've been and how often they've camped at KOA. If you are trying to personalize the interchangeable experience, this card system is a great way to do it. Every afternoon the company sends out what it calls a "Bull's-eye Target Report" so that the local manager knows all about his guests. KOA, just like McDonalds, even has its own university, where such tricks of the trade are exchanged.

And it works. Often this is because the people who manage KOAs are work campers, retirees who exchange labor for free hookups. These kindly folks have plenty of time and experience in RVing and often appear at your door bearing some goodie. As opposed to the often tired and out-of-sorts managers of standard campgrounds, KOA has some two thousand couples who are called KOA All-Star Work Campers. They know the system and travel around the country exchanging their bonhomie for free lodging. When I see that yellow shirt at my door, I cringe. They already know me too well.

For all of this, of course, KOA charges a premium price, about ten dollars more per night than the competition. After all, that's the reward for branding. Think bottled water. However, the RV owner is a relatively price-sophisticated consumer. The often 20 percent markup is usually fully understood, and so many consumers stay away. If you're not traveling with kids, the extra expense may not be worth it. Also, as Howard Johnson's and KFC have found out to their distress, if you let some of your outlets fall below par, the predictability of the brand experience can become seriously tarnished. There is still a lot of variation in the KOA parks—the mouse in the Coke bottle—that wreaks havoc with the brand.

BOONDOCKING

The problem that all commercial parks must face is that they compete not only with state parks (which are invariably better) but also with the parking lots of Walmart and Cracker Barrel (which offer much the same experience for free). Walmart is currently ground zero for a noisy battle over this service. Walmart's genius for garnering bad publicity (remember the stories of workers locked into the store after-hours and obsessive penny-pinching?) is matched by its coddling of the RVer. Take a look at your local Walmart in the middle of the night and you'll see what looks like a scene from an early cowboy movie: covered wagons circled 'til dawn. Then take a look at the never-ending legal squabble about allowing such "camping." The con argument is that the local township is losing out on transient tax money. That these protests are invariably spearheaded by the local campgrounds goes without saying. They usually don't say that, however. They usually say that camping at Walmart is not safe.

Compared with the alternatives, it's plenty safe to stay at Walmart. The parking lots are usually out in front, and the stores are most often at the edges of town. Walmart's security system is yours as well. It's a nifty marketing move as campers invariably go inside to shop, and the store has a special section just for their stuff. (One of their biggest sellers is a high-quality sewer hose with couplings that don't come apart.) The standard etiquette is to ask permission from the store manager and then not to use outside grills or furniture that might scar the parking lot. I know it's not *de rigueur* to say a nice word about Walmart, but in the RV world, the store is tops.

The practice of "camping" outside a campsite or in a campground without hookups is called *boondocking* (docking in the boonies) or *dry camping* and is, after all, the supposed reason the RV has all that self-sufficiency apparatus like generator, self-contained water, septic, and cooking equipment. People who frequent the parking lots usually don't

Figure 4.1: Act 3: Author (center) wally docking, 2010.

think of themselves as camping in a parking lot. They say they're "parking here to go camping elsewhere." In RV lingo, "Wally docking" is just a stop along the "asphalt prairie." In any case, Walmart is far preferable to rest stops on the interstate, where you definitely will be asked by a flashlight-toting state policeman to move along at two o'clock in the morning (except in Arizona, however, where rest-stop camping is perfectly legal).

Some observers have suggested that the next development in RV parks is to offer not more services à la KOA, but fewer. To lure some of the boondockers out from Walmart, they suggest that perhaps commercial campgrounds should offer no-frills camping for a minimal charge, say ten dollars a night. After all, if all you want is a place to sleep—no hookups, no restrooms, no tele, no splashpool for the kiddies—then why not have a special section for the only-overnight crowd?

THE RISE AND FALL OF OUTDOOR RESORTS

Meanwhile, some parks that promise exclusivity can charge a premium for delivering it. Usually this is because the park is close to some attraction, like Disney's Fort Wilderness Park. After the Disney Company built the West Coast theme park (Disneyland), they recognized the audience they had neglected—families who arrive in RVs—and decided not to make that same mistake with the Disney World resort in Florida. Fort Wilderness, separated from Disney World by a little lake, shows not only how attractive a landscaped park can be, but how deep the pockets of many RVers are. The place charges upward of eighty dollars per night and is invariably full, especially around school vacations. Needless to say, it is spotless.

More interesting to students of the Winnebago Nation are parks that cater to an exclusive audience not because of proximity to a theme park or a natural wonder but because of some consumer affiliation. I will discuss the Escapees organization in the next chapter, but a look at Outdoor Resorts may be instructive, for here we may see the strange dynamic that plays out between Fishtown and Belmont.

Near the end of the twentieth century, Robert Schoelhorn, recently retired CEO of Abbott Labs, made a typical early-retirement purchase with a fistful of severance dollars—a big motorhome. For weeks he and his wife drove around the West. She thought the rig was inelegant, and he thought it was poorly designed. Both, however, were hooked on the experience. Looking for things to do, he invested in a bus-conversion company named Marathon Motorcoach in Oregon. Bit by bit, he took over the company. He, and later his sons, transformed the high-end (million-dollar-plus) side of the RV industry. He put bling on wheels. If it was electronic and could be operated by a remote keypad, from heated floors to color-shifting optic lighting, his Marathon buses would have it.

Schoelhorn then set about providing resort space for his high-end clients. The idea made sense. Rolls Royce owners don't like parking next to dilapidated Corvairs. A curtain separates first-class passengers from coach class on airplanes; on ocean liners it's an airlock door. And since these big rigs are essentially vacation homes, why not have a string of parking spots where owners could drop by for a few weeks and then take off to another? To make it feasible, you could buy a claim on a lot in a half-dozen places, just like a time-share. You'd simply move from country club to country club. depending on whim and the weather. You'd be perpetually in a four-star resort and never have to unpack. Feel the urge to change golf courses? Just turn the key and step on the gas.

Belmont was finally getting separated from Fishtown, and the operation was called Outdoor Resorts. Most of its venues were in the Southeast. Aside from one in California and three in Florida, they formed a swath from the Great Smokies to the Atlantic shore. Essentially, once you bought your $1.5 million rig, you plunked down another quarter million for a place to park it, a snazzy place that moved along with you. But more important, perhaps, a place where only people like you would be staying. To buy into Outdoor Resorts you had to have a Class A rig, with no pull-behind trailers, no matter how big or how expensive.

Outdoor Resorts initially garnered a lot of attention. Television shows like *Lifestyles of the Rich and Famous* and Home & Garden Television (HGTV) were forever foregrounding parking lots filled with these monster McMansions parked next to golf courses or on the beach front. The *New York Times* predictably cocked an eyebrow in "The Ritz? No, It's an RV Park" (7/7/2007). In the go-go years at the fin de siècle, here was the epitome of spending run amok. Outdoor Resorts even offered a concierge service where a butler would come by with whatever was needed; a golf pro was on call to help with the slice; a masseuse made house calls. Face it: The "world's richest RV parks" did have a certain oxymoronic allure, especially for the entrepreneurial class. Belmont finally got a zipcode.

Outdoor Resorts has not been a smashing success; in fact, it has teetered toward insolvency, vastly cutting back on its planned expansion. Part of the problem may be that many of the fourteen sites are located too close together. What's the point of jet-setting from Scarsdale to Bronxville? Part of the problem may be that the bloom is off the RV rose and fewer people want to buy such "look at me, now criticize me" rigs.

But I suspect another problem is that the consumption community of super-rig owners really doesn't want to separate from the warm fraternity of others on wheels. It may be that the goal of moving up the RV pyramid is not, finally, to escape but to mingle with those who enjoy the same experience. Belmonters may want Fishtowners nearby. Remember those Beavers up in Alaska? They wanted us commoners to come by for a visit. As New York socialites can tell you, what's the point of getting all dolled up if only your buddies can see you?

UNSUNG, UNAPPRECIATED, UNDERFUNDED: THE AMERICAN STATE PARKS

Everyone knows about the handful of iconic national parks like Yosemite, Grand Canyon, Zion, and Yellowstone. Less well known are the 6,624 state parks. Many of these parks were created in the Depression to provide employment to the Civilian Conservation Corp and to repair the ravages of careless logging and farming. Many of the sites are beautifully laid out, and the buildings show the craftsmanship of an earlier age. Ironically, in the repeated recessions of the early twenty-first century, some states, most notably California, are shutting some of them down. Money coming in does not match money going out. And the cries of those affected are muted. As with libraries, where much of the work is done by volunteers, there are few lobbyists to protect state parks. The parks are expensive to maintain and the common good of protecting them is not clear to cost-cutting politicians. This is bad news for the RVer, as many state parks provide spacious lots in delightful settings at reasonable prices.

Of all the regions in the United States, the Southeast has the most extensive state park systems because land was cheap after King Cotton had gone, the yellow pines were overlogged, unemployment was high, and the sites were easy to maintain. Go through Georgia and Florida, across Alabama and Mississippi to Louisiana and you'll find beautiful bosky parks almost always tucked in loblolly forests beside unspoiled lakes and rivers. Usually no reservations are needed, and you can stay up to two weeks in one site. With very little planning you can cross the American South going from state park to state park and see some of the most pastoral countryside and meet the friendliest people. The Tin Can Tourists knew what we may have forgotten.

I don't mean to stint on state parks in other sections of the country, but New England parks are not really RV-friendly (often downright hostile); in the Midwest they are few and far between (and often dull); and in the West they play second fiddle to the superb national parks. You can drive across the Deep South and not find a single *national* park. Yes, there are federal sites, mostly dedicated to the Civil War and civil rights, but nothing of national magnitude. The states have had to fill in the gap. And they have.

Take Mississippi, for example. This state may be poor in many things, but not in places to camp in your RV. True, many of the parks give you the sense that there was a chunk of land near a town with an overlogged forest and a pond or a stream and the state said, ah, here's a park. After all, a generation or two ago, Mississippi was mostly swampland, cotton fields, and pine forests. But this makes for neat and tidy RV sites: flat but overlooking water. So in Roosevelt State Park there are more than one hundred sites; Archusa Creek has more than seventy; near the coast in DeSoto there are more than twenty, and so forth. When you cross over Southern state borders on the Interstate, there will be a welcome center eager to provide brochures listing all the state parks, complete with information about RV camping.

Another unsung peculiarity of the Deep South that rewards the RVer is that many of the major rivers near the Gulf of Mexico have been dredged and "controlled" by various government agencies. Whenever you get near rivers like the Alabama, Tennessee, Chattahoochee, Tombigbee, and especially the Mississippi, you invariably find locks and dams with campsites provided by the Bureau of Land Management. The campsites are often built on the very site occupied by the Corps of Engineers, sometimes with their old infrastructure intact, and are, in a word beloved by RVers, *free*. Their only competition along the Gulf shore comes from casino operators who provide first-class RV sites while asking little in return—only a few hours of your time and a peek into your wallet.

THE AMERICAN SOUTHWEST: RV VALHALLA

For the RVer, nothing compares with the Southwest. In his 2003 book *American Nomads: Travels with Conquistadors, Mountain Men, Cowboys, Indians, Hobos, Truckers, and Bullriders*, Richard Grant makes a provocative point: The southwestern quadrant of the United States has been a repository for lost souls since the first humans arrived. This is a place where people go to get gone, to get really lost. Ironically, it's in the geography; it's too open. It's in the air: There's too much of it. The endless land is most often blank; seemingly waiting to be filled in by whomever is crossing it, or better yet, whomever is crossing, and double-crossing it. This is a land of mirages. This terrain is overwhelming not because you are being shut in by mountains or trees or even green plains but because you are not being shut in. The endless vista stretches in every direction with no edges in sight. Everything that naturally lives there, as they say, will either bite you, sting you, or stick you. Being there can make you anxious. In Grant's words:

> Nomad space: too far from the river to irrigate, to dry for crops or cities to take root. Like the deserts of the Bedouin, the Mongol steppes, the Tibetan plateaus or the buffalo plains, this is a harsh, marginal, wide-open landscape, with long horizons and a paucity of water. This is the homeland of . . . the last free-roaming hunter-gatherers in the lower forty-eight states to be brought to heel, at the close of the nineteenth century. Fifty years earlier this had been the westernmost range of the Western Apache raiding parties, attracted by the emigrant caravans traveling to the California goldfields. This, on the evidence of dust devils, is a place where the earth itself feels compelled to rise up and move. [86]

Maybe the best image of the Southwest is the tumbleweed. The tumbleweed was once an above-ground living plant that disengaged with its roots and began to be blown about by the wind. As befits the geography, there are a number of RV tumbleweed unsettlements in this area worthy of inspection: the RV flashtown Quartzsite in Arizona and, just over the border in California, the RV squattertown Slab City. As I write this, a third tumbleweed settlement is rolling around, that is distant cousin to Lollapalooza, an art installation, a Druid Halloween, and a football fantown: Burning Man near Black Rock City, Nevada. A decade ago RVs were disdained; now they are so abundant that they have their own parking section. Since Burning Man is about much more than RVs, I'm going to pass it by other than to say that it has already become one of the central *crepe* cities (see the next chapter) in the world. As the returning participants grow older, RVs will doubtless appear in greater numbers. Burning Man may well become another RV-topia.

Quartzsite, Arizona: Medieval Canterbury for RVs

If you are traveling west on Interstate 10, about a third of the way between Phoenix and Los Angeles you'll cross an exit for State Route 95. Unless you need gas, you won't exit. Why should you? Drive twenty-five more miles and you'll be in California, where things are a little greenish, thanks to the Colorado River. But this exit looks truly desolate—and it is. You're in the middle of the Mojave Desert.

Off in the distance is endless blowtorched land, and right beside the interstate, along what is called "Business 10," is what looks like collections of abandoned metal huts. Yes, there's a golden arch, a bundle of gas stations, some truck stops, a honky-tonk eatery, but no real grocery store or franchise motels. It's painfully dry. At the honky-tonk you'll see the town's motto over the bar: "Two feet from Hell and 25 miles from water." There's usually too much sunlight to see into the far distance, but occasionally you can just make out the sawtooth mountain ridges to the northwest.

Come February, however, this place is jam-packed with RVs of all sorts. The only places I've seen like it are the 405 in LA at rush hour and the Big Dig in Boston, bumper to bumper forever. But the bumpers all belong to behemoths. A decade ago, people just drove where they pleased, moving around like tumbleweeds. The hardpack desert floor made an ideal surface, called "desert pavement," which resembled tile or cobblestone paving and could support an army tank. Ironically, the paving of the side roads along the interstate has only made congestion worse. As old-timers will tell you, the new curbs (and a police department) brought chaos to order.

The town is called Quartzsite, named after quartzite, a sandstone cemented with quartz. The *s* got added in long ago, apparently by a bad speller with a good sense of place. The town has a history every bit as quartzy as its name. Long ago the spot was a watering hole for the Pony Express and later for the Southern Pacific Railroad. Along the way, prospectors decided that the presence of quartzite was a sign that other precious metals were nearby. They dug around and found some colored stones but nothing precious. Then, in 1855, U.S. Secretary of War Jefferson Davis (soon to become the president of the Southern Confederacy) approved a plan to experiment with camels for carrying mail and war supplies in the desert. Camels were imported, and a successful expedition traveled between Texas and California. But the project ultimately failed, and the camel driver and some of his camels ended their days around Quartzsite. All that remains of the Camel Corps is a good-natured memorial to the Syrian camel driver, nicknamed Hi Jolly. Most of this godforsaken land is still owned by the U.S. government and administered by the Bureau of Land Management.

The place did not become a popular rendezvous until about thirty years ago, when snowbirds started landing there in the winter. They came in RVs, and they came to do something that retirees like: collect and trade colored stones and boondock on all that federal land for *free*. Many of them were just passing through en route to Yuma and the Mexican border towns where warm weather waited, as well as cheap medical care and prescription drugs. Cross the border in Los Algodones and you see what they're after: Within a four-block radius are more pharmacies, doctors, dentists, and opticians than any similar four-block area anywhere in the world.

From exchanging colored stones, trading in Quartzsite soon expanded to include everything from Bowie knives to machine guns, from dried-up animal bones to romance novels, from bootleg movies to bootleg drugs. The market for arthritic cures was robust. The tents and metal buildings on one side of the interstate, now called Tyson Wells, resembled a medieval town with barkers squawking and banners fluttering. But it was a medieval town with no youngsters. Over time the swapmeet/fleamarket/drugstore became known as the *Pow Wow*. On the other side of the interstate was another market called *the Main Event*, a month-long exchanging of new and used recreational vehicles.

When this place is humming with the sound of generators, as happens each winter, it looks a bit like Lourdes. It's where you go to find new life, redemption, relics (in both senses of the term). You redecorate your house, then you trade it in for another. At twilight, the desert is literally lit up in reflective aluminum. From the air, you can see the RV silver tops shining like a lake bed. At night the RV lights and campfires are aglow until at least nine o'clock.

For a few weeks at the end of January and throughout February, Quartzsite is the third-largest city in Arizona, a sprawling RV-opolis

Figure 4.2: Quartzsite in June and January, 2009, showing impact of RVs, misspelling of town name, and local animals (Free World Photography postcard).

of mechanical tumbleweeds. It is also the second-most-visited spot in the state, right behind the Grand Canyon. Even the staid *National Geographic* tipped its hat, calling Quartzsite "the world's largest parking lot." It even has its own zip code: 85346.

There were so many freeloaders that the Bureau of Land Management now charges a small fee to help clean up the mess. And you have to move around a bit so you are not legally a squatter. It's a happy place: the RVs rounded up like circled wagons, geezers out front on lawn chairs, generators whirring in the background. Quartzsite is a

poor man's Palm Springs, a septuagenarian's spring break at Daytona Beach, a country-music lover's Woodstock. During the season it's also an undertaker's dream come true. Lots of people expire here. Average age of the population: 66.5. Quartzsite has a Medevac heli-pad for quick transfer to the hospital over in Blythe, California.

To appreciate Quartzsite you have to leave the Canterbury swap-meet, cross the interstate, and join the pilgrims who are exchanging their RVs. It's like a massive rendition of Lazydays, except that it goes on for miles. All along Main Street from one interstate exit to the other are never-ending full hook-ups for those who don't boondock, as well as what appears to be an endless sales lot filled with "product" for those who want upgrades. On this side of 10, the RV is just another tonic, just another gemstone, just another animal bone to be traded from one owner to the next. A trip along Main Street will tell you much about the community that enjoys home on the road and comes down this road to change homes.

My guide was Mr. Sam Lincoln of Mr. Motorhome, and he is hands down the best RV salesman I have ever met. He's tall, tanned, and smoother than syrup. As he told me, he has to be good to work here. He has "to look an 80-year-old straight in the eye and sell him a $600,000 rig with a 30-year mortgage." It's seasonal work, and Sam spends the rest of the year in his own RV traveling around. He sells for fun. It's like a seasonal sport, he said. Even the dealerships are seasonal; they fold up in April and move on. They often own just the "dirt" and bring the rigs in from elsewhere when the trading starts. For instance, Mr. Motorhome is legally headquartered in California and sets up an ad hoc operation in Arizona. During the Main Event, they bring in the new inventory to prime the pump, but the big business is shifting the used rigs back and forth among the visitors. It's like a zero-sum game, says Sam, with Mr. Motorhome taking its cut to keep it humming.

The business, Sam said, used to be better. "There was almost no paperwork then," he smiled. Thousands of people would come—at the height of the season there are almost a million people in motorhomes, approximately 5 percent of all RV owners! They would see other RVs and contract "rig fever." Sam's job was to provide the cure. Envy, Sam tells me, is his best salesman. Here's how it works: Snowbirds would come, Sam told me, and they would start dry-camping out in the desert. They loved it. It was cheap. They met people with bigger rigs and became friends. During the daytime they were fine, but at night the newbies would occasionally freeze. Then they would come into town and use the campsites with the hookups. The campsites were mixed in with the RV dealerships.

That's when Sam knew they were his. After trading at the flea market, they would come over to Mr. Motorhome for a slightly fancier and warmer rig. It was just another swapmeet transaction—unmeasured, untaxed, just folks swapping stuff, and Sam acting as the facilitator. "I ended up at the bank," he said.

Yes, he admitted, he was a good salesman, but where there are seventy-five thousand RVs all in one place, his main job was to provide the "go-between grease." The big rigs, he said, the ones costing a half million, were the easiest to sell. When I said I was amazed that people would buy something like that at a swapmeet, he just looked skyward. Although the recession was on and money was supposedly short, he had had no trouble moving the big Class A motorhomes. These people, he assured me, only look as if they don't have money. "They have," he whispered conspiratorially, "blue hair, bad breath, and *all the money.*"

Sad to say, from Sam's point of view, the glory days for Quartzsite are over. There's a new mayor, new zoning, new paperwork, and a police force—all unnecessary from his point of view. This was RV-topia before the rules. Now it's just like selling in Sacramento. Once they started paving the roads, "*Adios,*" he said, kissing his fingertips. You could buy and sell anything, but now someone is always checking your paperwork. Plus, a different clientele has moved in. He asked me to consider the names of the RV parks in Quartzsite, the ones with hookups. Many of them didn't even have names. I was staying at a place called 88 Shades (which I supposed was named for what could be imagined in the way of palm trees). But now there was a new kind of campground on both sides of the Colorado River, just thirty miles away. Sam told me to check them out.

Next day I did, and Sam was right. On the Arizona side: Castle Rock Shores Resort, Havasu Springs Resort, Sandbar Resort @ Redrock, Winnetou Shores Park. On the California side: Bermuda Parks, Big Bend Resort; Back Meadow Landing; Emerald Cove Resort; Rio Del Sol Haven, Sunshine Resort. . . . The names did tell a different story. There were still plenty of boondockers in the desert, but the demographics were shifting. Nesting birds were pushing out the migratory ones. His stock in trade, the "Geritol gypsies," were being pushed aside by the new breed of stay-at-homes. A sure sign of change: Indian casinos with their high-rise hotels were starting to appear up State Route 95. RV parking in the rear. Free.

Slab City, California: The End of the Road

If Quartzsite is the Emerald City of Oz, a magical stop on the yellow brick road for many RV enthusiasts, then Slab City is the Roach Motel, the place you drive into and maybe never get out of. It's been the end of the road for hundreds of RVs since the 1950s. The road in is not the transcontinental interstate, as with Quartzsite, but a dirt spur two miles from the dreary town of Niland, California.

The RV park (a considerable overstatement) sits on an abandoned military base once called Ft. Dunlap. Back before World War II, the fort housed wooden barracks used for training soldiers for the North Africa campaign. Before that the land had been ceded to the California State Teachers Retirement System as part of a federal grant in 1853 for public education. Since the war, day-to-day administration of the some 600 acres has shifted through various governmental agencies like the proverbial hot potato. No one wants to hold title to the land because all that remained when the army backed out were the cement slabs that supported the barracks (hence the name—the Slabs) and some unexploded ordnance. In addition, the navy has kept some adjacent land in the Chocolate Mountains onto which they drop real and pretend bombs (the *Enola Gay* practiced here before dropping the atomic bomb on Hiroshima). Some of the real ones haven't exploded, at least not until scavengers tinkered with them.

To appreciate the macabre nature of the Slabs, you need still more local knowledge. Niland is close to a huge inland sinkhole called the Salton Sea Basin. This vestigial ocean bay got closed up eons ago when tectonic plates shifted—it's atop the San Andreas Fault. The resulting fetid swamp was well on its way to becoming yet more desert when a freak accident happened. In 1905, a dike along the Colorado River burst during violent floods and the entire river poured in for months, filling up the ancient sinkhole. Desperately needing its rail bed over the sink repaired, the Southern Pacific Railroad Company dumped tons of earth back onto the dike, thereby trapping the freshwater.

Coincidentally, the Hoover Dam across the Colorado River was completed, thereby preventing more water from spilling into the sink. So by the early twentieth century, the Salton Sea had been partially filled with freshwater, with no more coming in and no drain channel to allow the water out. For a while in the late 1940s, it looked as if this inland lake was going to become a new tourist mecca. Developers hurried in to plat the new lakeshore houses. The shoreline was huge. Palm Springs was going to be rebuilt, this time for the common man. If you think the 1920s Florida land boom was scurrilous, it was tame compared with what was happening here.

The problem was that all that water was essentially orphaned in a highly saline basin, and, over time, as the hydrologists had warned, the salt began to leach back into the water. No one listened to the scientists. This was the Imperial Valley, home to some of the most fertile soil in the world. All you did was add water and a touch of Miracle Gro and step back: Crops exploded. So for generations the irrigation water from the Colorado has flowed down through the crops and emptied into the Salton Sea.

This made for a dangerous combination: The salty water, now rich in nutrients from the runoff, provided perfect living conditions for certain kinds of ocean fish like tilapia while freshwater fish gradually disappeared. This fertility has had some unintended consequences. Bacteria levels are high, and algae blooms are frequent. Blooms can cover huge portions of the sea, and when the algae die off, they decompose, taking oxygen out of the water and causing a horrible stench. As the oxygen leaves the water in the extreme heat of summer, millions of tilapia surface, gasping for air, flop over, and die. The flotsam of dead fish, some of which carry avian botulism, soon attracts hundreds of thousands of birds. In 1997, the disease killed ten thousand endangered brown pelicans.

This place is eerie. The Salton Sea Basin makes Love Canal look like an environmental romp in the hay. Even Sonny Bono, whose political district this was, couldn't figure out what to do other than to change its name in 1998 to the Sonny Bono Salton Sea National Wildlife Refuge. You could flood it with freshwater, you could flood it with salt water, you could leave it alone to putrefy, or you could try to drain it. No matter what you do, though, it's a toxic mess. And that's why no one cares about the entire region, why towns like Niland are in a state of advanced decrepitude, why the California state park on the shores of the sea is being closed, why even the Hell's Angels, who used to frequent taverns on the shore, have better places to go, and why the Slabs RV settlement has been left alone.

When I asked the park ranger at the Salton Sea State Recreational Area for directions to the Slabs, he rolled his eyes and asked if I really wanted to go there. There was always something going wrong at the Slabs, he said, nothing important, but always something out of whack. In fact, he said, the southern part of the state park was now closed because someone kept stealing the photovoltaic panels that provided power for the composting outhouses. The vandals might have come from the Slabs; he wasn't sure, because they use the panels to power their RV batteries. Also, in the past few days there had been a minor robbery of the collection money that is set aside for Leonard Knight, the artist who is still creating Salvation Mountain. These were not big events, misdemeanors really, but they typified what was now happening at the Slabs.

He seemed to find stealing donations from this Leonard Knight more upsetting than the pillaging of the solar panels. In any case, many people who visit the Slabs in their RVs now spend the night here at his state park, where they pay a fee rather than boondock at the Slabs for free. "Draw your own conclusions," he sighed.

I had not heard of Salvation Mountain before, nor did I know of Leonard Knight, but clearly he was a central part of the Salton Sea Cultural Basin, and, as I learned, to appreciate the Slabs you should know a bit about his extraordinary work. It's not that Salvation Mountain and Slab City necessarily fit together, but they are on the same road, literally and figuratively. They are both on the margins of a culture at risk. In a way, they both turn their worlds upside down. And they depend on each other.

You approach the Slabs from the west, leaving lonely State Highway 111, heading out past Niland on a dirt road. There are no directional signs, no souvenir shops, no local pride in what should be a tribute to freedom-loving RVers. Off to your right you see a massive mound—about 30 acres—of packed sand and baled hay coated in layer upon layer of painted adobe. In fact, the paint—some 60,000 gallons—literally holds the bas-relief of flowers, flags, and gigantic words together. From afar it looks like a child's ice cream confection with the squirty print of a birthday cake.

As you get closer, you see that across the front it implores, in creamy 3-D script: *Jesus I'm a sinner please come upon my body and into my heart.* Higher up the mound of flowing contours all in caps is: *love.* Higher still is *god is*, so the whole sentence *god is love* can be seen. On top of the cake, like a single candle, is a large cross fixed to the undulating mountain by a stable monument base. The sense you get from first seeing this mound of rolling curves and flowing dips is that it's vaguely protoplasmic.

When art historians discuss Salvation Mountain, they invariably invoke Grandma Moses, Dr. Seuss, and Simon Rodia, the sculptor who created the Watts Towers. Like much folk art, it looks childish, loud, Crayola-bright, and joyful. But when you get close, you see that it is intricate, proportional, balanced, and really well organized. The artist, now in his seventies, is usually on the scene and more than willing to give you the story. It's simple. Some thirty years ago he was visited by the Lord. He first tried to make a balloon to express his thanks, but it wouldn't fly. Then he came to the desert and realized he could make the balloon in adobe and paint. For years he has lived in his own makeshift RV that he has painted in 3-D just like the hay bales. The RV is part and parcel of Salvation Mountain and in a way sets the stage for the Slabs next door.

As Leonard gleefully will tell you, it has not been easy to be chosen. A decade ago he was visited by the EPA, which bored holes in his mountain and proclaimed it a "toxic nightmare." The lead from all that paint was draining into the subsurface. Clearly, they had not considered what was draining into the ground up at the Slabs. The EPA suggested destruction of the entire Salvation Mountain. Leonard's many supporters lobbied the state, and finally Congresswoman Barbara Boxer had the site enshrined as "primitive art." Ironically, that act is also protecting the Slabs.

I spent an afternoon with Leonard. He is now in declining health and would rather work the crowd than work on the mountain. He had a helper who scampered around arranging interviews and generally acting as curator of this massive mound of religious excitement. You are free to walk around, over, and under the mountain. The installation is amazingly clever, with little grottos and turnarounds built into the stacked hay bales. While we were talking, kids were riding over the top of his masterpiece on all-terrain vehicles, and halfway up the mountain I saw my dog taking a pee on the path. I was aghast; Leonard, unfazed.

Leonard's slightly upside-down approach sets the stage for the Slabs. His favorite word after *salvation* is *freedom*. He has included the American

Figure 4.3: Salvation Mountain, near Slab City (Lukas & Suzy VanDyke *www.lukasandsuzy.com*).

Figure 4.4: Leonard's RV (Lukas & Suzy VanDyke
www.lukasandsuzy.com).

flag on the mountain because it represents freedom, even though some of his devout visitors say he's mixing church and state, sacred and profane. He's unfazed. We must be free, he says, to do what we must do to be saved, and this country is the place to do it. America: home of the free and the saved. So he lives in his converted 1939 White fire truck (which is decorated as intensely as the hay bales) because, who knows?, he may want to move. The rig doesn't move, of course; it's larded with coats of paint and putty. But the RV, the home-on-wheels, is the point. It offers the illusion of escape, the gypsy wagon at the ready. He's American, and his Prairie Clipper is out behind the barn. Escape to what? Salvation.

Up the road from Leonard's brilliantly plastered waves of grain is an apocalyptic chapter in the Book of American Roadside Revelation. You know you are getting close when you pass a cement pedestal with a large hand-painted welcome to Slab City sign. About a half mile ahead, across hard-packed desert, are the famous cement slabs left by the departing army of George Patton. Up on them now is a new encampment, this time of folks who want a life of unfettered freedom, a group of tumbleweeds and dirt devils whom the general would have had a hard time whipping into shape. They want freedom from all: freedom from state-supplied electricity, water, and sewage as well as freedom from any tariff for an overnight or even over-lifetime stay; freedom from nagging spouses and child support; freedom from mail delivery, freedom from, well, you name it.

The Slabs is the largest free camping site in the country. As a utopia of "do your own thing," it is well worth a trip for those Panglossians who promulgate the faith in "least government is best government." This place does not celebrate the more famous Burning Man joy in an untethered world; it lives it. Burning Man tries to find new order in the desert for a week or so; the Slabs tries to get away from order by going into the desert for an indefinite time. Burning Man is intensely self-conscious: How'm I doin' takin' my clothes off? It's recreation. Slabs is more pragmatic: I'm naked; my clothes are worn out. It's survival. Slabs is Burning Man with a vulture overhead. It looked to me like the end of William Golding's *Lord of the Flies*.

I was repeatedly told that the Slabs has changed. In the early 1960s, this was a place where you could see the $300,000 rig parked in peaceful

Figure 4.5: Slab City welcome sign (Frank McKenna Photography, San Diego California).

tranquility next to the dilapidated school bus. Here was boondocking in its idyllic form. Snowbirds could fire up their generators while Slabbers could harvest battery power from solar cells. Potable water was trucked in, and sewage was either dumped down the gopher holes or trucked out. The community was connected by CB radio, which broadcast a nightly program of local events, including dances, pot-luck dinners, book clubs, and board games. To the people who first observed this New Harmony and reported on it in the *LA Times*, *New York Times*, *Harper's*, and *Time* magazine, the magic was palpable. In the wake of such good press, the Slabs also started appearing on the endless lists of cheap places to retire. It was part of what easterners call "Weird California," by which they often meant Belmont and Fishtown side by side.

After all, the Slabs was, in a sense, the apogee of American Romanticism, each person finding salvation on his own slab, hoeing his own bean row, as Thoreau supposed, and coming together only when it fitted individual needs, not group demands. What law there was was the law of unreflecting generosity. The limits of individual freedom were indeed the edges of one's desire. Sure, the state was hovering over the slabs, but there was so much confusion as to who actually owned the land that no one knew who could legally kick the squatters out, or even force them to pay for their "externalities." (There were a few kids going to school in Niland, there was a continual ambulance service to hospital, and there was the garbage problem.)

No wonder that in Sean Penn's 2007 adaptation of Jon Krakauer's *Into the Wild*, a central scene takes place in the Slabs. Here we see Christopher McCandless meeting other RV vagabonds who will induct him into the fraternity of enlightened earth wanderers. The Slabs is portrayed as utopian, an unfettered life in discarded school buses under the warming sun. At the Slabs, Christopher changes his name to Alexander Supertramp, and he is finally with his own people. But, alas, he must push on to his fate, which just happens to be a strange turn on his time at Slabs: He spends his final days holed up and freezing in a discarded school bus in Denali National Park.

Perhaps it was the attraction of the movie that caused a shift in clientele at the Slabs. For a while younger people came, stayed, and then moved on. Gray hair notwithstanding, there is a deep strain of adolescence in the RV life, as there is in American Transcendentalism. Experiments in American utopia from Brook Farm, Amana, Fruitlands, and the Shakers all bump up against the fact that finally someone has to take out the trash. The City on the Hill, or, in this case, the City in the Sand, slowly started to crack from underneath. Of course the Slabs was never self-consciously constituted as a commune of freedom-loving individuals. It had no manifesto other than, "If you don't like it, move out."

But when you talk with Slabbers, you realize their language is the lingo of RVers filtered through Leonard Knight. They are all living private lives in which the refrain of heading out to the Promised Land is often repeated like a mantra. But while the kids may come and go, most of the old-timers are not heading out. Like Leonard's RV, they're stuck. And without medical care, many are living lives of discomfort, even pain. Utopias have a nasty tendency to flip into dystopias. Remember *Fahrenheit 451, Brave New World, Nineteen Eighty-four, The Handmaid's Tale, The Giver, Battle Royale, Lord of the Flies.* . . .

Although numbers are hard to gauge, at one time there were about two thousand full-timers at an average age of just over fifty-five. Now I would guess there are half that many and still fewer in the summer. As many observers have noticed, most of the permanent settlers of the Slabs are, again like Leonard Knight, solitary men with minor adaptation problems. Although there are many interior neighborhoods (Canadians in *Loonie Hill*, occasional nudists in *Skin City*, northerners in *Snowbird, East Jesus* for artists, *Poverty Flats* for what you'd expect), the core is called the *Badlands*. And it's called that not because it's hostile, but because life for these residents is . . . bad.

More telling is that the ratio of men to women in this group of die-hards is about five to one. That's the opposite of most retirement communities. Like many such communities, there are groups for the singles to join (Loners on Wheels, the Wandering Individuals Network, Birds of a Feather), but the groups come together not to find mates but to find helpmates. Many of these Badlanders are here because they ran out of money and gas, but some are here to hide from the law. Most common offense: not paying child support. They have no interest in starting a new family; they are more concerned with staying alive.

Although *Into the Wild* made Badlands famous, another movie, the *Mad Max* franchise, gives a better picture of the feel of the place—except these people are not mobile, they're stuck. They spend their days doing the simple things: getting water in and getting waste out. There are no dumpsters, no places to take trash, and hence the place looks like a dump. Dogs run free, and there are a lot of them. When you drive through this section of the Slabs, you see that around each derelict RV is a patch of privacy often marked by camo netting and tires filled with sand. There is little interest in human reproduction; in fact, the aged population is rapidly decreasing. The old-time Slabbers are dying off, literally, going the way of their antitype, the New England Shakers. As I wandered through I couldn't help but think that this place was a profound upside-downing of the usual American catchphrase, "So much to

Figure 4.6: RV on slab (Lynn Bremner, DesertUSA.com).

do, so little time." At the Slabs, there was so little to do, so much time. These are Easy Riders on a rough road.

No one knows what will happen to the Slabs as the older generation passes on. Some self-professed artists have appeared, thanks to Salvation Mountain being protected as a National Treasure, and part of the Slabs is turning into an artists' collective. The anarchist mentality still makes it attractive for a revival of experiments in life outside the lines. I saw tie-dyes worn with no embarrassment. Music is important, and there is an active collection of players and even a performance stage called The Range. Drugs, especially meth, promise yet another subculture, complete with its own manufacture and distribution. Wandering around, I couldn't get out of my mind the grizzly scene at the beginning of the critically acclaimed TV series *Breaking Bad* in which an old Winnebago is used as a mobile meth lab.

Whatever it becomes, the Slabs will probably retain its primal connection with the RV. After all, you really can't live here without perching on those concrete pads. And there are plenty of discarded RVs around the country that have enough gas left to make the trip out to Salvation Mountain before breaking down. Slabs will have a future of some sort. People will continue to come to camp, although no one can predict what that camping will be like.

BUT IS THIS CAMPING OR PARKING?

Especially after seeing the Slabs, many people might understandably bridle when the words *RV* and *camping* are used together. What's camping when it entails hooking yourself up to all the things you are supposedly leaving home to be free of? Or is camping living on a concrete pad in the middle of nowhere? When you go *camping*, my friends tell me, you take a bedroll and some matches and you either backpack or paddle. You go from tame to wild and then back to tame. That's the point. You don't drive there, open the awning, turn on the AC, and then close the door and watch the tele. I know they are right. Many RVers I've spoken to agree. They prefer words like *traveling* or *living*. There should be a word that describes the process of heading out in an RV, be it to Disney's Fort Wilderness Campground or to the Slabs.

You might think that as an English teacher who has spent upward of three years and 60,000 miles puttering about North America I should be able to bring peace to this semantic hairsplitting. I know when I pass those *camping* signs on the interstate that something is horribly wrong. I've pulled off and spent the night there: I know it's not camping. But *glamping* (glamorous camping) in *glampsites* does not do it for me. Nor would a sign at the next exit saying *soft camping*. Or even one saying *slabbing*. The English have a term, *caravan camping* or *caravanning*, which depends on knowing that caravan and small RV are synonymous. We don't have this usage. And terms like *boutique camping* or *posh camping* or even *land yachting* are a bit over-the-top and really not accurate. *Winnebagoing* is too much on the take.

If there is one thing we've seen in this chapter—from staying in the typical RV campground to staying in the national/state park system, to boondocking in the asphalt wilderness of Walmart, to staying in swanky lots with concierge service, to becoming part of such *unsettlements* as NASCAR infields, football games, Quartzsite, and the Slabs—the place to stay is as variable as the rigs in which to get there. A friend has suggested *comfy camping*, not because it's all that comfy but because in each case being in the rig is relatively better than the alternative. At least you are not on the ground: *grounded*. True enough, but I wouldn't hold my breath waiting for the signs along the interstate to change. Maybe the lack of specific language pays proper tribute to the variability of the experience.

chapter five

THE RISE AND FALL AND RISE AND FALL OF THE RV IN AMERICA

...

On May 20, 2012, the *New York Times* published a somewhat flighty article on RV life titled "Just Me and My RV" in which writer/photographer Andy Isaacson described roaming around northeastern California in a rented RV. It was a pleasant and fair-minded piece typical of the Travel Section. In this genre, the writer usually boards a plane, heads off to a distant place, and then tells us a bit of what he saw, what he ate, how much it cost, whom he talked to, and how much fun it was. Often there's a map next to the text so that you can see where our correspondent went and where he stayed. The following week a few letters appear in this section chiding the author that he missed such-and-such place that really is the letter writer's favorite. This tradition continues in the online edition of the *Times*, only with more entries.

MR. WINNEBAGO, TEAR DOWN THIS OBJECT

THE
RISE
AND
FALL
AND
...
OF
THE
RV
IN
AMERICA
128

After Isaacson's article appeared, 105 comments quickly followed. True to form, there were the listing of omissions, warm reminiscences of RV trips, and much discussion of which is cheaper, RV travel using campgrounds or car travel using motels. The tone was generally cheery. But there was also a series of comments the like of which I have never seen in years of reading the Travel Section. Some comments were about Iasscson's opening paragraph: "I have spent the night in a Wal-Mart parking lot. I have driven through a national park with a trail of cars in my rearview mirror. I have learned how to dispose of my waste through a plastic hose, and I have filled my gas tank more times in one week than I thought were possible." These words touched a nerve with letter writers. Here, have a look:

From Marc in Colorado:

From Columbus to Lewis and Clark to Kerouac the distant unknown and the discovery that "IT" is in the journey and not the destination has shaped the character of America. But as you celebrate your personal pilgrimage and liberation from the ordinary—and I do so genuinely wish you all the "enlighten-ment" we fellow travelers seek and venerate—please allow others to find their own way in their own time: PULL OVER! We too enjoy the view and the back of an RV is not what we had in mind. Thank you.

From Reiser from Everywhere:

"I have driven through a national park with a trail of cars in my rearview mirror." Yep, I think I saw you today in Rocky Mountain, quite literally a studio apartment on wheels where none belong. Get off the road!

From D. Dodd in North Hero, Vermont:

"I have driven through a national park with a trail of cars in my rearview mirror." So pull over & let them by!

From Grannychi in Grand Rapids, Michigan:

Having been nearly forced off the road or side-swiped on countless occasions by SUV-renters who had no feel for their vehicle's
width, I rather dread meeting novice RV drivers on the road.
Just a bit of practice, please.

Michael Jacques in southwestern Pennsylvania:

Ick. I've always hated RVs; it's not like they just became uncool
after the recession. They're traffic hazards. They're environmental
nightmares. They're ugly.

Jelafleur from Woonsocket, Rhode Island:

Did you ever stop to consider that RV's and dinosaurs have a
lot in common?

And then this most provocative comment from **Dancing Scorpion
in Arizona:**

Yes, I'm aware that Mr. Isaacson, the advertised writer and
photographer, has a living to get but, really, I'M PERPLEXED
BY THIS FEATURE IN THE PAPER. The aware reader may
have noticed that while many of the corporations are doing well
(by firing personnel, raising prices, cutting production corners,
etc.), ordinary Americans still find themselves very much mired
in a recession, contrary to government reports stretching the
truth from revision to report revision. Why ordinary Americans
such as "RVers" would spend $4–5 a gallon for gas to travel in
a troublesome tin can with low m.p.g. and soaring mechanical
costs and insurance is truly a mystery. Everything about travel
has entered the fantasy zone of over the moon pricing and inconvenience, so either "RVers" haven't a clue how to spend their
money wisely or are the filthy rich the world has come to despise.
I think a case can be made that the NYT is really a reactionary

THE
RISE
AND
FALL
AND
...
OF
THE
RV
IN
AMERICA

129

THE
RISE
AND
FALL
AND
...
OF
THE
RV
IN
AMERICA

130

publication, producing stuff over and over for its readers that was appropriate forty years ago, when the roads were open and road travel didn't threaten to break the bank. The readers it chooses to target are too old, too broke, or too tired to care anymore. Mr. Isaacson, are you listening!

This comment spurs Rich Truesdell from California to defend the article saying, "The great thing about America, up until now, is that we are free to make our own decisions about where and how to live, what we spend our money on, and how and where we travel," to which the Dancing Scorpion stings:

PLEASE, MR. TRUESDELL, LET'S GET my participation on this thread straight. My criticism of the author was for a singular unwarranted act of materialism and hedonism in time of war and relentless recession. And the willingness of the NYT and the author to flaunt such behavior among those who must suffer these calamities, in the paper of national record. Really, what don't you get about that? Bragging on your own materialism and hedonism is astounding, and brings to mind that there is good reason to question anymore the lacking common sense of ordinary Americans and decision makers. Is there any reason to question why America has become a parody of itself? And, by the way, my comments were not about the open road and the associated costs of travel "back in 1976." Finally, no one is preventing you from acting as you wish; but certainly no one has to find anything to admire about what you do, either.

Lest you think that the Scorpion's bite is just the reaction of a disgruntled Marxist from Fishtown, here is Bill Bryson, a favorite of Belmontians, saying much the same thing in *The Lost Continent: Travels in Small Town America*. Bryson lets loose as he is driving through Appalachia:

All morning I had been troubled by a vague sense of something being missing, and then it occurred to me what it was. There were no hikers such as you would see in England—no people in stout boots and short pants, with knee-high tasseled stockings. No little rucksacks full of sandwiches and flasks of tea and baker's caps laboring breathlessly up the mountainsides, slowing up traffic. What slowed the traffic here were the massive motor homes lumbering up and down the mountain passes. Some of them, amazingly, had cars tethered to their rear bumpers, like dinghies. I got stuck behind one on the long, sinuous descent down the mountain into Tennessee. It was so wide that it could barely stay within its lane and kept threatening to nudge oncoming cars off into the picturesque void to our left. That, alas, is the way of vacationing nowadays for many people. The whole idea is not to expose yourself to a moment of discomfort or inconvenience—indeed, not to breathe fresh air if possible. . . . *RV people are another breed—and a largely demented one at that.* They become obsessed with trying to equip their vehicles with gadgets to deal with every possible contingency. Their lives become ruled by the dread thought that one day they may find themselves in a situation in which they are not entirely self-sufficient. (84–85, italics mine)

I mention these reactions because there are few objects in the American cornucopia that generate as much scorn as the RV. Dancing Scorpion would never write to the *Times* and complain that the traveling correspondent has just burned up a ton of finite fuel to fly to some far-off spot to write his piece. And Mr. Bryson, who spends much of this time flying between the U.S. and his home in England, would not be wasting ink if he didn't feel superior to the RV owner. When he lets loose with, "RV people are another breed—and a largely demented one at that," he is venting sensations widely shared. Bryson's annoyance is, I dare say, directed at the very Americanness of the RV, the self-sufficiency of it, the nose-thumbing of a culture whose often conflicted love affair with the internal combustion engine occasionally goes AWOL. Yes, what he says is true—they are road hogs—but what he misses is the fun of it, the pleasure of it, the escape of it, and, in a way, the daft Romanticism of it. Okay, so William Wordsworth would not have bought one, but Lord Byron certainly would have. And did. In 1816 Byron crossed

THE TOURING

Figure 5.1: Albert Levering, *The Touring Car of the Future, Puck* (magazine centerfold), June, 28, 1905 (Library of Congress) with Dining Hall, Kitchen, Servants Hall, High Finance and Recupera-

F THE FUTURE.

tion Apartment, State Rooms, Hair Dressing Studio, Gossip Den, Nursery, and Gymnasium on the roof.

THE
RISE
AND
FALL
AND
...
OF
THE
RV
IN
AMERICA

134

Europe in a huge campaign-style coach modeled on the one used by his hero Napoleon. He, and others, slept and drank in it. Rather like the Puritans' problem with bear baiting, which, according to the arch Victorian Thomas Macaulay, was not that it gave too much pain to the bear but that it gave too much pleasure to the audience, the imagined release of RVing is partly what makes it upsetting. Have a look at figure 5.1, which shows how joyfully the English of the early twentieth century pictured the future thrill of autotouring in *The Touring Car of the Future*.

So I wonder if the current Belmontian response to the supposed thrills of the nomadic life is not at the heart of much of the unease that surrounds this object. That it seems to cost a lot of money and that it seems to be a bit of fun is, perhaps, hard to take. Worse, of course, it hogs the highway. If you look at how the object is portrayed in popular culture, you may see something quite interesting. The RV has great attraction for children (think Barbie's RV from Mattel) and great attraction for those in retirement, but it often poses a problem for those in the middle. I wonder if "taking off" and getting "outta here" is an irritant for those who are stuck in place, those who are riding alone to their jobs in their gas-guzzling cars and who are perhaps secretly counting the days until they too can slip the harness.

THE RISE, SHINE, EVAPORATION, AND FALL OF THE RV IN POPULAR CULTURE

I say this because if you look at how the RV is portrayed in popular entertainment, you see that it was an object of much interest and even yearning until about the 1960s. (I say this overlooking that the first famous RV—the Joad family Hudson in the 1940 *Grapes of Wrath*—may have been an escape vehicle but the escape was hardly drawn from dreams.) But then, as the epynomic Winnebago started to be mass-produced, the allure of escape in the house-on-wheels grew double-edged. Once almost every Tom, Dick, and Harry could have a moveable bedroom— and many did, thanks to banks' willingness to consider them "second homes," the object of yearning became an object of annoyance. By the 1970s the RV had become a metaphor of middle-class uncouthness and was well on its way to becoming an symbol of wastefulness.

Just two movies will demonstrate this arc: Lucille Ball and Desi Arnez's 1953 movie *The Long, Long Trailer* and Robin Williams's 2006 film *RV: The Movie*. Both were comedies starring the generation's central comedians, both were expensive with high production values, both featured adventures crossing the Rockies, and both were box-office successes. Yet they show that a real shift has occurred: the RV in the 1950s was aspirational; fifty years later it had become laughable.

The Long, Long Trailer is beautiful to look at. It should be: the movie was produced by Pandro Berman, who did all the Fred Astaire movies, and it was filmed by Vincent Minnelli, who made musicals for MGM. These men knew how to make *lavish*. So their making a Technicolor extravaganza about trailers tells much about what was happening in American culture after the war. This film literally sparkles. The trailer is an eyeful of lemon cream with stripes of coruscating chrome. And this trailer—the brand is never mentioned but the Redman New Moon logo is shown often enough to make the point—is a testament to what Thomas Hine has called *populuxe*, the new world of rounded surfaces, the layering of Formica and plastic to create a spangling world of excitement.

Of course Lucy wants one. She loves things that shine. Plus the trailer has all the labor-saving devices she doesn't have in the dingy apartment. And Desi wants one too. This way they can be together. Oddly enough, although he does a lot of singing and finger-snapping, in this film Desi is not a band leader but a roadway engineer. His job makes no sense until you realize that this movie is really a celebration of roads and what can appear on these roads. So Desi makes them, and Lucy uses them.

Forget the plot. There really isn't one. This is a film dedicated to a new phenomenon: the ability to move your house around the country whenever, wherever you want. Lucy, not Desi, wants to buy the trailer even if it costs $5,345 (one-third down and years to pay) and even if it means having to buy a new car. Once Desi gets over the sticker shock, and once they are married, the first thing they do is drive the rig back to the family home, where all can gawk at their good fortune. Then it's off from trailer park to trailer park, where they invariably meet the "nicest people," who also have these newfangled things. When they miss the trailer park, as they must when Lucy is doing the cartography,

Figure 5.2:
Lucy and Desi go camping,
The Long, Long Trailer, 1953
(lobby card).

they do a little boondocking. Cue the rainstorm and a chance to use a
jack. Predictable pratfalls.

But the real focus of the movie is what it's like inside the trailer.
For one thing, it's spacious. While Desi is up front driving the con-
vertible (sometimes it's a Lincoln, sometimes a Mercury) singing some
momborama tune, we watch Lucy homemaking in back. The fun begins
when she starts to move around and we get a lesson in why riding in a
moving trailer was soon to become illegal. The best scenes are when
she's cooking while Desi is crooning (and doing 60, as repeated cuts to
the speedometer show). To wit: Lucy cooking in the trailer opens with
her tossing dressing and cheese on the salad and ends with her being
tossed along with the salad. Then she opens a bag of flour. The scene

ends with Lucy finally exiting the trailer into the arms of Desi covered in lettuce and flour and tears. She spends the next day at the beauty parlor.

The most famous scene in *The Long, Long Trailer* has become a set piece in countless RV movies: crossing the Rockies. We watch the rig going up, up, up and then *almost* over a mountain pass. Although the sequence is now a cliché, the filmgoers who first saw Lucy in the trailer while Desi is weaving across the lanes, just at the edge of sending the trailer over the embankment, were understandably thrilled. It's wonderful cinematography and really scary, even without 3-D. At the summit, this huge mass of metal and wheels (Desi calls it "40 feet of freight train") almost goes careening over the road shoulder. Up front, Desi is oblivious; behind, Lucy is saucer-eyed and screaming.

THE
RISE
AND
FALL
AND
...
OF
THE
RV
IN
AMERICA

138

The young lovebirds have a little fight as Desi learns that the reason for the topsy-turvy trouble is that Lucy has been loading up the trailer with souvenir rocks and tons of canned food—shades of the Tin Can Tourists perhaps. It's the extra weight—not Desi's driving, or any flaw in the trailer—that almost sends them tumbling off the mountain pass. After a pout or two, the newlyweds make up and the movie is over. It's not clear what happens to the star of the film, the lemon-meringue recreational vehicle, but it has served its purpose. America has been introduced to this new object of desire, and it sure is great. To make the point stick, a spanking new trailer from the Redman Trailer Company was often parked on the street in front of major theaters for opening night.

And we in the audience have learned our lesson: Build more roads. See the USA. Listen to Ike: We need an interstate system. Trailers are nifty, even though they take some care in operating (in one scene Desi is instructed in how to apply the brakes—trailer first, then car). We are instructed to be careful cooking in a moving trailer; we have met "trailerites," as they are called in the film, and they are good people always bringing over Epsom salts and advice for young lovers; we know now not to add too much weight to the rig or things can go screwy, and, most important, if Lucy and Desi can do it, you can too.

In the next half century this tone will shift from enthusiastic acceptance to, if the Dancing Scorpion and Bill Bryson are trustworthy observers, biting denunciation. I don't believe the arched eyebrows are wholly related to the RVs' environmental "externalities": their road hogging, gas guzzling, or their ungainliness. Remember, these critics have no qualms about traveling by airplane (as opposed to the more environmentally friendly Greyhound or Amtrak) and then renting a full-sized car. And big trucks do more road hogging. I believe something far more interesting is at work in our modern response to the wheeled estate.

If entertainment culture can be trusted as a gauge of popular opinion, then briefly looking at portrayals of who owns RVs, and how they use them, may tell us something of how we feel both about the object and about those who drive it. In the last half century, there have been about a hundred films in which the RV played a role. And this is not counting the way that the subject is treated on television, other than to say that, as might be expected, Homer Simpson drove a humungous RV over a cliff à la Desi. And that the Partridge Family spent their entire 1970 season driving around in one that looked as if it had been painted by Mondrian. Enough said, the stereotype that RVs are for dolts and kiddies is well in place on the small screen.

The movies, however, tell a more interesting tale, and to a considerable extent that's because if you want to transport your protagonist from scene to scene, the RV is perfect. It's a living room on wheels with a front window that acts almost like a movie screen. There's even a litcrit genre to describe this kind of episodic story, and it's called the *picaresque*. The hero is usually a young man, called a *picaro*, who has a series of encounters with the confusions of growing up. Think Tom Jones, Huck Finn, or even Harry Potter. But the original template for the picaresque protagonist is Cervantes's cranky, aging Don Quixote, and that's exactly who you find starring in the RV movie.

If you ask someone to name a movie in which an RV figures prominently, they will probably forget the titles but remember the actors: Robert De Niro, Jack Nicholson, Robin Williams, Chevy Chase, and Albert Brooks. So, clearly, whatever story is going to be told, it's not going to be about a kid finding out about life, but a mature male learning about things he may have missed earlier in life. And so, like Don Quixote, he's probably going to be playing the fool. In a word, he's *quixotic*.

And indeed in the Focker franchise (*Meet the Parents*, 2000; *Meet the Fockers*, 2004; *Little Fockers*, 2011), *About Schmidt* (2002), *RV: the Movie* (2006), *Christmas Vacation* (1989), and *Lost in America* (1985), that is exactly what happens. The middle-aged American male is off on an adventure, to be sure, and he's using this kind of transport because he's a doofus. The RV is the ideal capsule in which to observe him. We look in as he looks out. Here's just a thumbnail view of what happens:

- In *About Schmidt*, Jack Nicholson plays a weary insurance agent whose wife has died and he's off in the ironically named Winnebago Adventurer to recover his lost self. He putters around the Midwest having experiences in RV parks, in hot tubs, and on the highway. He's a sad sack, a gray man, and the RV is both a palliative and an escape. In fact, at the end he prefers sleeping in the rig to going back to an empty home.

THE
RISE
AND
FALL
AND
...
OF
THE
RV
IN
AMERICA
139

THE
RISE
AND
FALL
AND
...
OF
THE
RV
IN
AMERICA

140

- In the *Focker* franchise, Robert De Niro plays a tightly wound ex-CIA operative who appears in his big Class A motorhome ("It's not a trailer, it's a Fleetwood!") and is a busybody pest. He means well perhaps, but he's a nudge. His RV is not just a place to stay but a command center for his foolish intrusions into his daughter's life. Once again: RV owner = dolt.

- Not much need be said about *Christmas Vacation* other than that it comes from the *National Lampoon* series starring Chevy Chase. The goofy brother-in-law from Kansas (Randy Quaid) arrives in a dilapidated RV and, based on our watching of the earlier films, we know some real stupidity is coming our way. We are not let down. Emptying sewage into public spaces plays a prominent role.

- The most sophisticated of the genre is understandably the one that made the least money, Albert Brooks's *Lost in America*. Here the middle-aged male takes off to find himself in America. He's an adman in LA who does not want to be transferred to New York. So he buys the Winnebago. As critics pointed out, it makes no sense, but it doesn't have to. There's the frantic scene on the interstate when he runs out of gas, and the requisite stop in Las Vegas, where he runs out of money. It's Desi and Lucy all over again, with Mr. Brooks often playing the Lucy part. This film abruptly ends *in medias res* because there is really no ending to this kind of trip: It just goes on and on.

In many respects the most recent entry, *RV: The Movie* (2006), starring Robin Williams, is a condensation of all the attempts to tell this story. This is the middle-aged RV saga with all the clichés in place: the *picaro*'s frustration with his job, the long-suffering family, the problems with above-ground sewage, the deep allure of the gypsy life, the road hogging, the awkward ending, and even a scene lifted from *The Long, Long Trailer* (and *The Simpsons*) with the motorhome suspended on a precipice in the Rockies.

In *RV: The Movie* Robin Williams plays "Robin Williams," his usual stage persona—the man with too much on his mind. Typical of the genre, he's about to be "repositioned" and so takes his family off for an

Figure 5.3: Robin Williams goes camping in *RV: The Movie*, 2006 (print ad).

THE
RISE
AND
FALL
AND
...
OF
THE
RV
IN
AMERICA
142

adventure. Of course they don't want to go, and of course the RV he gets is really ludicrous—a huge rental unit with an image of the owner of the rental company slathered across the side in garish streaks of green with blotches of orange. (The inside joke is that this is the likeness of Barry Sonnenberg, who directed the movie.) "But we're not campers!" says the long-suffering wife. "This RV is a rolling turd," says his 'tween daughter.

As now expected in the genre, sewage is central, and having it spew out all over our *picaro* takes up most of our time. Robin is helped by Jeff Daniels and his family, who are full-timers in an old-time bus (a classic Flxible). They know how to handle the black water. We see how wonderfully this family gets along—the kids are home-schooled, or bus-schooled, and they eagerly do the RV chores. By watching them, Robin sees what's wrong with his family: He's not there for his kids, so of course they are "acting out." In the climactic scene, Robin realizes that family is more important than his job writing inane reports. So he confronts his employer saying, "If you ever want to find your family, go for trip in a RV," and he's summarily fired.

En route back to his family in the RV, he gets stuck on the Lucy/Desi mountaintop, is rescued by a new employer who appreciates Robin's candor, and this rather horrible movie grinds to a halt. The gears have been worn out. What could have been a passable farce is ironically flawed by the fact that by the time this movie was made—2006—all these scenes, especially the sewage and mountaintop ones, had been done numerous times before. *RV: The Movie* is not so much a movie as a mélange of stock footage.

Although the movies that best demonstrate our reaction to the RV have been part of the middle-aged picaresque genre, the motorhome has played a role in other stories as well. Here are just a few: You'll see it in the horror film (*Dead and Breakfast, Slither, Troll 2, Friday the 13th Part 6, The Hills Have Eyes* . . .); the action adventure thriller (*Rambo, Independence Day, Terminator 3: Rise of the Machines, Escape to Witch Mountain* . . .); cartoons (*The Incredibles, Cars, A Bug's Life The Wild Thornberrys Movie* . . .); road comedy (*Borat, The Jerk, Stripes, Blues Brothers, Space Balls, Beavis and Butthead Do America* . . .); dramas (*What's Eating Gilbert Grape?, Tin Cup, Best in Show* . . .) and, well, you get the point. When you want to show something a little silly, roll out the RV.

Figure 5.4: Tom Swift goes camping in *Tom Swift and His House on Wheels*, 1929 (book cover).

A DIFFERENT STORY:
THE RV IN AMERICAN FICTION

THE
RISE
AND
FALL
AND
...
OF
THE
RV
IN
AMERICA

144

I've gone on about these movies because they show how deeply this object—the motorized house on wheels—is now embedded in the American popular consciousness. And it's been this way really since the first automobile came off the Ford assembly line. In real life and in fantasy *auto camping* has become central to our ideas of crisis and escape. Maybe what these movies tell us is that while children and retirees should escape, middle-aged men should just quit fussing, keep punching the time clock, and only dream about freedom.

There is some history in this. Not by happenstance does Tom Swift, way back in the time of the Lampsteed Kampkar, make his own RV. In *Tom Swift and His House on Wheels* (1929), our hero, or should I say, our grandparents' hero, designs and builds a motorhome. He intends to use it on his honeymoon, but it's pressed into service to rid the neighborhood of highwaymen. We are told that it looks like either a circus wagon or a canal boat. Powered by a V12, it can reach speeds of more than 100 mph on "special grooved non-skid tires" but is comfortable cruising at 50. Behind electric headlamps and powerful windshield wipers is a monster mobile weighing over two tons. The "house" part has more than four spacious rooms, including a galley with electric stove and refrigerator, both powered by an onboard "dynamo."

Like the proper Victorian manse, there are two entrances, one front and one rear, with the rear entrance gained by climbing up drop-down stairs. These stairs can be folded away so street urchins cannot hop aboard, as they do on the trolley cars. (You should always pay your way and not hitch-hike on others, advises a young Mr. Swift.) There is a parlor at the front entrance to meet the guests. In the world before the sewage scenes become *de rigueur*, there is simply no mention of a bathroom. Presumably, Tom uses under-the-bed potties, and we are told that the windows have shutters for privacy.

In the same year—1929—a slightly older version of Tom Swift, Sam Dodsworth, has a similar yearning. He's a tinkerer too, but he builds assembly-line machines. In the book by Sinclair Lewis bearing his name, Dodsworth is retired, having sold his car company to a smarmy financier, Alex Kynance. However, the one machine he still hankers to create is an RV. He doesn't use that term; he calls it by its English name, a *caravan*. Here Sinclair Lewis has him musing:

> He had fallen into rather a rigid routine. Most days, between office and home, he walked to the Union Club in winter, drove to the golf course in summer. But tonight he was restless. He could not endure the fustiness of the old boys at the club. His chauffeur would be waiting there, but on his way to the club Sam stopped, with a vague notion of tasting foreignness, at a cheap German restaurant.
>
> It was dark, quiet, free of the bouncing grandeur of Kynances. At a greasy oilcloth-covered table he sat sipping coffee and nibbling at sugar-crusted coffee-cake.
>
> "Why should I wear myself out making more money for myself—no, for Kynance! He will like hell take my caravans away from me!"
>
> He dreamed of a very masterwork of caravans: a tiny kitchen with electric stove, electric refrigerator; a tiny toilet with showerbath; a living-room which should become a bedroom by night—a living-room with a radio, a real writing desk; and on one side of the caravan, or at the back, a folding verandah. He could see his caravanners dining on the verandah in a forest fifty miles from any house.
>
> "Kind of a shame to have 'em ruin any more wilderness. Oh, that's just sentimentality," he assured himself. "Let's see. We ought to make that up—" He was figuring on a menu. "We ought to produce those in quantities for seventeen hundred dollars, and our selling-point will be the saving in hotel bills. Like to camp in one myself! I will not let Kynance have my ideas! He'd turn the caravans out, flimsy and uncomfortable, for eleven hundred, and all he'd think about would be how many we could slam on the market. Kynance! Lord, to take his orders, to stand his back-slapping, at fifty! No!"
>
> [*Dodsworth*, chapter 3]

I mention Tom's rig and Sam's dream because, like the long, long trailer of the Arnez family, this was the world before the self-propelled things were actually mass-produced. Once they appeared, however, and once Winnebago became a synonym for the wheeled home, the dream got benightmared. Now the object is a toy for kiddies or, as Bill Bryson implies above, a menace in the hands of the drooling proles from Fishtown.

THE
RISE
AND
FALL
AND
...
OF
THE
RV
IN
AMERICA
145

THE
RISE
AND
FALL
AND
...
OF
THE
RV
IN
AMERICA
146

Figure 5.5: Barbie goes RV camping.

Let's deal with the kids first because they still dream the dream. One of the more popular accessories for Barbie and Ken was the Mattel RV Party Bus. The product description on the box tells all you need to know:

> There's no place like home and even on the road Barbie doll and friends enjoy all the comforts of home! This RV has three complete room areas and lots of transformation fun with over twenty travel and play pieces. The living room has an entertainment center with a "flat screen TV," swivel driver's chair, and a sofa that opens into a bed. There's a pull-down second bed and more! The kitchen area includes a refrigerator, microwave oven, built-in sink, and pull-down dinette table. There's a bathroom with a toilet and built-in sink. Pull down the back of the motor home for a fabulous hot tub that lights up and has fun party music, too.

THE RV IN URBAN FOLKLORE

And now for what's happened to the adult version, here's a revelatory bit of contemporary folklore. As an indication of how lots of people feel about the aspirations of Tom Swift and Sam Dodsworth, consider this story, current a few years ago: A doltish couple was driving their big Winnebago across Texas. The driver put on the cruise control and went back to the bedroom for a nap. Big crash. Winnebago, Inc. was sued because the salesman supposedly said that the rig would "practically drive itself."

Like the stories of alligators in the New York sewers, Coca-Cola dissolving a toothbrush left in a glass, or kidneys harvested on the black market, this Winnebago urban legend gets currency from playing on already in-dwelling suspicions. This story has many variations (predictably featuring foreigners, minorities, and women), but one version was so believable that it actually won the (nonhoax) Stella Award for Outrageous Lawsuit (named to honor the woman who sued McDonalds for serving too-hot coffee). That version went like this:

> In November 2000, Mr. Grazinski purchased a brand-new 32-foot Winnebago motor home. On his first trip home, having joined the freeway, he set the cruise control at 70 mph and calmly left the driver's seat to go into the back and make himself a cup of coffee. Not surprisingly, the Winnie left the freeway, crashed and overturned. Mr. Grazinski sued Winnebago for not advising him in the handbook that he could not actually do this. He was awarded $1,750,000 plus a new Winnebago. [www.StellaAwards.com/bogus.html]

The fact that the RV has entered the world of urban folklore (cited in the Jan Harold Brunvand books and even joked about on the Winnebago website) as well as the toy world (there is even a book entirely made up of RV toys for tots—*RV & Camper Toys: The History of RVing in Miniature*) tells us that something profound has happened to the RV. What started in dreams of freedom ended, at least for some, in nightmares of piggishness. Those letters to the *New York Times* are not flukes. Many, many people feel this way. RVs are big, ugly, ungainly, gas-guzzling, scenery blockers driven by road-hogging geezers who belong in an assisted-living facility, presumably one owned by Ralph Nader and presided over by Nurse Rached.

THE
RISE
AND
FALL
AND
...
OF
THE
RV
IN
AMERICA
147

THE
RISE
AND
FALL
AND
...
OF
THE
RV
IN
AMERICA
148

So what happens now? Do these things sink in the ooze of history like the maladaptive dinosaurs to which they are often compared by some readers of the *New York Times*? Or do they squirm around a bit and somehow reinvent themselves lest they become extinct by their own inability to adapt? Should I have written a tearful eulogy rather than a mild appreciation? If the history of human yearnings is a guide, chances are they adapt. Their DNA is too powerful. As long as humans want to travel and not sleep on the ground, the RV will continue to mutate. In fact, mutations happen every thirty years or so, even without the critics.

First off, the RV power source is going to change. Just as the manufacturers have gone from horse power to gasoline to diesel, they are soon to go to compressed natural gas. The increasing supplies of cheap natural gas (NG) are going to change the fuel of first big trucks and then, in the process, RVs. Cummings Engine, Volvo, and Caterpillar are already producing NG engines for heavy machines. A major reason that Navistar, the large truck builder, bought Monaco, the ailing RV manufacturer, is that the RV is going to go the way of the truck and bus. The analog is no longer with car camping but with adapting truck/bus technology to RVs.

Once the pipeline companies like Chiniere Energy and the Williams Companies succeed in building the fueling stations along the interstates, refueling will be easy, although time-consuming. Of course this also means that RVs will not be able to wander far from their fuel docks, which will be another problem. The big-three American automakers have already resolved this problem for pickup trucks by making them bi-fuel. GM sells a Chevy Silverado, Chrysler has a Dodge Ram, and Ford makes its 650 pickup, all of which are currently able to automatically switch from NG to gasoline. A conversion kit for about $3,000 allows you to do this with your small RV, provided it is gasoline—not diesel—powered.

And it is here, in providing the alternative power, that electric power may finally become successful. Many Chinese, Indian, German, and American companies have been experimenting with new battery configurations. Oddly enough, the main stimulus has come not from hybrid cars or buses but from mining companies, which need safe and powerful trucks to carry ore from inside the earth. Sometimes the batteries have a liquid core that can be replaced or recharged, sometimes the cores are solid, but the key is that the fuel cell can be removed and/or recharged.

As soon as batteries are capable of maintaining a range of around 350 to 400 miles, the electric RVs will appear. Already a Thor Motor Coach Avanti 3106 has been so configured, although there have as yet been no production runs. Providing recharging stations may create a boon for RV parks. Many of them now have ports for recharging electric cars, but it takes time. So the advantage for the RV user over an automobile or truck traveler is obvious: You spend the night sleeping in your rig as your batteries are being recharged. GE is promoting its WattStation, which attaches to the RV campground hookup and provides a full charge of DC current in six hours. National parks and state parks would also provide charging stations as well as such places as Camping World. And of course, if charging does become ubiquitous, then towing a small electric car makes even more sense.

These possible adaptations overlook the power source already in place—solar. Considering the flat roof space that often goes to waste on RVs, it's predictable that companies will be making voltaic panels part of the roof unit. Although the panels are now an aftermarket item, some manufacturer will find a way to make the entire roof into an efficient energy receiver. After all, an 80-watt panel that takes only half of my roof generates about 30 amp hours a day, about a third of what my battery does. Not only is this backup power good for long-term outings, it's enough to keep the generator off much of the time while boondocking. Kampgrounds of America, ever eager to position itself as the national campground, has started what it calls a "Solar Kolony." This is a section of the park where its cabins are powered exclusively by the sun (with a backup propane generator, just in case). Thus the terrestrial motel room becomes a mimic of the RV. Many KOAs now have charging stations for electric cars.

THE
RISE
AND
FALL
AND
...
OF
THE
RV
IN
AMERICA
150

The RV is also going to have to change its form. No more box. It needs a new outline. The gypsy wagon went from horse-drawn to engine-driven, then from looking like a parlor on wheels to looking like a ranch house on wheels. Let's face it: Most RVs today look dreary, which may be why they get those flashy paint jobs. To get a better form, the RV needs a new consumer. The current consumers are too old and dull. Moving from empty nests, they want a mimic of what they are leaving behind (washer/dryer, ice maker, drop-down televisions, comfy chairs…). Sociologists call this "compensatory domesticity."

And that may explain why the contemporary RV looks the way it does: It's trying to get it both ways, home away from home. It's simply too homey. That's why the awning that can be extended to welcome neighbors, why the green indoor/outdoor carpeting often spread near the doorway, why the ersatz fireplaces, potted plants, massive couches,

Figure 5.6: Some variations on the RV life: Stacked trailers (Al Hesselbart collection at RV/MH Hall of Fame and Museum) and (opposite page) *Camper Bike*, Kevin Cyr, 2008: art installation of a Chinese production model.

THE
RISE
AND
FALL
AND
...
OF
THE
RV
IN
AMERICA
151

twinkle lights, and, most perplexingly, the huge television set that comes sliding out of the cargo bay so it can be watched from lawn chairs. What's happening is that the old-time home has been dehydrated and then reconstituted so that it is essentially a split-level ranch house compressed and then expanded thanks to the slide-outs and yard art.

But as the demographics change, the mobile-nest prototype may change as well. The Recreation Vehicle Industry Association (RVIA) asserts that the fastest-growing group of RV owners is now made up of young families between eighteen and thirty-four years old. If the RV really is moving out of what's called Phase 3 (retirement) consumers and into Phase 2 (active individuals), then the lines of thing itself should change. No longer will "getting away from it all" mean "taking it all with you." Something else may happen, something more experimental. And the outlines for this change may well come from the places where RV life is just taking hold—Australia and China as well as the American Southwest.

There's precedent for this flux. Architects have long dreamed of unbolting their buildings from the earth. In the early twentieth century, Le Corbusier and the Italian futurists went gaga over steam trains, ocean

THE
RISE
AND
FALL
AND
...
OF
THE
RV
IN
AMERICA
152

liners, biplanes, and anything that moved. Why should housing always be fastened to the ground? After all, humans for centuries have lived in yurts, hogans, teepees, pods, and desert tents. The French Utopie group experimented with pneumatic architecture that could be blown up and deflated. Archigram, in London, responded with the Walking City, which literally got up on its legs and wandered about. Both of these groups took *movement* as a necessary part of interesting housing.

Now a new generation of designers is experimenting with variations on the gypsy architecture. All kinds of unfolding mini-homes with fewer than 1,000 square feet are on the market. Nils Moormann's *Walden*, Sustain Design's *Bunkie*, and Tumbleweed's *Tiny Houses* are all moveable compressions. You buy the kit and then assemble it, but then you'll need a crane to move it about. Other innovations are *parasitic dwellings*, such as the Loftcube, which you assemble on a rooftop, stay in for a while, and then take apart (or hire a helicopter). And there's a little aluminum-clad box called a Micro Compact Home, which opens up like Origami. To assemble, you plug it into an electrical outlet and up it goes. A selling point is that Micros fit together like Legos. You can attach ten of them and have a little apartment house like the famous Habitat of the 1967 World's Fair.

But why do the wheels have to come off? Maybe it's time that we pay more attention to one of the real visionaries in small-space architecture, Wally Byam, who back in the 1930s also realized the importance of wheels. The designer of the Airstream trailer, Byam was also a successful lawyer and publisher of do-it-yourself magazines. Ironically, because his reputation never transcended his signature product, he has never really been appreciated. His vision was for far more than the single sculpted trailer. He imagined putting these trailers together to make a self-contained habitat, a moveable city. He never got to that stage, but his idea of these things moving separately in a caravan by day and then hooking up at night was a step in the right direction. The Airstream trailer, like its cousin the RV, got stuck in the rut of the independent self-contained mimic of home. And that rut was not of Byam's making; it is a function of who was buying them.

There's a lot of interest today in creating new houses that are easily moved. A new generation of "green" architects has been influenced by

Buckminster Fuller and his Dymaxion House. Bucky's house was a pop-up geodesic dome supported by wires from a central mast. When you wanted to expand it, you just popped open one of the sides. Bucky even tried to fit one on a Volkswagen bus so it could dock with others. No success. But he was obsessed with what he called "ephemeralization"—the importance of making do on the fly. The key was not to make the individual unit self-contained but to make it connectable with others—in other words, just the opposite of how the RV industry developed. RV manufacturers only wanted to sell the individual things, not worry about how to connect them. Bucky even coined the term *drop city* to describe how a community could be opened and closed with the least amount of waste. People drop by, they connect, they stay, they fold up and leave.

If this sounds a bit like the RV park, Quartzsite, Burning Man, and even the Slabs; perhaps it should. These *flash cities* are not that far from Bucky's *drop city*. The problems are with the current RVs, how-ever. Our cars are smart, our clothing is smart, our food is smart, our temperature controls are smart, but our RVs are stupid. They are too self-contained. As with what happened with the station wagon, this

THE
RISE
AND
FALL
AND
...
OF
THE
RV
IN
AMERICA
153

Figure 5.7: RV tailgating starts in the mid-twentieth century and becomes a *crepe* city in the early twenty-first century (Recreational Vehicle Industry Association).

THE
RISE
AND
FALL
AND
...
OF
THE
RV
IN
AMERICA

154

new generation of buyers may smarten them up. They may not want all that "compensatory domesticity." Instead, they may want some kind of experimental community, some sort of social network, some kind of mobile neighborhood.

And they are already getting parts of it, thanks to the Internet. Almost every RV park has wi-fi. Skyping is second nature to many RVers. They are all over the social networks. High-speed computing has made working on the road as easy as working at home. With satellite technology you can have continuous communication as you move about. If you want to see what cities of tomorrow may look like, just amble around RVs tailgating at a football game. Their owners share plans electronically, they drive to a prearranged spot, they park, they move around, and only maybe do they attend the game. Then they disconnect and separate. They become urban, then they turn rural, and they do it at will: It's a kind of technological arcadia that allows a rolling community created by desire, gasoline, and electricity.

You can already see ordered flux in the behavior of the Escapees, a loosely strung-together organization of about two hundred thousand RV owners, many of them full-timers. They have a variety of campgrounds around the southern United States that are owned in a number of ways. A member may literally own a lot, he may own a limited right to use a lot, or he may simply stop by and hope a lot is free to rent. But what distinguishes this group is that when they pull in and meet each other, they hug. I've seen it. True, it's contrived, but it's sincere. They know each other not by shared experience, but by shared lifestyle. If they were wearing tie-dye you might mistake them for hippies. It's a bit of a shock to stay in one of their parks and watch people who haven't met before behave like old friends. I don't mean to make too much of this, but clearly they are committed to generating a deeper level of community than the usual *here today, gone tomorrow* experience of the RV campground.

In "Nomadic Urbanism: The Senior Full-time RV Community" Deane Simpson, an architectural student, makes a provocative point (*Interstices: A Journal of Architecture and Related Arts*, {2008}: 34–46). The most radical experiments in contemporary urbanism are being realized

Figure 5.8: The city as egg: boiled (ancient), fried (early modern), scrambled (modern), and crepe (post-modern). After Cedric Price's *city as egg* analogy (Susan G. Duser).

THE
RISE
AND
FALL
AND
...
OF
THE
RV
IN
AMERICA
155

not by young long-hairs smoking dope in communes and growing kale but by their balding parents dawdling in RV parks, drinking Merlot and watching sunsets. Millions of these *leisure nomads* are promising to create a new kind of city, an urban phenomenon called "an unsettlement." People come together not to settle down as much as to settle out.

Simpson makes a provocative addition to the famous egg analogy developed in the 1960s by the urbanologist Cedric Price. According to Price, ancient cities were like *hard-boiled* eggs, with a dense center protected by defensive walls. Think Italian hill towns. The cannon rendered these walls obsolete and put the yoke at risk. The next version of the city was like a *poached* egg, with a core surrounded by expanding rings of residential and industrial areas. The railroad station was at the center of this town. Think Bruges in the Flemish region of Belgium. But the car destroyed this hub by making it easier to live and work outside the downtown. Now the modern city is the *scrambled* egg in which roadways have removed the sense of city proper and made exurbia the sprawling norm. Downtown, midtown, edgetown are all mixed up. The center will not hold because there is no center. Think Atlanta, LA, Singapore—in fact, all over.

Simpson goes a step further by suggesting that the next city is the *crepe* city, the wafer-thin Japanese *usuyaki tamago*, the city that comes and goes, literally moving around like a crepe flipped in a pan. In a sense it's like the covered wagons of the pioneers, clustering around at night and then pulling apart by day. The *crepe* city is the opposite of sedentary; it is transient, rootless, an unsettlement. Think the nighttime parking lot at Walmart. Magnify it by a hundred and it's the NASCAR infield or a football game. By a thousand, Burning Man. By a hundred

THE
RISE
AND
FALL
AND
...
OF
THE
RV
IN
AMERICA
156

thousand, Quartzsite. As I write this, a sizable *crepe* of RVs is forming in the Bakken oil region of North Dakota, causing all kinds of trouble in part because it has grown so quickly.

Who knows what other forms it will take, but we saw a *crepe* city creeping around the Gulf of Mexico in 2005. This time it came on the heels of a disaster, Hurricane Katrina, and it was tossed together by FEMA. The *crepe* itself was almost as disastrous as the storm. As many RV owners observed, they could have done a better job of organizing the living situation. Not only were the FEMA "Emergency Living Units" a hazard unto themselves (formaldehyde and shoddy workmanship), but FEMA had little sense of how a transient community finds order. They just plotted the rigs in endless lines without much sense of how humans moved to food, water, sewage, and community. As recent disasters have shown, FEMA has learned fast.

With the advent of global warming and possible changes in weather and water levels, FEMA may well consider joining forces with RV owners to work out some kind of borrowing program so that, during emergencies, FEMA could contact local RVers to lend (or rent) their rigs. FEMA would supervise the *crepe*. I, for one, would happily drive my rig to a spot and set it up for temporary use. As knuckleheaded as this sounds (and I can predict the thousands of reasons against it), it's a better use than looking at the thing unused in the backyard while people go homeless. This almost happened after Hurricane Sandy when the New Jersey Campground Owners Association (NJCOA) essentially created a small satellite town for workers from utility companies, tree service companies, and insurance adjusters. But, alas, not for those made homeless by the storm. Co-operation between FEMA and RV owners would certainly be a huge PR bonanza, maybe even taking a bit of the sting out of Dancing Scorpion.

We may not agree on how we feel about the thing, but no one denies that it's become part of our common culture. How else to explain that Alex Trebek on the television show *Jeopardy* (12/8/2010) asked the contestants three questions from a new category: *the RV*. Alas, the contestants put the category off until the end of the round and time ran out, but you should get most of them right.

- $200 clue: The GMC motorhome from the 1960s and 1970s was among the first models to have this innovation that helps with traction by putting the engine's weight over the wheels that do the work. (Early GMC motorhome displayed.)
- $400 clue: I'm behind the wheel of the first motorhome from the company whose name has become a synonym for motorhome. Since 1967, they've sold over 400,000 of them. (Clue giver shown inside an early model Class A motorhome.)
- $600 clue: One of the first times a movie star received a fancy trailer as a perk was in 1931. Paramount gave a Chevy house car to this sexy star as she left the stage to make movies like *She Done Him Wrong*. (Black-and-white photograph of the actress was shown in tandem with the clue.)

THE
RISE
AND
FALL
AND
...
OF
THE
RV
IN
AMERICA
157

I'm sure you answered correctly (front-wheel drive, Winnebago, Mae West).

This thing has become part of our shared knowledge because it's become part of the rhythms of American life. It's an irony worthy of mention that Romanticism, which starts as a nineteenth-century reaction to the rise of industry and mass production, should find its modern reincarnation in what seems its opposite: a motorized cabin not in the woods, but in the concrete wilderness. It's the machine in the garden; technology in the pastoral ideal. And it's a further irony that this thing may become a characteristic component in cities of the future.

So, of course, we know about it. It's a distillation of who Americans are: mechanical yet dreamy, independent yet needful of hook-ups, heading out yet gas-dependent, solitary yet clubby, buying things to be free of things, adventurous yet home-bound. Who cares if taking off, hitting the road, getting gone, ultimately sends us around the barn back to where we started? As anthropologists now tell us, the nomadic life did not always precede the sedentary; sometimes it followed it. We got to these shores by being restless. We haven't stopped even though the frontier has given out. The RV is how we pretend to take civilization into the wilderness even though the wilderness is no more. It's a simu-

THE
RISE
AND
FALL
AND
...
OF
THE
RV
IN
AMERICA
158

lacrum, as my colleagues would say, of the entire American experience. The yearning to move is ancient and primordial: Gypsy fever, hitch itch, is not easily cured. We will never happily sleep on the ground, but we rejoice sleeping a few feet above it. Maybe once we had the car, the RV was inevitable. Or, better yet, once we had the wheel, maybe the Winnebago was sure to follow.

ACKNOWLEDGMENTS

I guess it goes without saying that I loved writing this book. How often can you combine doing something, with writing about it, with deducting it from your taxes? I came by my passion for things on wheels honestly. Every September in the early 1950s I used to go down to the showrooms to look at the new models from Detroit. In grammar school I distressed my parents by being able to spot the Chevy Impala or Chrysler Imperial from a block away. What a waste of a brain, my mom would say. Now, approaching seventy, I find myself doing the same thing with RVs. "Look at that nifty Allegro Breeze. Is that the 28- or the 32-foot model?" I say to my wife as we are driving on the Interstate. She gives me the same look my mom did.

I mention this because, although I want to thank people for helping me, I often don't remember their names, only what they were driving. I think of them as those farmers from Iowa who were driving the Holiday Rambler. Or, if I forget the rig, I remember them by campsite, like that nice couple in that parking lot near Kennecott, Alaska, who knew too much about bear attacks, those workcampers in Newfoundland who had us over for beers and cutthroat Uno, or those friendly couples at a gay RV park in central Texas who had festooned their sites in twinkly lights. I never got any names. But I want to thank them anyway. Meeting them made this project such a joy. I tell people who want to start RVing that they don't have to read the owner's manual. Just drive into the RV park, stand in front of your rig, look pathetic. Descending swarms of locusts barely describe what happens next.

However, I did get a few names. Jon and Louise Fairbank in Vermont showed me how much fun it was to putter around. They had a VW Rialta, and for me it was indeed "a little world made cunningly." Bob Cohan, my old chum from graduate school days, owned a vintage Airstream trailer that had mahogany-like wainscoting inside. It looked like an English men's cigar club. We took a wonderful trip across the American South together. Joe Taylor in Louisiana, whose wife lets him use her Fleetwood Southwind, has graciously shown me around the Sportsman's Paradise. And I especially want to thank all the people whose names I got because they took time to educate me. David Castaneda, the Chief Learning Officer/Vice President/Director/Manager of Corporate Education at Lazydays RV Park; Sam Lincoln of Mr. Motorhome in Quartzsite; Al Hesselbart, resident historian at the RV museum in Elkhart, Indiana; Mahlon Miller, bishop of the Mennonite group near Nappanee, Indiana, and CEO of NewmarCorp.; Bob Phebus, the Marathon motorhome marketing manager for the Southeast; Dave Kelly, Marketing Director of the Florida RV Trade Association; and Leonard Knight, artist-in-residence at Salvation Mountain. All of these men went way, way out of their way to help me.

Although I've learned a lot from being on the road, I have also been greatly helped by people who have written about it from inside the library. As I mentioned earlier, there has not been much academic interest in the RV. There is an overflowing reservoir of stuff written on the car: in real life, in films, in books, on TV, in videogames, as tattoos. And in the last decade, there has been a gusher of books on highways, on the selling of travel, and on what is called in academic jargon, *automobility*. But still only droplets have fallen on my chosen subject. No matter; here are the best books, or at least the ones, I've enjoyed most and learned from.

The best general book that sets the stage is Warren Belasco's superb 1979 *Americans on the Road: From Autocamp to Motel, 1910–1945*. It's filled with insights, interesting facts, and a great annotated bibliography on various subjects like Gypsying, Trains, Autocamping, Hotels, and Motels. Belasco paved the road for most of the subsequent studies of *mobilis Americanis*. The best history *qua* history of the RV is *Home on the Road: The Motor Home in America* (2000) by Roger B. White, transportation curator at the Smithsonian. Growing out of the 1985 exhibit "At Home on the Road: Autocamping, Motels, and the Rediscovery of America," the book is much more than a catalog *raisonné*. I personally like *Homes on Wheels* (1980)—written by another wide-eyed college teacher, Michael Rockland—because it's a jaunty stroll around these objects with someone who really enjoys them. The text is accompanied by some curious, often downright spooky, photographs by Amy Stromsten. Al Hesselbart's *The Dumb Things Sold Just Like That: A History of the Recreational Vehicle Industry in America* (2007) is almost an oral history of just what the title says, the *industry* that makes these things. So if you want to know who first figured out how to empty sewage or who mastered the door latch, this is the place to go. Al is a generous man with his time, knowledge, and photographic collection. Go to almost any big RV convention and you'll see him there giving his slide show to a fascinated audience of users. Also at such shows, at least until a few years ago, you might find one-time Baptist minister turned RV evangelist David Woodworth, another human encyclopedia. In a sense both of these men update Carlton Edwards, a historian of the mobile home industry at Michigan State, whose privately published *Homes for Travel and Living: The History and Development of the Recreational Vehicle and Mobile Home Industries* (1977) is the Ur-text of industrial data, full of charts and graphs but not much in the way of interpretation. From a slightly different angle, a valuable collection of essays is Kate Trant's

Home Away from Home: The World of Camper Vans and Motorhomes (2005), which outlines the cultural and social history of RV camping in the US, the UK, and Europe, and so gives a global perspective to what we often think of as a North American phenomenon.

As befits an object that is so striking (or distressing) to look at, there are some really dreamy book collections of photographs. Donald F. Wood, *RVs & Campers 1900–2000: An Illustrated History* (2002) is great for old rigs and where I got many of the ads for camping in your car. Jane Lidz, *Rolling Homes: Handmade Houses on Wheels* (1979) and Baron Wolman, *Vans: A Book of Rolling Rooms* (1976) both show how the personal touch has long been part of homemaking on wheels. You may buy the house on wheels, but then you have to make a home of it. The glossiest picture book is Douglas Keister, *Mobile Mansions: Taking "Home Sweet Home" on the Road* (2006), which is really a coffee table book, just right for a small RV coffee table. To enthusiasts it's our Book of Kells.

Dovetailing with my own approach, I am especially indebted to those cultural anthropologists who have found insight into the human condition by studying modern gypsy life. In a way, the first of these was Wally Byam, who in *Trailer Travel Here and Abroad* (1960) discussed the central paradox of a community of separatists without ever having to invoke the exhausted Alexis de Tocqueville. More contemporary and really important for me is Dorothy and David Counts's *Over the Next Hill: An Ethnography of RVing Seniors in North America* (1996, rpt. 2001). What I especially like is that these field anthropologists came to look, as it were, and stayed to pray. They now spend much of their time on the road. Because of this they can report inside out and outside in. Thanks to all their interviews and questionnaires we have a much better appreciation of exactly who is in these rigs and how they are living this nomadic life. The research may be a little old but the conclusions are in no way dated. The Counts are especially good explaining the allure of the Escapees organization.

In the context of self-generated interpretations, the RV world is full of enthusiastic amateurs who contribute fresh insights and provocative observations, often via self-publishing. I can't think of another *lifestyle* that has produced so much chatty commentary from participants. Some of my favorites are Kay Peterson, *Home Is Where You Park It* (1977); Ken

Halloran, *Travel Tales: An Old Retiree, His RV, His Dog and His Woman* (2006); Doreen Orion, *Queen of the Road: The True Tale of 47 States, 22,000 Miles, 200 Shoes, 2 Cats, 1 Poodle, a Husband and a Bus with a Will of Its Own* (2008); Nick Russell, *Meandering Down the Highway: A Year on the Road with Fulltime RVers* (2001); Ron and Barb Hofmeister, *Movin' On: Living and Traveling Full Time in a Recreational Vehicle* (1999); Alice Zyetz and Steve Zikman, *RV Traveling Tales: Women's Journeys on the Open Road* (2003); Lisa Oliver, *Out on the Road Again: Living Life Full Time in an RV* (2012); and my hands-down favorite (in part because they include some pretty funny commentary from their dog), Mark and Donia Steele, *Steeles on Wheels: A Year on the Road in an RV* (2002). So while academics may have passed RVers by, these autodidacts have built up quite a library of their own. Perhaps my New York agent was correct when he mused that people who live in RVs don't buy books. But they certainly know how to write them.

INDEX

Page numbers in italics refer to illustrations.

at Slab City, 121; solar power and, 149. *See also* wally docking; Walmart

Bounder: as brand name, 15; club for owners of, 65, 88

Bounders of America, 65

Bounders United, 65

Boxer, Barbara, 115

branding, brands: as badge, 62, 97; future possibilities of, 17; imagined past and, 11–12, 14; Native American culture and, 12–13; wanderlust and, 15. *See also* brand names of RVs

brand names of RVs: American Spirit, 14; Ameriscape, 12; Bigfoot, 12; Big Horn, 12; Bounder, 15; Brave, 12; Cherokee, 12; Chinook, 12; Escaper, 15; Flagstaff, 12; Free Spirit, 12, 15; Frontier, 12; Fun Runner, 15; Grey Hawk, 12; Grey Wolf, 12; Gypsy, 15; Heritage, 11; Hitchhiker, 15; Hobo, 15; Independence, 12; Lakota, 12; Mallard, 15; Montana, 12; Nomad, 15; Out Back, 12; Outfitter, 12; Prairie Schooner, 12; Scamper, 15; Searcher, 11; Seneca, 12; Superchief, 12; Sundance, 12; Surveyor, 12; Trail Blazer, 12; Voyager, 11; Wanderer, 15. *See also* branding, brands

Breaking Bad, 124

Brimmer, F. E., *Autocamping*, 6–7

Briny Breezes, 86–87

Brooks, Albert, 139, 140

Brunvand, Jan Harold, 147

Bryson, Bill, 130–31, 138, 145

Bumppo, Natty, 11

Burbank, Luther, 77

Bureau of Land Management: land owned by, 104, 107; Quartszite and, 107–8

Burning Man, 120; as destination, 15; as flash-city, 105, 153

Burroughs, John, as Vagabond, 5, 28, 42–43, 77, 80, 81

Busch Gardens, Florida, as destination, 70

bus conversions, 3, 5, 29, 34–35, *35*, 53, 76. *See also names of bus manufacturers*

Byam, Wally, 152; Airstream design and, 30, 152; sense of community and, 65, 72

By Motor to the Golden Gate (Emily Post), 25–27, 35

Byron, Lord, 131, 134

California, 38, 107, 109, 111; Andy Isaacson in, 127–28; Mojave Desert, 106; Mr. Motorhome in, 110; Outdoor Resorts in, 102; state parks in, 103. *See also* Slab City, California

Camp Club USA, 90

campgrounds, *40*, 41–42, 81, 104. *See also* Kampgrounds of America; RV parks

camping: for fun, 5; as not RV travel, 9, 125–26

THE KING OF
MULBERRY STREET

Also by Donna Jo Napoli

THE KING OF MULBERRY STREET

DONNA JO NAPOLI

WENDY
L A M B
BOOKS

Published by
Wendy Lamb Books
an imprint of
Random House Children's Books
a division of Random House, Inc.
New York

Visit us on the Web! www.randomhouse.com/kids
Educators and librarians, for a variety of teaching tools,
visit us at www.randomhouse.com/teachers

Library of Congress Cataloging-in-Publication Data
is available upon request.

ISBN: 0-385-74653-9 (trade)   0-385-90890-3 (lib. bdg.)

Printed in the United States of America
October 2005
BVG   10 9 8 7 6 5 4 3 2 1

ACKNOWLEDGMENTS

Thanks to Professor Umberto Fortis of the Archivio Renato Maestro in Venice for allowing me access to the materials about the history of Jews in Italy and for discussing them with me and recommending other readings. For comments on earlier drafts, thanks to Paolo Asso, Carolynn Laurenza, Paolo Munson, Helen Plotkin, Richard Tchen, Jeff Wu, and my editorial team: Suma Balu, Jack Lienke, Alison Meyer, and, especially, Wendy Lamb. Thanks also to Mary Reindorp's eighth-period sixth-grade language arts class at the Strath Haven Middle School in 2003–2004. And, as always, thanks to my faithful family.

But most most most of all, thank you to Thad Guyer, whose insights put me back on emotional track.

To Thad Guyer and the spirits of my grandfathers

THE KING OF
MULBERRY STREET

CHAPTER ONE

Surprise

I woke to Mamma's singing in the kitchen.

I pulled the sheet off my head. Mamma had tucked it over me to keep out mosquitoes and malaria.

The room was stifling. I got up from my bed of two chairs pushed together and opened the shutters. I straddled the windowsill, one leg dangling out, and savored the fresh air.

In the alley below, mothers hurried along on errands. I hoped someone would see me—the brave boy on the sill—so I could wave. A child from the market walked beneath me with a basket of flat beans on his head. They looked good.

There was a saying that no one starved in farmlands. My city, Napoli, was surrounded by farmlands, yet we'd been hungry for months. People went

1

to bed trying not to think of food. Maybe Mamma sang to ward off that empty feeling.

I looked back into the room at Uncle Aurelio and Aunt Sara's bed. Baby Daniela's cradle sat on the floor. Aunt Rebecca, a widow, and my little cousins Luigi and Ernesto slept in another big bed.

Uncle Vittorio snored in the cot farthest from the kitchen, our other room. He cleaned streets, a night job, and slept by day.

I was nine, the oldest child in our home. Before I was born, a diphtheria outbreak killed all the other children and one aunt. So our friends celebrated at my birth. My grandmother, Nonna, told me they roasted a goat. They celebrated even though Mamma had no husband and I was illegitimate.

Nonna was the tenth person in our home. In winter we crowded into the kitchen to sleep around the oven, but the rest of the year the kitchen was Nonna's at night. Her cot was beside the credenza with the mirrored doors and lion feet that my grandfather had carved. She said his spirit lived in it, and she slept in the kitchen to be near him.

She also slept there so she could protect our home. She was tiny, but she knew dozens of charms against evil.

Now Baby Daniela made gulping noises. Aunt Sara scooped her from the cradle with one arm and rolled onto her side to nurse.

I got down from the window and walked into the kitchen to find warm bread on the table. Mamma kissed me, her anise-seed breath mixing with the smell of the bread. "Beniamino, *mio tesoro*—my treasure." She fit my yarmulke on my head and we said prayers. Then she tore a hunk off the loaf for me. I chewed in bliss.

Nonna's slow footsteps came up the stairs and I ran to open the door. She handed me a full basket of clothes.

Mamma got up in surprise. "For Sara?"

"And you," said Nonna with reproach in her voice.

Mamma wiped a drop of coffee from her bottom lip. "I'm going to find an office job," she said in a flat tone. "Soon someone will hire me. Then you'll all be glad."

"*Magari*," said Nonna. It was one of her favorite words. It meant *if only that were true*. "In the meantime . . ." She jerked her chin toward the basket.

Aunt Sara took in clothes for mending. At least, she used to; lately it seemed that people couldn't afford it. She'd be happy for this pile of work.

Mamma motioned to me to set the basket under the table. "How did you collect so much?" she asked Nonna.

"I was early and beat the competition."

"You don't have to go out that early," said Mamma. "You don't have to work so hard at your age."

"*Magari*." Nonna dropped onto a bench with an "oof." "Maybe I'll crochet today."

Nonna made baby clothes to sell at Hanukah and Christmas. It was my job to keep her yarn balls in order, piled just right. I went toward the yarn cabinet.

Mamma caught my arm. "Get ready. We're going out." Her smile surprised me; the night before I'd heard her crying quietly in the dark.

I raced into the corridor, to the water closet we shared with the neighbors on our floor. When I came back, I heard Nonna say, "Give up this idea of an office job. No doctor or lawyer will hire an unwed mother—and a Jewess, at that—to greet clients and keep records. You should work in a restaurant, cleaning up."

Mamma said, "You don't know. People will appreciate how well I read if they'll only give me a chance."

They hushed when I came in, as though they thought I didn't know it was my fault Mamma couldn't get an office job. But right now that didn't upset me. Mamma was in a good mood and errands were fun.

I pulled my nightshirt off and Nonna folded it, while Mamma held out my day shirt and pants to step into. As we went through the doorway, Mamma's fingertips grazed the box mounted on the doorframe that held the *mezuzah*. She boosted me up so I could touch it, too, though I scarcely looked at it. I didn't need its reminder—for I knew the Most Powerful One was unique and perfect.

Our alley opened onto the Via dei Tribunali, full of merchants and buyers and laborers on their way to work.

Men hooted obscenely and called things to Mamma as we passed. This happened to any woman alone; the prettier she was, the worse it got. Mamma was beautiful, so I was used to this. But I still hated it. Heat went up my chest. Even nine-year-olds knew those words. I glanced up at her, wanting to apologize for not being big enough to make them stop. But she didn't seem offended; she never did. She neither slowed down nor sped up, her leather-shod feet making quick slaps, my bare ones silent.

Mamma pointed at a small boy in the Piazza Dante. "That's Tonino's son," she said. "Tonino just sent money in a letter from America."

That spring, Tonino had left for America, where everyone got rich. "Good," I said. "Will they join him there now?"

"Not yet. He hasn't made much money." Mamma's hand tightened around mine. "But he will. He works in a coal mine."

We turned left down the wide Via Toledo. Gold numerals on black marble over the doorways told when the fancy shops were founded. Through glass windows I saw carved picture frames and chandeliers and shiny dresses. We passed a store filled with artificial roses, camellias, carnations, dahlias.

Mamma hesitated at the flower shop. I smiled up at her, but she stared at nothing, as though she was about to weep. Then she turned quickly and moved on. "Watch where you walk," she said.

The streets were dangerous for my bare feet. I looked down.

Mamma went into a cobbler's. That was odd; we never bought outside our neighborhood. From the doorway I peered into the cool dark. She talked to a man at a workbench cutting leather with giant scissors. He hugged her. She wrested herself free and beckoned to me. The man shook my hand and went into a back room.

Mamma called, "Wrap them, please. They're a surprise."

A surprise? I perked up.

"Come look first," he answered. "It'll only take a minute."

I waited while she went into the back.

She came out carrying a parcel wrapped in newsprint, tied with yellow string. The man handed me a licorice.

5

We continued down Via Toledo. I watched that surprise package. Mamma held it in the hand farther from me, and when I changed to her other side, she shifted the package to her other hand. It became a game, both of us laughing. Mamma turned right, toward our synagogue. Napoli had only one synagogue and no Jewish neighborhood. Uncle Aurelio said the Jews of Napoli were the world's best-kept secret. The Spanish had kicked them out centuries before. But no matter how many times they were kicked out, they always snuck back.

We were as proud of being Jewish as of being Napoletani. My cousins were named after famous Jews: Luigi after Luigi Luzzatti, a Venetian and the first Jewish member of the House of Parliament; Ernesto after Ernesto Natan, one of Roma's most important businessmen. Uncle Aurelio lectured us cousins on the possibilities—*le possibilità*. "You can do anything if you put your heads to it and work hard. It doesn't matter what adversity comes; we are Jews—Napoletani Jews. We never miss a beat."

At the Piazza dei Martiri I climbed over the fence onto the back of a stone lion. Other kids' mothers didn't let them. But Mamma said that if the city didn't want kids playing on the lions, they shouldn't make statues just the right size for climbing on.

We turned down the alley A Cappella Vecchia and into the courtyard. Napoli's buildings were mostly three or four stories high. Around this courtyard, though, the buildings had five floors. Passing under the thick stone arch, I felt as though we were leaving the ordinary and coming into someplace truly holy.

"I love this courtyard," I said.

Mamma stopped. "More than you love the synagogue itself?"

I didn't want to answer. Maybe my preference for the openness of the courtyard meant there was something lacking in my soul.

She squatted, put a pinch of anise seeds in my palm, and looked up into my face as I chewed them. "Stand here and think of why you love this place. Then go spend the day doing exactly what you want." She straightened up.

"What do you mean?" Usually my family needed me to run errands.

"Visit all your favorite places. And, please, visit Uncle Aurelio and Aunt Rebecca at work." She put her hands on my cheeks. "I don't have money for you. But don't go home to eat at midday, because if you do, Nonna or Aunt Sara might give you a chore. No chores today. See Napoli. See all that you love."

I nodded in a daze of happiness. I would visit Aunt Rebecca at midday. She was a servant to a rich family and she always snuck me meat from their table.

"Stay well. You know how to be careful. I'll see you at dinnertime." She kissed my forehead. "Stay well, *mio tesoro.*"

CHAPTER TWO

Dirty

As I walked, children passed me on their way to school. I didn't go to school; Uncle Aurelio didn't like how Catholic teachers put religion into the lessons. So he taught me numbers and Mamma taught me reading. Mamma said I needed more than that and I was smart enough not to let the Catholic teachers influence me. She had just about talked Uncle into letting me go to school in autumn.

Crowd noises came from Via Toledo. I ran over to see men in gloves and top hats and horses in black cloth hoods with white rings around their eyeholes marching down the road. A funeral. A flag waved the family crest from the top of the coach that carried the women in the dead person's family. It must have been someone important.

The casket rolled by with lilies on top. Lilies in

summer. Somehow Catholic funerals had real lilies, no matter the season. If only I could take one—just one—for Mamma.

I made my way to the next road, where I begged a ride from a horse-drawn cart to the stables where Uncle Aurelio worked.

He smiled when I came in, but we didn't speak. He was scraping the rear hoof of a mare. When he finished, Uncle Aurelio walked outside with me. "So what's the message? Who sent you?"

"I just wanted to see you. I'm on my way up the hill."

"To Vomero?" He winked. "Going to snitch food from the midday meal?" He put his hand on my head, in the center of my yarmulke. The weight made me feel solid and safe.

I climbed onto the next cart going toward Vomero. At the base of the hill, I took the stairs up to the piazza and looked down and out over my town and the bay and the two humps of Mount Vesuvio beyond. The buildings shone yellow and orange, and the bay sparkled green, dotted with fishing boats and merchant boats and sailboats. A huge steamer docked in the port. I saw bright market umbrellas in piazzas, and a train slowing to a halt at the station, and oxen pulling carts on the bay avenue.

I turned to face the wide Vomero streets with sidewalks under the wispy fringe of acacias. A couple strolled along, arms linked. Everything was calm—so different from the Napoli below. Vomero was rich; rich people didn't have to hustle all the time. The people here owned the sailboats on the bay. The women played tennis in white dresses to their ankles, with sleeves to their knuckles; the men cheered for

9

their sons at soccer matches. Their lives were a mystery of leisure.

A boy sat on a barrel beside a cow and filled pails with milk for servants to carry back to the big, airy houses. Aunt Rebecca stood waiting. When her pails were full, I carried one while she carried the other.

Aunt Rebecca was not lovely like Mamma or Nonna. Everyone had been delighted when she got married and devastated when her husband was killed in a street fight. No one expected her to remarry. But her looks were in her favor when it came to being a servant. Rich women didn't hire pretty servants; their husbands might like them too much.

Entering the house, I heard the noises of *tombola*—bingo—from the parlor. Aunt Rebecca went on to the kitchen, but I stopped and peeked.

"Look." One of the three girls on the sofa pointed at me.

I stepped back into the hall, out of sight.

"It's just a servant's boy," said a second girl.

"Make him play with us."

"He's dirty."

I wasn't dirty. Or not that dirty.

"It's more fun with more people. Get him, Caterina."

We played *tombola* at home, like every Napoli family. But what boy would play with girls? I hurried to the kitchen and set the milk pail on the counter. Aunt Rebecca looked sideways at me from her chopping. I put a finger to my lips and ducked behind the pantry curtain.

"Where's your nephew?" came Caterina's voice.

"I thought there was a noise on the cellar steps," said Aunt Rebecca. Not a lie—just a crafty answer.

"Why would he go down there?"

"I could use a bucket." More craftiness.

I heard steps cross the room. "Are you down there, boy?" Caterina called. "Come on up. We want you."

I burst from the pantry and ran out the front door. I didn't stop to pant till I reached the bottom of the hill. Stupid me, now no lunch.

I passed the window where Nicola sold hot, almond-speckled *taralli*—dough loops. My mouth watered, my stomach fluttered.

Oh, for a coin to buy a dough loop.

Instantly, I thought of the convent. I set off running to the church of San Gregorio Armeno and clanked the iron knocker on the side chapel door.

My favorite nun answered. "Ah, Beniamino, what a pleasure." She kissed my cheeks. "What brings you here?"

"Perhaps you might need help?"

"Of course. You're getting bigger. You should help us more often while you can still fit through the passageways. Come."

I followed her to the floor hatch that opened to the ladder down to the grotto. She put a key in a pouch, then added a backup candle, two matchsticks, and rough paper. She hung the pouch around my neck and gave me a candle. "Two bottles today."

That might mean double pay. I held the lit candle sideways between my teeth and went down the ladder. Twenty-two rungs. That was nothing. Some grottos were two hundred steps down.

The grottos and the channels between them formed the ancient water system, connected to the old aqueducts aboveground. Greek slaves had built it a thousand years

11

before. The grottos had been closed for nearly a century, but they were still used as wine cellars; and thieves climbed down them, then crawled up old, dry wells into the atriums of fancy homes when the people were out. I'd never seen a thief here, but other boys claimed they had.

Once I saw a lover, though. Lovers of rich married women came and left like thieves. I knew the man was a lover, not a thief, because he smiled as we passed. A boy told me lovers came to the nuns, too. But they couldn't come to my nuns—not unless they were as small as I was—because of the awful tunnel.

At the bottom of the ladder I took off my yarmulke and left it safely under the last rung. I followed the passageway to where the ceiling came down so low I had to crawl. I held the end of the candle in my mouth now, so that the flame led the way. The walls were wet from the humid air. My hair stuck to my neck.

I'd gone through this tunnel many times, but it always seemed endless. I was afraid I'd die there.

Then suddenly I was out. I stood and breathed, and oh, what was that terrible smell? Something lay in the channel ahead. I held out my candle to see better. A body! I screamed and the candle fell. I crawled to the wall. I sat and pulled my feet up quick under my bottom. I wedged the backup candle between my knees and struck a match on the rough paper. The flame fizzled out and the dark swallowed me. My hands were wet from the damp air, so I blew on them frantically. I struck the other match; it flamed and the wick took. Blessed light.

I pressed my back against the wall and stood on tiptoe to look again. Rats ripped at the naked, bloated body of a man.

12

My eyes burned. The month before, an old man had stabbed a man on our street. A week later a young man had shot another in the piazza. When the stabbing happened, I was with Mamma. She whisked me home and held me till I slept. For the shooting, I was alone. I bit my knuckles to keep from screaming. The shooter walked up to me, and I recognized him—he lived nearby. He knocked my yarmulke off with the tip of the gun and hissed, "*Bastardo* Jew." *Bastardo*—a name for mongrel dogs, not people.

I ran home, but I didn't tell Mamma. She would have cried. I didn't cry then and I battled away tears now. Boys didn't cry.

I kept my eyes straight ahead till I got to the locked grotto that held the convent's special wines. I took two bottles and walked back. Fast, fast past the body. Hardly breathing.

At the tunnel I tried to tuck the bottles into my waistband. They wouldn't both fit. The idea of leaving one behind and passing through that tunnel two more times to fetch it was unbearable. So I lay on my back in the tunnel with my hands cradling the bottles on my belly and with the candle in my mouth. Little by little I scooched headfirst the length of that tunnel, as hot candle wax dripped on my chest through my open collar.

When I got to the ladder, I kissed my yarmulke and stuck it on my head. I climbed up with one bottle and put it on the convent floor, then went down for the other before I could think twice. I set it beside the first, crawled out, and stood.

"What's the matter, child? You smell awful."

The nun's worried face undid me; I cried. Loudly, as

13

though I was crying for everyone who had ever died and everyone who ever would. And I thanked the Most Powerful One that there were only nuns to watch me disgrace myself like this.

Soon five nuns huddled around me, wiping me with a wet cloth, offering water and bread with chocolate. I rinsed my mouth. "There was a body," I said.

"Oh. That. Ah." My favorite nun smoothed my hair gently. None of them was surprised. The cemeteries were full, so after funerals, men dug up the corpses and dumped them in the grottos.

I ate as they talked. Chocolate, such good chocolate, speckled with nuts.

My favorite nun lifted the pouch from my neck. "A candle is missing." She touched my cheek. "Munaciello stole it."

Munaciello was a spirit who hid things. Children blamed him, not adults. I felt charmed, though her words were just kindness, to keep the head nun from charging me for that candle.

The head nun gave me three coins. Three! "Beniamino, special one." She was about to tell me to become Catholic. Mamma hated my coming here because of that. But for three coins, let her blab. Besides, she called me special. Everyone said my cousins Luigi and Ernesto were special because they were named after famous men, but only Mamma thought I was special. "A boy with no earthly father is always special," said the nun. "Jesus Christ was just so. Your right place is here, child."

Despite the praise, I knew she felt sorry for me; I was Jewish and fatherless. What a fool she was to feel that way.

14

Being Jewish was best. And Nonna had taught me not to be jealous of children with fathers. *"Chi tene mamma, nun chiagne"*—Whoever has a mother doesn't cry. A proverb. That's all I needed, all anyone needed: a mother.

My favorite nun handed me half a lemon dipped in sugar. "That extra coin can't lessen the horror behind, but it may make the prospects ahead better, right?" That was why she was my favorite—she spoke straight. "Come back soon, sweet one."

I sat on the step and blinked at the sunlight. The lemon made my mouth fresh, but I couldn't shake the feeling of being dirty. The odor of the corpse clung to me.

I walked slowly through the empty streets; people had gone home for the afternoon rest. The three coins pressed into my fist. I needed something to put them in so I wouldn't lose them.

I took a side street, where a girl sat on a chair outside while her mother combed her hair. At the next corner a woman dressed in rags picked lice from the head of a boy at her feet. They were all poor. Maybe poorer than us.

I came out into the marketplace. In front of an oil store a family had set out a table under a canopy of grapevines. Their meal was over, but two men leaned back in their chairs, talking.

A fine gentleman came into the square, and a man and two boys appeared from nowhere. The man plunked down a shoe-shine box and the gentleman put a foot up on the box. One boy stood behind the gentleman and reached a stealthy hand under the loose hem of his fancy coat. He pulled out a handkerchief and stuffed it under his own shirt.

15

The thief looked hard at me.

The man finished the shoe shine, and he left with the boys.

People were robbed all the time; still, I went all jittery.

My family would hit me if I stole. Nonna especially. She'd recite: *"Chi sparagna 'a mazza nun vô bene ê figlie"*— Those who don't beat their children don't love them. Then she'd hit me again. And the Most Powerful One, He'd never forgive me.

The men at the table were still talking. Had they noticed? I'd noticed, but the thief had glared at me to make sure I'd never tell. Like the man with the gun who'd said, *"Bastardo* Jew."

I felt dirtier than ever. In the trash I spied a matchbox. I slipped the coins into the box and tied the ends of my pant strings around it, then tucked it in at my waist. Now to get clean.

I ran along the bay to a cove. Boys were jumping off a fishing boat. They were naked, like most boys at the beach, but these boys were probably always naked except in church. They were *scugnizzi*—urchins, the poorest of the poor. No one trusted them. One stood on the gunwale and jabbed with a pole under the water. A seagull circled, screeching greedily.

They didn't look at me, but they knew I was there. They were aware of everything that happened; *scugnizzi* always were. If I hid the matchbox, it would disappear while I was swimming.

I was so filthy. I had to swim. Where else could I go?

Vesuvio, of course. Up to the rain-filled craters near the volcano's peak. I hitched a ride on the coastal road and lay

16

on my back in the empty wagon, arms and legs spread wide. The sides were high; I saw only clouds. The air smelled of sea. I felt tiny—a speck of nothing, suspended without time or care.

The wagon turned inland and stopped in front of the monastery at the base of Vesuvio. Then I climbed on foot.

Some of the crater lakes were so hot they bubbled. I stopped at the first one that wasn't steamy, and I hid the matchbox under a rock. Then I took off my clothes, swished them in the water, and stretched them to dry on a rock while I swam. The water was heavy like oil and stank of sulfur. I scrubbed my skin nearly raw with bottom silt, the black volcanic ash.

When I came out of the water, my pants were gone. I had two pairs—one for the Sabbath, one for other days. Now one was gone. But the matchbox was undisturbed.

In my wet shirt I walked with slow, heavy steps down-hill. Mamma would be furious, Nonna would smack me, my uncles would shout. It wasn't that I was indecent; my shirt came to my knees. But how much did pants cost? And I was supposed to be smart; no one should have been able to steal from me.

It was late by the time I got to the coastal road and hitched a ride on a cart. When I finally jumped off, I ran to the kosher butcher. I bought three coins' worth of liver, for couscous, a rare treat, and raced home, where Mamma burst into tears and hit me on top of the head.

"Eh," said Nonna, "*E figlie so' piezze 'e core*"—Children are pieces of your heart. She smacked me on the back of my head.

17

"Your uncle is searching the streets for you," said Aunt Rebecca. "Instead of eating. You had us sick with worry."

Ernesto pointed at my legs and laughed. Luigi joined in.

"Your pants," said Uncle Aurelio. "What happened?"

I shrugged and avoided his eyes.

The room smelled of tripe. I lifted my nose and sniffed.

"Your foolish mother spent a fortune on a feast," said Aunt Sara, nursing Baby Daniela. "And you didn't even show up."

I held out my bundle, a silent plea for forgiveness, and the women went into action. Aunt Rebecca minced the liver, Nonna peeled onions, Mamma grated old bread for the meatballs. They had to cook the meat now, or it would spoil.

"You're just like your mother," said Aunt Sara. "It's stupid to sell your pants for money for meat."

"I didn't," I mumbled. "It was a thief. I went swimming."

"*Scugnizzi.*" Nonna threw up her hands.

Aunt Sara sighed. "You know better than to swim without a friend to guard your clothes."

"He couldn't help it; Munaciello robbed him." Mamma smiled and I smiled back in grateful surprise. "We'll leave the dishes in the sink tonight. Munaciello needs something to eat."

"You just want to get out of work," said Aunt Sara. "Munaciello never eats when we leave the dishes dirty overnight."

"He's a spirit," said Mamma. "He eats the spirit of the food, not the food itself."

18

"You think you're too good for menial tasks."

"Enough," said Uncle Aurelio. He wagged his finger at the meat. "So where'd you get the money?"

"The nuns. I did a chore."

"The church is rich." Uncle Aurelio winked. "Next time be here for dinner. With your pants on. Now eat."

I filled my bowl with thin tripe slices and soft beans and ate greedily.

Nonna dumped hot meatballs into a bowl. She pointed toward the door with her chin, telling me to bring them to the Rossi family next door. If you received unexpectedly, you had to give unexpectedly. It was how friends behaved.

I delivered the meatballs, then raced back.

Uncle Vittorio came in only seconds behind me. "Ah, you're home, Beniamino," he said. "Now I can eat and go to work."

Mamma wiped sweat from her brow and raked her fingers through her hair. "Beniamino and I will sleep in here tonight. Nonna will sleep in my cot." Before Nonna could protest, Mamma put up her hand. "We'll guard this home with our lives."

So I lay on my chairs in the hot kitchen as Mamma whispered stories to me. I don't know which of us fell asleep first.

Once in the night I woke to Mamma's almost silent crying. Her back was to me, and her shoulder barely moved in the moonlight. I put my hand between the wings of her shoulder blades and pressed. She stopped, as she had the night before and the night before that. When we woke, I'd ask her what was wrong.

CHAPTER THREE

Shoes

I woke to Mamma's hand over my mouth. "Don't say anything," she whispered in my ear. "Don't make noise."

She dressed me in my synagogue pants and shirt. I loved those pants; they had pockets. And the shirt didn't have a single mended spot. She lingered over the buttons. I raised my hand to help and she firmly pushed it away. Then she sat me on the kitchen bench and put socks on my feet. Socks. And then, miracle of miracles, shoes. My first pair of socks, my first pair of shoes. That was what she'd had in that package the morning before. The big surprise. I stared through the faint dawn light and wiggled my toes. If I held them up, they just grazed the leather, there was so much room. The smell was heavenly: clean leather. Shoes got passed from the rich down to the poor. They always held a bump here from the first owner, a dent there from the second, scuffs along the toes from the third. But these were absolutely new—all mine.

She tied the laces in a bow and whispered, *"Antifurto,"* and with the two bow loops she made an extra knot against thieves.

From beyond the door came the muffled sounds of sleep. I wished the others were awake to see my shoes. Especially Luigi and Ernesto. It was all I could do to stay quiet.

I put on my yarmulke, took Mamma's hand, and walked proudly out the door. She lifted me and we touched the *mezuzah* together.

Though she hurried me, I walked carefully. I tried to make sure that nothing would dirty my shoes. It was hard because the light was feeble, the ground was covered with trash, and we walked fast. I kept imagining Luigi's and Ernesto's reactions. I would take care of these shoes so that they could be passed like new to Luigi.

The leather-smacking sound of my own footsteps was a surprise. The strangeness of walking on the street without feeling it underfoot almost made me laugh. Gradually, though, the giddiness wore off and I looked around.

The people out and about so early were mostly men who worked the farmlands. They had to walk an hour or two to reach their jobs. They carried bread in one hand and, if they were lucky, cheese in the other, eating as they went.

I smelled the sharp pecorino and wanted it. Without songs filling me as I woke, I was hungry. That morning Mamma hadn't sung. She'd acted as if we were sneaking out, on a secret treat.

The tenseness of her shoulders told me she was excited. I squeezed her hand in happiness. "Did you get a job?" I asked. "In an office? Are you starting today? Am I helping you?"

Mamma looked at me, her eyelids half lowered. "They hired someone else." Her voice broke.

I squeezed her hand again. "You'll get the next job."

She gave a sad "humph." Then she pulled me faster, the long shawl over her head and shoulders flapping behind. In this hot weather no one but an old crone would cover her head. Mamma must have been sweltering.

"Mamma, where are we going?"

She gripped my arm and pulled me along even faster through neighborhoods I'd never been in before. Long strands of spaghetti hung from poles in front of a pasta factory. Men dressed only in towels around their waists set more poles of pasta to dry in the sun. Other men wrapped dried strands in blue paper. Shopkeepers swept steps and washed windows before opening. The air was coffee. Men came out of coffee bars with powdered-sugar mustaches, licking pastry cheese from their teeth.

A group of women stood around an empty washtub and looked at us. Mamma snatched my yarmulke and tucked it inside her shawl. Why? Those women hadn't said anything. But Mamma's face was flushed.

The seagull screams grew louder. The first fishermen had already returned to the beaches near the port. They gutted fish and threw the innards to the swooping birds. A stooped man grilled fish tails for sale. My mouth watered.

Mamma stopped, as though she had heard my stomach call out. She ran onto the sand and talked to the man. He fashioned a cone from newsprint and filled it with fish tails. He squeezed on lemon and laced them with salt.

Mamma whispered a prayer and we squatted side by side. Normally, we'd sit to eat, like any Jew; we weren't horses. But there was nowhere clean. The Most Powerful One would understand—squatting was almost sitting. Mamma draped her shawl over my head, too, and we ate. Those fish tails were amazing.

I chewed and stared at my shoes. Life could hardly get better.

When we finished, we walked along the water. A steamer loomed in the harbor. I'd seen it the day before from the high piazza on Vomero, but up close it was overwhelming—a giant iron monster. We walked onto the dock. Mamma went down on one knee and smoothed my shirt across my bony chest and wiped my hands and face with the inner hem of her shawl.

From somewhere under that shawl she pulled out a little fold of cloth. It had a string tied around it. Another surprise? With her thumb, she tucked it inside my right shoe, under the arch of my foot. It was so small, it fit easily. "Your job is to survive."

"Wha—?" I opened my mouth, but she put a finger over my lips.

"First of all, simply survive." She stopped and swallowed and for a moment I thought maybe she was sick. "Watch, like you always do, watch and learn and do whatever you have to do to fit in. Talk as little as possible—just watch and use your head." Her eyes didn't blink for so long, they turned glassy. "Nothing can stop you, *tesoro mio*. Remember, you're special, a gift from the Most Powerful One. As soon

23

as you can, get an education. Be your own boss." Then she said, "Open your mouth." I opened my mouth and she spat in it. "That's for long life." She stood up. "Don't undress with anyone around. Ever. Swear to me."

"What?"

"Swear, Beniamino."

I swallowed her saliva. "I swear, Mamma."

We held hands and walked the plank onto the ship. I looked beyond to the two mounds of Vesuvio, red in the rising sun.

A man stopped us.

"We've come to see Pier Giorgio," said Mamma.

"He went to visit his family in Calabria."

"Then we'll wait for him."

"He's not coming on this trip," said the man.

Mamma sucked in air. "That can't be." She pulled me in front of her and pressed her hands down on my shoulders so hard, I thought I'd fall. "I paid," she said. "I paid Pier Giorgio."

"For what?"

"Passage to America."

America. I reached up and put my hand on hers. That was why she had said those crazy words about survival; she was afraid of the journey. But it was worth it; we'd find our fortune in America, like Tonino. We'd send money home, enough for everyone to come and join us.

I would have whispered encouragement, but the man was arguing with her. "This is a cargo ship," he said for a second time. "No passengers."

"That can't be," said Mamma. "It's all arranged."

The man sighed. "How much have you got?"

"I gave it all to Pier Giorgio. My son's passage is paid."

"Go to another ship. Give him to a *padrone*—an agent—who will pay his fare in exchange for work once the ship lands."

"My son will never be anyone's slave."

"Then he's not going to America."

I looked up at Mamma to ask her what was going on. But she put a hand over my mouth and stared at the man. "Yes, he is." She took off her shawl. The cloth of her dress seemed thin and shabby, like gauze. In an instant my strong mamma changed into someone small and weak. I wanted to cover her up.

The man rubbed his dirt-caked neck, leaving a clean streak of olive flesh. Then he took us down a ladder. We stepped off at the first inside deck, but the ladder kept going down. "Go hide in the dark, boy, past those barrels and boxes. Don't make a peep till you feel the sea moving under you. Even then wait a full hour before you come up. Promise."

I looked at Mamma. She nodded. "I promise." I took Mamma's hand, to lead her to the right spot, but he slapped my hand away.

"Your mother has to hide in a different spot, for safety. Hurry up now. Go."

My eyes stung. I blinked hard. This was nothing, nothing at all, compared to being in the grotto under the convent with the body and the rats. This was simple.

I felt my way into the dark. When I looked back, Mamma and the man no longer stood in the circle of light that came in above the ladder. I went farther. Finally, I sat. But the floorboards were wet. They smelled of vinegar. So

25

I climbed onto a barrel lid. Other smells came at me—
machine oils and salted foods and wine and olive oil. And,
strangest of all, hay.

Soon men climbed up and down the ladder, disappearing below or above, mercifully not stopping on this deck.

My skin prickled, but I didn't rub my arms. My bottom
went numb from not changing position, but I didn't flinch.
My tongue felt fat against the roof of my mouth, but I
didn't open my jaw. There were noises from the deck above
as though hundreds of people were up there. And there
were quiet sounds, too, now and then in the dark nearby.
The labored breathing of a frightened person. Mamma. I
wanted to call out to her. But I had promised not to.

After a while, scraping sounds came from the deck below, then the whoosh of fire and the roar of the steam engine. I heard a clank and all light ceased.

Only babies were afraid of the dark.

A horn blasted over and over, and I felt the movement
of the sea. We were going. Going to America.

I waited in the dark. More than an hour, it had to be
more. I waited in the heat that grew until I was drenched
with sweat. Then I whispered, "Mamma."

CHAPTER FOUR

Whispers

"*Zitto*—quiet," came a hot hiss of sour breath. A man's voice.

I twisted my neck and peered into the dark. I couldn't see him, but someone was near. "Where's Mamma?"

"Halfway back to hell by now," came the raspy voice.

Catholics talked that way—hell this and hell that. I got off the barrel and felt my way in the direction of the ladder, calling loudly, "Mamma."

"Stop," said the man. "Come back and shut up. Someone might hear you."

Yes. "Mamma!" I pressed forward. I'd find her and we'd climb to the top deck and see America.

Something caught my pants at the hip. I pulled and the cloth came free with a small rip.

"They'll throw you overboard," said the man.

That stopped me. I swam good; I wouldn't drown, no matter how deep it was. But I didn't know which way America was. And what if they threw Mamma overboard, too? With her shawl on, she might sink.

A long time passed, enough for my shoulders to ache from holding them tight and still. Think—use my head, like Mamma said. People couldn't just throw other people overboard. Weren't there laws against things like that? And even if there weren't, someone would have to have a terrible reason to do such a terrible thing.

I slid my foot forward silently. My path was blocked. I pushed at crates. "Mamma." I whispered as loud as I dared. "Mamma, Mamma."

"Don't doubt me, boy. We're too far from port to turn around. If they find us, we'll be food for the fish. There's no other way to get rid of us."

"Why would they want to get rid of us?" I said.

"No one has pity on sick stowaways. We could infect the ship; then they wouldn't let anyone debark in America. They won't take that chance. I hear that if a sailor lets a sick guy on, they throw him overboard, too."

I wasn't sick. Neither was Mamma. We wouldn't get thrown overboard.

I had to get away from this sick man. I tried to climb over the crates. Impossible.

Mamma was nowhere near. Even if she hadn't overheard our conversation, she would have called out for me by now if she was down here. But she knew where I was. She'd come find me.

"I shouldn't be a stowaway," said the man in a tired

28

voice. "I paid my passage. I was supposed to go to America in steerage, on a regular ship. It took years to earn the money." He stopped talking. Too bad. At least his voice was a kind of company.

The boat pitched and made my stomach lurch.

The man groaned. "Leave it to me to pick up cholera, so they wouldn't take me, even with a ticket. But last night I heard people saying this cargo ship was heading to New York. I was practically crawling, but I snuck on."

I shook my head, though he couldn't see me in the dark. "New York? I thought we were going to America?"

"New York is America, boy. Don't you know anything? New York is paradise. The opposite of your little hovel in Napoli. The opposite of where your mamma is."

"Mamma is here. On the boat."

"No, she's not. She stuck you here so you can go to America and make a life for yourself."

"Mamma's hiding. She's on the top deck."

"Are you crazy? No hiding places up there."

"Then she's on the deck below. She's here!" I pushed hard at the crates. I threw myself against them, over and over. Finally some tumbled away, me with them. I stumbled forward till I finally grasped the ladder. It was as though I was in the grotto all over again—the panic I felt at the bottom of the ladder, the relief that came as I climbed.

At the top was a metal hatch. I heaved my back against it and it opened. Sunlight streamed in, all wonderful. The cool sea air swelled my lungs. "Mamma," I hollered. "Mamma, where are you?"

A man pulled me from the hole. "What do we have here? A talking rat?"

29

Talking? Mamma had said to talk as little as possible. I dangled by one arm from the man's hand, the breeze knocking me about.

"No, a silent rat," said the man who had told me where to hide. He came running over and shot me a warning glance.

I pulled myself free and gingerly walked a few steps along the deck toward a herd of cattle with pigs snorting among them. It was their hooves I must have heard before—that was what had made me think there were a hundred people on board. Beyond them was the terrifying sea in every direction. Green, swelling and falling, on and on forever.

Find Mamma. But the railing was two levels of pipes, with so much space below and between them that there was nothing to stop me from flying into the water with the next pitch of the ship. A mast rose thick and sturdy off to my left with a high pile of oily cloth folded beside it. I went toward it, my shoes slipping on the wet deck, arms reaching. I made it!

I climbed onto the pile of cloth, clung to the mast, and looked around. I saw men. Men, but no women. Not a single one.

CHAPTER FIVE

Brooms

"Come on." A hand tugged my elbow.

My arms and legs were wrapped around the mast as if I was a monkey. My bottom was on the oily cloth, getting dirty, which didn't matter, since I'd wet my pants. I had yelled for Mamma, then cried myself to sleep.

"Get up."

I hated all these men. They had seen me cry. And none of them would bring me to Mamma.

"Food," the man said, lifting his eyebrows. "Come."

Food? His face looked nice, almost kind. But I looked at the sea beyond the open deck and hugged the mast tighter.

He grabbed my shirt and pulled me down. "You'll get your sea legs soon," he said. "For now, take the middle path." And he let go.

I stood unsteady, arms to both sides. Path? All I saw were animals packed against one another and thick ropes coiled high. And pipes and rigging and barrels and lifeboats and the big white funnel horn.

"Follow me." The man went straight toward the animals. Just then, the ship rolled and I fell on all fours. He grabbed me by the arm and we staggered through the animals. The cows had to be thumped hard to get them to move. The pigs grunted and threatened to charge.

We came to a second mast and a set of steps up to a raised area near the prow of the ship. A circle of men sat there, stripped to the waist. They made space for us.

Fresh bread passed from hand to hand. Then came dripping mozzarella, so new my fingers left dents.

"This'll be the last mozzarella till America," said a man.

I caught the white drops of its milk in my hunk of bread. Slices of salami came around, wet to the touch. I didn't take any; they were made from pig. But I let myself smell my fingers after I'd passed it on: spicy and lemony. Then came tomatoes.

If the men had prayed before they ate, I hadn't seen it. And no one covered his head. They didn't act like my family—they didn't talk about how good the meal was and how thankful they were, even though this food was plentiful and delicious.

"Where's Mamma? She's hungry, too."

"Your mother again?" said a man. "Eat, and we'll worry about her later."

Nonna's proverb came to me: *"Chi tene mamma, nun chiagne"*—Whoever has a mother doesn't cry. I held my breath to stop the tears, but they came anyway.

The men jabbered on, not looking at me. I should have been grateful, but their ignoring me only made me feel more alone. They talked about the trip: two weeks if we were lucky and didn't hit storms. It could be three weeks. Four.

All that time at sea. How far was America, anyway?

They passed around a bottle of wine, each one taking a swill. When it came to me, I hesitated.

"What's the matter, aren't you weaned yet? You want milk?" asked a man jokingly.

They laughed.

I tried it. It was strong—not like the sweet wine we had at Passover. I didn't like it, but I was thirsty. I drank again, then passed the bottle.

But now they were all looking at me and talking about me, as though they'd suddenly been reminded I was there. The man who had brought me over from the mast said, "I'm Carlo. You get an extra tomato since you didn't eat the salami."

"I'll save it for Mamma."

"Don't worry about your mother," said the man who had spoken before. "Just eat."

"Why should he eat more?" said a man gruffly. "He's another mouth to feed—a useless mouth."

Still, Carlo handed me a tomato so ripe and sweet, its juices burst in my mouth. I finished it and wiped my chin with my palm, then licked my hand.

"At least he appreciates a tomato," said one man. And the others laughed again.

They went around the circle introducing themselves. Then they asked my name. Beniamino was a typical Jewish

33

name. These men weren't Jewish—not the way they'd devoured that salami. I remembered Mamma taking my yarmulke off. I shrugged.

"A talking rat with no name," said Eduardo, the one who had lifted me from the top of the ladder. A cigarette bobbled between his lips as he spoke.

"He must have slipped in last night early," said Carlo, "because we had someone guarding the plank from midnight on."

I glanced at Franco, the man who had snuck Mamma and me onto the boat this morning. He was looking at me, his face tense.

". . . quieter than a rat," Carlo was saying. "More like a mouse in church. What shall we call the mouse we see at Mass on *domenica*—on Sunday?" He clapped. "Let's call him Domenico."

"In America, though, he'll need an American name," said Eduardo. "Joe would be better."

"Or just make Domenico short—Dom—like the Americans do," said Carlo. "After all, he's a little fellow."

They laughed. Most of them had lit cigarettes by now, and they were blowing their smoke into the breeze.

"What'll it be, little mouse?" asked Eduardo. "Joe or Dom?"

"Dom," I said.

"See?" said Eduardo to Franco. "A talking mouse."

"What do they call you in America?" I asked Eduardo.

"I don't need an American name," he said. "I'm not staying when we land. You'll go off to Mulberry Street. But us . . ." He looked around at the circle of men. "We go back to Napoli—*bella* Napoli. So, little mouse, little Dom, let's

34

talk." He leaned away from me as if to get a look at my whole self, while he picked salami from between his teeth. "Is your mother really hidden on this ship?"

I stole a glance at Franco. He closed his eyes briefly. But he didn't have to, because I'd figured it out. He'd get in trouble if I told; he'd brought two more mouths to feed onto this boat.

I looked down at my hands. As soon as these men went about their business again, I'd find Mamma. On my own. And I'd bring her food. Franco would give me food for her.

"If there's a woman on board," said Carlo, "I'll be mighty happy."

The men chuckled.

"If there were other stowaways, we'd know by now," said Franco.

I remembered the sick man. "There is someone else," I blurted.

"What! Who?"

"I don't know. He talked to me, but he didn't tell me his name."

"Where is he?" asked Eduardo.

"One deck down. He was hiding in the dark near me."

Eduardo got up.

"Wait." I grabbed his ankle. "Be careful. He's sick."

Eduardo's cheek twitched. "Sick how?"

"Cholera."

He jerked free from me.

"I don't have cholera," I said. "I swear."

"Did he vomit?"

"Yes."

Eduardo's mouth twisted into a grimace. "Then he's dying."

And now they were all arguing. Everyone had heard of a different way to deal with cholera. The only thing they could agree on was that someone had to find the man. And soon.

No one volunteered.

They played a game—guessing the number of pigs on deck. The loser, a big man called Beppe, touched his forehead, his chest, his left shoulder, then his right. Aha: the sign of the cross. Catholics did that a lot. Beppe held up the medal that hung around his neck and said, "Help me, Sant'Antonio." He kissed it and disappeared down the hatch.

He came back up, holding an oil lamp. "He's breathing. But he's too far gone to answer."

One man got an oilclotch. Another got three brooms and handed them out. Beppe went back down the ladder with the lamp, leading the way to the sick man.

"Get up," said Beppe.

No response. He must have been playing dead, hoping they'd go away.

"They won't hurt you," I said. "They'll feed you. They fed me."

He didn't answer.

Two men spread the oilcloth beside him and stood holding tight the top and bottom ends. Three other men used the brooms to push him onto the cloth.

He groaned and his head lolled to one side. The black bristles of his new beard were streaked with yellow and red. "Water," he breathed roughly.

They carried him up onto the deck near the railing. Then two men lowered buckets over the side and filled them with water.

"Don't swallow," said Beppe. "It's seawater. To clean you up." And he doused the sick man with bucket after bucket.

The man's chest rose and fell. His face was clean now, and his black beard glistened.

"I've got fresh water for you," Beppe said. "Open your mouth wide."

The man opened his mouth but kept his eyes closed.

Beppe poured water into his mouth.

The sick man gulped and opened his mouth again.

Beppe poured a little more.

The sick man lay there with his mouth open. He didn't swallow this time. His chest stopped moving.

Someone nudged him with a broom. "He's gone."

What? He was right there. The man nudged him harder. "He's not gone," I said. "He can't be." I went closer.

Eduardo caught me by the pants and pulled me to him.

They argued about whether they should search the man's pockets for identification, since his family would want to know. But no one was ready to touch him.

They all made the sign of the cross. Then the men with brooms came forward and the rest stepped back. I knew what they were going to do before they did it. I didn't scream.

He was gone, oilcloth and all.

He was there, and then he wasn't.

They swabbed the deck. Some went down the ladder with buckets and mops to swab below, too.

I stood and watched, my legs splayed so I wouldn't fall. The spot where the man had sunk, the man who was now food for the fish, was far behind us, covered by the turbulence of our wake. He was dead when they threw him over. He was dead, he was dead, he was dead. They would never throw over a living person. They would never throw over Mamma or me.

"Your pants could use some cleaning, too, Dom," said a voice.

It took a moment before I realized the voice was talking to me. I was Dom. I looked up at Franco, who held a bucket.

"Take your pants off and dip them in here."

Never undress with anyone else around—Mamma had made me swear. And now I knew why; she had said it for the same reason she had taken my yarmulke. She didn't want people to see my circumcision and know I was Jewish. I shook my head.

"You smell, boy."

"I don't care."

"But we do." Franco wrinkled his nose. "Take off your shoes."

Why? My shoes were way too small for these men. "No."

"Suit yourself," he said. "Do you like the water?"

"I swim," I said. Then I tensed up. What did he mean?

"Oop la." And he sloshed the whole bucket right at my middle with a smile.

I stood dripping, my new shoes soaked. Before I could think straight, I raised the back of my forearm to him, fist curled tight, in the angry gesture every Napoletano recognized.

CHAPTER SIX

The Plan

I sat on the deck cleaning squid for Riccardo, the cook. I didn't like squid—they weren't kosher. The first time I cleaned them, I had to fight off revulsion. But cleaning squid took all my attention, and that was good because then I couldn't think about Mamma.

For two days I searched the whole boat for her, over and over. When I didn't find her and Franco wouldn't answer my questions, I imagined he had her in a cage off the boiler rooms. So I told Carlo. If anyone could stand up to Franco, it was Carlo. He helped me search. Everywhere.

She wasn't here.

I was alone on this ship. I hugged myself hard and pressed my back into the wall and listened to the buzz in my head. I was dizzy the rest of that day. Dizzy and nauseated.

Franco had left Mamma in Napoli. That coward. I hated him. Poor Mamma. My poor, poor mamma, frantic with worry for me.

But I had a plan. When we got to America, I wouldn't get off the cargo ship. I'd turn right around and go back to Mamma. In my prayers, I asked the Most Powerful One to tell her that, so she wouldn't cry too much. In the meantime, my job was to fit in. The first time I went into the galley and asked what I could do to help, Riccardo ignored me. So I watched. Then I shelled peas. When he saw how quick I was, he gave me all sorts of tasks.

There were tons of jobs on this ship. I looked around and did whatever needed doing. I was living Uncle Aurelio's lecture—I'd been smacked with adversity, and I'd picked myself up like any good Jew.

I swept out the poultry coops on the top deck and gathered eggs. I got my share of pecks on my hands and arms and even on the back of my neck. Fabrizio taught me how to milk the cows. And I cleaned the cabins, the galley, the bakery, the wheels and pipes and tools and water-distilling machine. I loved cleaning that machine, with the shiny compasses, wheels, and complicated gauges in the helm. I washed dishes, swept rat droppings, scrubbed the toilets. I brought the coal trimmers water while they shoveled, and raced up the ladders to the top deck to dip the rags for wiping their foreheads into the bucket of cold seawater.

The crew came to count on me. It was part of my plan. If they needed me, they'd take me back with them gladly. I couldn't tell them my plan, because stowaways were illegal. But when they discovered me on the ship on the way back, they'd be glad.

Eduardo said I reminded him of his son. He woke me in the morning and asked if I needed anything at night. And Carlo liked me, too. He made sure I got my fair share of food.

Each afternoon, when most of the crew took a nap, I sat in a corner far from everyone and practiced my private ritual. I untied the string around the tiny bundle Mamma had tucked in my right shoe and unfolded the cloth. Inside were four tassels, each made of eight strands of yarn, seven white and one blue, tied into many knots. The first time I opened the bundle, I recognized them instantly. They were holy tassels—*tzitzit*—from my grandfather's prayer shawl. I held them and let memories wash me clean.

My grandfather Nonno had had a beautiful prayer shawl—a *tallit*. My uncles had beautiful ones, too. But theirs were combinations of blues and greens and yellows. Nonno's was a mix of extravagantly bright swatches of red silk fabrics stitched together with fine embroidery. And it was so long that even with his arms hanging by his sides, it draped down a full hand's length past his fingertips.

From the four corners of that shawl hung these tassels. In synagogue, I used to stand beside Nonno and hold a tassel and count the knots. When we got home and he took it off, he let me help him fold it. I smoothed the tassels and wondered what secret message the Hebrew letters across the top of the *tallit* held.

Nonno died when I was five. We buried him in his *tallit*. But Nonna saved the tassels. When I turned thirteen, I'd get my own prayer shawl at my Bar Mitzvah, with these tassels at the corners.

Mamma had put them in my shoe for safekeeping.

I fingered the knots. Then I rubbed my shoes with that small piece of cloth. Not because they were dirty. No, no. They were perfectly clean. I didn't wear them; they were too slippery to walk around the ship in. And it would have been impossible to keep them dry. So I stored them in a bale of hay. I rubbed them every day—at first to make them soft again, because they'd dried hard after Franco had thrown the water on me, but later just as part of my ritual.

While I worked, I thought of Mamma. Mamma, who had wanted a better life—the life of people who wore shoes even when they were children. We'd have been together on the trip to that better life in America if it wasn't for Franco.

When I got back home, I'd go to school. Then in a few years I'd have my Bar Mitzvah and Nonna could attach these tassels to my prayer shawl and I'd get a good job. The first thing I'd do with my money was buy us ship tickets. We would live Mamma's dream, that better life.

In the meantime, being on this boat wasn't so bad. Sometimes I'd stand at the rail, holding tight, and look out at sea, pretending to be a pirate scouting for ships to raid. There were lots of dolphins, and Riccardo taught me how to spot whales. Sometimes, when we threw garbage over the side, sharks came close enough to the surface to give me goose bumps.

I finished cleaning the squid now and carried the bowls to the galley. Even when the sea was rough, I kept my footing. All it had taken was one storm to teach me perfect balance.

The crew usually ate out on the poop deck, where I'd

had my first meal with them. This was the best part of the day; the men talked till the stars came out. I headed there now. The men were already sitting around.

"Maybe I'll stay this time," said Franco. "Maybe I'll join the line on Ellis Island and make my fortune in New York."

"You can have it," said Ivo. "They speak too much gobbledy-gook there. English, bah."

"English?" said Franco. "They don't speak English in America. They speak English in England."

"Shows how much you know. In New York they speak English and German."

"And Irish," said Carlo.

"What are you all, idiots?" said Ivo. "Most Irish people speak English. Just in a funny way. Like the people from Avellino speak Napoletano funny. Nah," he said. "You can have New York. You go ahead, sound like a dumb immigrant your whole life, with everyone laughing at you. I've heard the ship officers talk about it. People even laugh at them when they go into town. For me, if I was going to jump ship, why, I'd go to South America any day. They speak Spanish there. It's like Napoletano, I hear. It's easy."

"Or Africa," said Salvatore. "In Tripoli, they respect Italians so much, they learn Italian rather than making the Italians learn African. That's where I'd go."

All this talk of different languages was news to me. I'd thought everyone everywhere spoke pretty much the same, except that Jews spoke Hebrew in synagogue, Catholics spoke Latin in church, and Muslims spoke Arabic in the mosque. Maybe when I got rich, I'd take Mamma to

South America instead of New York. If English sounded awful, who needed it?

That night as I lay in my usual spot on the floor under Eduardo's bunk, he leaned over. "Hey, Dom? You awake?"

"Sure," I said.

"Tomorrow, when we land . . ."

"We land tomorrow? Already?"

"Already? We're ten days overdue because of those storms. Anyway, when we land, you have to stay out of sight in the bunk room till I tell you. I'll find a way for you to sneak off. But you have to be quick about it. The captain said we're leaving the same day we arrive because we're so far behind schedule. So you have to do what I say when I say it. Understand?"

"Yes."

"Do you have people waiting for you in New York?"

"No."

"That's what I was afraid of." He gave a brief whistle. "There are plenty of kids on their own in America, but it's hard. Harder than in Napoli. Head for Mulberry Street."

"Why?"

"That's where Napoletani live. You'll understand them, know what's going on. I have a cousin there, but he's a son of a gun. Otherwise I'd tell you to look him up."

"Okay," I said, "Mulberry Street." What did it matter? I wasn't going anywhere but home to *bella* Napoli.

"Stay how you are, Dom, exactly how you are—make yourself useful. You know how to do it. But don't trust anyone."

"Except Napoletani," I said, "Napoletani on Mulberry Street."

44

"Especially don't trust them. Napoletani cheat everyone. Remember that."

"But you don't have to cheat in America," I said. "Everyone's rich."

"What a sack of lies. My cousin, jerk that he is, told me the truth. It's tough all over, especially at the bottom, where you'll be. Take care of yourself, Dom, because no one else will."

I didn't answer.

"In bocca al lupo," he said—In the mouth of the wolf. It was a roundabout way of wishing me luck without challenging fate.

"Crepi," I answered—May it burst and die—the standard response.

"And don't forget your shoes," said Eduardo. He pulled his head back up.

Snores came from many bunks.

I rolled on my side. We would be in America the next day.

A match struck, and the little flame lit the cigarette between Franco's lips. His face appeared old, all the crags deep in shadow. Smoking wasn't allowed anywhere except on the open deck. But there was no one awake to notice. No one but me.

"Go put your shoes on," said Franco.

"What?"

"Eduardo's right. You're sleeping with them on tonight. So you'll be ready in the morning."

I put on my shoes, careful to place the cloth with the tassels under my right arch, and crawled back beneath Eduardo's bunk.

Eventually, Franco's cigarette went out. Then the smell

of the smoke faded. There was nothing but the quiet noises of sleepers and the background rumble of the boiler and engines.

I stared into the dark.

The funnel horn woke me. I was groggy from too little sleep, but I jumped up. I raced to the open deck to find everyone else working even though it was barely morning. We were pulling into a gigantic harbor. People and horses and wagons jammed the shore. Another cargo ship unloaded sheep in clumps of three, lifting them with pulleys from the deck, swinging them over the railing, and plopping them onto the dock. Bells clanged, horns blew, the air shook with bleats and shouts.

Someone smacked the back of my head.

"Get to the bunk room till it's time," said Eduardo. "You'll only make trouble for everyone if they see you now."

So I ran, but not to the bunks. I hid in the dairy cow house. I strained to see between the slats, but I couldn't make out much. The noise went on for hours.

I had slept through breakfast, so I patted my favorite cow and squirted hot milk into my mouth.

The heat of the cows and the milk in my belly and the roar of the world outside . . . I'd gone to bed so late . . . I dozed off.

When I woke, I peeked between the slats. The men were already loading things for the return trip. Lined up nearby were crates marked with the post office symbol. I'd always wanted to get a letter—and to write one. I knew exactly what went into a letter, because I listened when Uncle Vittorio read the mail for women in our neighborhood. Many of the men didn't read, either. Mamma could have read for them, but no one asked her to. The women said Mamma was uppity to know how to read like that.

Mamma Mamma Mamma. I pressed the heels of my hands against my eyelids to stop the tears. This was a trick the journey had taught me. Sometimes I sat for hours with the heels of my hands against my eyelids.

Then the horn blared and the plank was drawn up and the ship pulled away from the dock. I was going home. I whooped for joy.

The door of the cow house opened. "It's you!" Franco's shocked face was in mine. "You idiot! We're leaving already."

"I'm going back to Napoli."

"A promise is a promise." Franco dragged me out. "You said you knew how to swim. So swim." And he threw me overboard.

CHAPTER SEVEN

Waiting

The water was farther down than I'd thought. Far enough for me to scream, far enough for me to think I was dead. I hit it with a smack and went under so deep, I couldn't see anything.

I put my hands over my head and swam upward as fast as I could. My hands split the water and slammed down to push me up, up. I gasped to fill my burning lungs.

The swirl of water from the screw-propeller engine of my own ship pulled me under. I swam away with all my might, broke the surface, gasped, got sucked under all over again.

But then my ship was gone, and I was alone in the water. With another ship coming in to harbor.

I swam for the dock and latched on to a piling

pole. Barnacles cut my hands and arms. I shouted. I imagined the huge ship crushing me against the pole as I screamed for help.

The ship made the water rise and fall and swirl. It splashed over my head and pulled me. If I let go and swam under the dock, I might get sucked down again and not have the strength to swim up this time. So I held on with my whole body, despite the barnacles, curling myself as tight as I could, praying that none of me stuck out past the dock's edge.

The bang of the ship against the dock sent a shudder through my pole, but the ship didn't touch me.

I was cold. Bleeding. Exhausted.

And alive.

Shouts of joy came from the ship as people walked down the plank.

I called out. The people were looking around in wonder at the new world in front of them; surely someone would glance down between the ship and the dock. Just one person, that was all I needed. That man in the suit, or that woman in the fancy dress. I kept calling. My throat grew hoarse. But who could hear me?

Soon the passengers were gone and the crew unloaded luggage. No one was looking around in wonder anymore.

I cried out again. My neck hurt from straining. I let my head fall.

After a long while, a holler came from above. I looked up. A man on the dock jabbered at me frantically.

"Help," I tried to shout, but it came out as a croak.

"Italian?" he screeched.

A man with a large mustache appeared and looked down at me. "What are you doing there?" His words sounded strange—but I understood.

"I fell."

"Can you swim?"

"Yes."

"Swim under the dock. I'll throw you a rope on the other side." He disappeared.

The first man still jabbered at me.

I didn't move.

Eventually the Italian man came back. "Go. Go to the other side. It's not safe to pull you up on the side with the ship. Understand?"

"I'll wait," I said.

"For what?"

"Till the ship leaves."

"Only first and second class were allowed to disembark. The rest of the passengers won't be processed for days."

I had no idea what that meant.

"Did you hear me? The ship won't leave for three days, at the least."

I whimpered.

"Stay put. I'll find someone who can swim." His face disappeared again.

In a little while gasping breaths came from under the dock.

"Here," I called out. "I'm here."

An older man swam to me. He grabbed the pole, then cursed as he pulled his bleeding hand away. He carried the end of a rope between his teeth. He took it out and offered it to me.

I didn't let go of the pole. I couldn't. I was stuck.

The man grabbed my ear and twisted.

"Aiii!" I let go of the pole with one hand and clawed at him.

He looped the rope around my chest and gave a yank, and I was jerked away through the water. I spun; water went up my nose and down my throat. I was drowning. Then I was suddenly out in the air, swinging like a clump of seaweed on a hook. I landed in a heap on the hot dock.

Someone asked me in plain language who I was, but my eyes were closed against the bright sun and I wasn't sure I could open them. My bones ached from being in the cold water; my teeth chattered.

I could hear men talking, trying to guess how I'd gotten down there, who I was. That had to be my passenger ship—it was from Napoli, and my speech told them I was, too. And I had to be a boy from a good family with shoes like that. I must have fallen off the plank when the first- and second-class passengers disembarked. Someone would surely pay a reward for their saving me. They argued about who deserved the reward. Then they worried that instead of a reward, they'd get blamed for my winding up in the water. That ended that.

Someone wrapped a padded crate cloth around me and rubbed my back and arms and legs through the cloth. Gradually, warmth radiated from my middle. But I still wouldn't open my eyes. I wanted whoever was holding me to keep holding me.

He carried me, bumping through crowds. I took a peek. Everyone was rushing. They talked funny. And they carried canes and wore so many clothes—jackets and hats.

51

Even the men working the docks had on shirts under that beating sun.

He carried me into a brick building filled with people in nice clothes, packed together. Men in uniforms stood beside them, holding on to giant handcarts of baggage. He spoke to a man who called out strange things through his megaphone. Another man came running and took the megaphone and announced in plain language, "Who's missing a Napoletano boy?" He pointed at me.

"What a nightmare for his parents," a woman said. "Take him back to the ship right away."

A man touched the rip in my pants, the one I'd gotten my first day on the ship. It had grown so big, I could put my hand through it. "You're third class." He wagged his head. Another man pulled me by the hand back to the dock and up onto the ship and left me there.

What? Just like that?

The crew was still unloading luggage, and no one seemed to have noticed me. I scrambled over by a mast, out of the way, and watched. The heat of the day slowly dried me. The drier I got, the better I felt. Life was looking up; I was back on a ship. A passenger ship. This might even be better than my cargo ship.

I wandered into a room with a bed and desk and many ledgers. One lay open, listing name after name. This was the record of passengers. I had to stay out of the way of whoever kept it.

I walked out quickly, my heart thumping, and went straight to a group of lifeboats along the side. I held on to the rail and looked down and tried to blend with the background.

Time passed, and no one came to chase me away.

The smell of food got me wandering again. I hadn't eaten since that squirt of cow's milk. A crew member glanced at me, then stopped his work to look again. I ran to the closest hatch and scooted down below deck.

I sank into a sea of people. Most were quiet, putting their energy into the struggle to breathe in this heat. Some grumbled that they weren't allowed up on deck. The only people left on the ship now were third-class passengers. A man said there were five hundred and twenty of them, all in a stench of vomit and feces.

Here in the dark, no one could see beyond arm's length. But there was bread with lard spread, salty and delicious. And all I really needed to do was stay on this ship.

Home to Mamma. It was just a matter of time. My mamma.

The officers allowed us to sleep on the top deck. Babies cried, men cursed.

I was too wound up to do anything but wander among them. I found a man and two boys wearing yarmulkes, but I couldn't understand them. So I hung around Napoletani and listened. They pointed at a statue in the harbor and fell to their knees in prayer. I thought often of Uncle Aurelio and his speeches about *le possibilità*.

The next day the quarantine station officers came on board. People had been warning one another about them. They checked for typhus, yellow fever, smallpox. The trick was to stand at attention, look alert, and, no matter what, not cough. I was grateful to know the trick. Some who didn't were taken off someplace. It was rumored that they went into observation far away, and if they got sicker, they

53

went into isolation somewhere even farther away. After that, who knew what became of them?

That second night, I took my shoes off and spread out my socks to air. I carefully tucked the cloth with the tassels inside one sock, and I used, instead, the corner of the padded crate cloth that I carried everywhere to rub the shoe leather soft, because it had dried hard again after being in the water. When I went to put my shoes back on, I couldn't find my socks.

My *tzitzit*—my tassels!

No!

I felt all over the floor around me. I ran through the clusters of people, looking everywhere. I tugged on women's skirts and asked for help. I looked and looked and looked.

No no no.

My grandfather's prayer shawl tassels were gone. America had thieves, like Napoli—but worse ones. Far worse.

I stared out over the buildings of New York and pressed the heels of my hands against my eyelids. Still the tears came. I brushed them away as fast as they fell.

Some of those buildings seemed as tall as Vesuvio. But they didn't make me feel uplifted, like the high building of my synagogue in Napoli. Instead, I felt tiny and weak.

I turned my back to them and looked at the statue the others had prayed to—the grand Statue of Liberty.

I didn't want liberty. I stood there snuffling. All I wanted was to go home.

CHAPTER EIGHT

On Land

When it was time to disembark, men put gold chains around their necks, then ties and vests and coats, and they combed their mustaches. Women pinned their hair and put on jackets and fancy shoes with big wooden heels and any number of rings. Even the children sprouted boots and coats. I was a *scugnizzo* compared to them. And I was the only one missing a label—they all had a big number three pinned to their jackets, for third class. I tucked my shirt in my pants and smoothed the front of it.

The men carried baggage in both hands. So did the women, unless they were carrying a child or two. Some had an infant strapped to their chest. Everyone clenched their health certificate in their teeth.

I held my padded cloth and tried to blend in. I had a plan. As we filed along, I was going to duck into the cow house. It had worked last time—almost. All I needed was to stay on this ship until it left for home.

But when I opened the cow house door, the woman behind me shouted, and a man from Napoli pulled me back into the crowd. He said, "What? You want to go to England? America is better." Stupid me, to think that because this ship had left from the port of Napoli, it would return there.

Now I needed another plan.

The crowd carried me along, deafened by boat horns blasting from every direction, down the plank, around crates and animals and wagons on the pier, into the customs building. When it was my turn, the officer simply waved me past, and again the crowd carried me, this time onto a barge, men going to one side, and women and children to the other. They piled the baggage between us.

In less than half an hour we were ferried across to Ellis Island, and our shipload of passengers merged with shiploads from all over the world. No one understood anyone else. We went into a giant building. I'd never seen a building with wood walls. In Napoli only shacks were made of wood, not homes, and certainly not official buildings. On the bottom floor was a baggage area. Everyone was told to place their belongings there, but no one wanted to. The official kept saying that they could fetch them after they'd passed through the registration room upstairs. Still, no one put anything down.

The official lost patience; he barked at us.

Everyone's eyes darted around. Then they opened their bundles and layered extra clothes onto already sweating bodies. Around their necks they hung picture lockets and saint medals and keys to the homes they'd left behind. They loaded their pockets with bone fans and wood pipes and rolling pins and little bottles and all kinds of documents. A woman from Napoli took out needle and thread and sewed letters from her dead husband into the hem of her skirt. She said they were love letters. Some people locked their fingers around the handles of their suitcases and simply refused to give them up.

Mamma's voice called, *"Tesoro? Tesoro mio?"*

I whirled around and watched a boy run to the fat, short woman who had stolen Mamma's voice, stolen Mamma's name for me—treasure. She said, "Grab hold of my skirt and don't let go, no matter what."

That was what Mamma would say to me. My heart raced. I had to bite my hand to keep from screaming.

I threw my padded crate cloth onto the baggage pile and joined the crowd on the stairs. Everyone was talking and telling everyone else to hush so they could figure out what was going on. I stayed close to Napoletani. If they understood anything and repeated it, I would understand, too.

At the top of the stairs doctors checked fingernails and the backs of legs. They opened collars and felt necks. Women shuddered, their faces tight with fear, for they'd never been touched like that before. The doctors made everyone take off hats and kerchiefs, and they parted hair to inspect scalps. Men with pompadours were yelled at, as though they were trying to hide something in their puffed-up hair. Then the doctors took out metal hooks—like the kind people used to button their shoes—and looked inside lower eyelids. All that took only seconds.

Children screamed constantly. Doctors wanted to make sure any child over two years old was healthy enough to walk alone, but the children clung to their mothers. So the doctors ripped them away and walked off several paces with them, then set them down to go shrieking back.

I watched everything closely. Watch and learn and fit in—that was what Mamma said.

Almost everyone was pushed on into the giant registration room. But now and then the doctors made a mark with colored chalk on a person's clothes. The mark was always a letter; I saw *S, B, X, C, H, L, E, K, F, G, N*. Sometimes there were two letters, *Ft, Pg, CT, Sc*, or sometimes an *X* inside a circle. All the letters meant something bad, because they were written on people a doctor had spent extra time with. A man took off his coat and turned it inside out to hide the mark on his lapel.

The doctor who inspected me took five seconds. He touched the scabs on my arms from the barnacles on the piling pole at the dock and said something to me in English. I stood at attention, without coughing—I remembered the trick. Then he said something to the woman behind me and she shrugged. Two women in white uniforms—nurses—came up. One pulled me to the side. She did things with her hands, sticking up one finger, then five, then three, or forming an O with her thumb and index finger. The other woman mimicked her. Then the nurse turned to me and made a shape with her hand. She waited. I looked at her. The other nurse mimicked the shape. They both looked at me. And I got it; I made the shape. The first nurse took me through several shapes. Then she drew shapes on a piece of paper and I had to copy them. She smiled at me and patted me on the back and pointed for me to go join the lines in the registration room.

I'd passed another test. Though what it meant was beyond me. I got in line and looked back at the nurses. They were still watching me, with suspicious eyes now. So I moved ahead through the line, out of their sight, till I found two men speaking Napoletano. I stood behind them and looked up at their faces as though I knew them. After a while I snuck a glance back; the nurses were testing someone else. I heard a man say they were testing for idiocy. So they'd thought I was an idiot.

This was the first time in my life I'd ever stood in a real line. Napoletani waited for things in clusters. But here, there were three strict lines. I was in the one on the left. I couldn't see the front, so I kept my ears open and I looked out the side windows at the Statue of Liberty. She was green in this light, and her torch was bright gold. A barge pulled in with more people. Where would they all fit? I looked at the floor. It was tiled, like any floor in Napoli. But it was dirty. Why was everyone coming to a place where people worked in wood buildings with dirty floors?

The lines moved slowly, but finally I could see an inspector at the head of each one. The inspector for my line questioned everyone in English. When they answered in another language, he called over a man in uniform who could speak every language in the world. The men in front of me called him a translator. Everyone handed over documents and pulled money out of pockets and hems of coats. The inspector asked questions and handed it all back, including the money.

A woman in the next line cried to her husband. She

wasn't from Napoli, but I could understand her. Their child had gotten a chalk mark on his jacket because he was sick. The nurses said they'd have to take him away. She was afraid to let him go. At the same time she was afraid that if she didn't, they'd all be sent back. I wanted to tell her they'd be lucky if they were sent back. As soon as I reached that inspector, I would tell him everything and be sent home.

The two Napoletani in front of me practiced what they were going to say.

One of them played the inspector: "Do you have a job?"

The other answered, "Yes, at . . ."

"No!" said the first one. "It's illegal to have a *padrone* who got you a job ahead of time. You say, 'No.' "

"But we paid all that money. We have a *padrone,* right?"

"Of course we do. He's waiting for us when we get out. Okay, second question. Where are you going to live?"

"I don't know."

"No! You say, 'At my cousin's on Mulberry Street.' With as little money as we have, unless we say we have a place to stay, they'll send us to the Board of Inquiry, who will send us back to Napoli. Listen, you be the inspector. Ask me what I'll do in America."

"What will you do in America?"

"Anything. I will take any job I am offered. See? That's the right answer. Ask me about money."

"What about money?"

"We have to have enough. That's what I just said. Show the inspector all your money." He sighed. "They have to let us stay—we can't go back to starving. Look, I'll answer first.

60

Listen and you say the same thing when it's your turn. Understand?"

"I understand."

I doubted the second man understood anything. But I understood. And I was happy. I had no money. They'd send me home for sure.

Finally, the inspector talked to the two men. The translator spoke our language pretty good. The inspector checked their names against the ship's list. He asked if they could read, if they were sick, if they were married, if they'd committed crimes, what their occupations were, if they were anarchists—on and on, ending with how much money they had. The men couldn't write, so the translator wrote answers for them.

I glanced over at the next line. The inspector there asked a woman if she was married. He asked her that shameless question with her child holding her hand, right in front of her husband. She stiffened at the insult and her husband objected in a fierce voice.

Mamma had to put up with insults because of me all the time. And it dawned on me: right now, wherever she was, she didn't have to. Anyone new who met her didn't have to know she had a child. They could ask, "Do you have a child at home?" and she could answer, "No." She could get an office job—the right kind of job for someone who could read. Maybe she had one already.

That would be good. If she had a job, she couldn't cry all day about missing me. And when I got back, she could keep the job, because her boss would realize by then how smart and useful she was. Life would be better.

61

The man behind me pushed me forward. The inspector spoke to me in loud English. It was clear he was annoyed. He must have been talking to me while I was thinking about Mamma.

"I want to go to Napoli," I said.

"Ah," said the translator, "another from Napoli. Where are your parents?"

"Everyone I know is in Napoli."

"No no, I'm talking about here. Where are your parents in this room?"

"I'm alone. I want to go to Napoli. I have no money."

The man lowered his head toward me. "What's your name?"

Should I tell the truth? Beniamino, the name I was born with, or Dom, the name the cargo crew had given me?

"You know your name, boy. What is it?"

I shook my head.

"A lost child," said the translator.

"There are lots of lost children," said another translator. He stood in front of the middle line, and the way he talked, I knew he'd grown up in Napoli. "Put him out on the front steps. His agent—some tricky *padrone*—will find him."

"I don't think he has one. He must have come on that big ship—the *Città di Napoli*. That ship's careful not to break the law; they don't let on children who belong to a *padrone*. He must have lost his family."

"Then his father's in this crowd," said the Napoletano translator. "Don't worry. The father will find him."

"He'll stay with you, then, Giosè."

"I'm as busy as you are. I can't worry about a little

scugnizzo." The Napoletano translator turned away and spoke to the people at the front of that line.

"My inspector says you have to keep him beside you till his father shows up," my translator said, then gestured to the man behind me to come forward.

"I'm not babysitting him," said Giosè.

"Look," said my translator. He pointed at my shoes. "This is no urchin. The father will be grateful. Maybe I should keep him myself to get the reward."

Giosè blinked at my shoes. I might not have had socks, but my shoes looked beautiful. "What am I supposed to do with you? All right, you've got shoes. You're somebody's little *signore*. Get over here and stand behind me."

I stood behind Giosè. My arms hung at my sides like dead fish. It was too hard to keep fighting. Soon enough they'd realize I had no father here and they'd have to send me home.

The lines went on forever. Giosè told me that more than five thousand people would pass through these lines that day. I knew that was huge.

The immigrants were almost all men, some in their teens. They talked about how wonderful they knew America was and how they would send for their wives and mothers and sisters soon, as though Giosè would be impressed and treat them better. But he didn't really look at them, and he did a lot of sighing. Many of the men held books and read to one another.

When Giosè went to the bathroom, I asked the man at the front of the line, "What are the stories about?"

He smiled proudly. "These are no stories. This book is

teaching me how to speak English. Listen." He spouted off gobbledy-gook. Then he waited.

It took a second before I knew what he wanted; I clapped.

He pressed his palm against his chest. "I'm a skilled artisan and now I speak English. I'm going to get a good job making beautiful furniture." His breath was foul, and I found myself staring at a tiny black bug jumping in his hair. I stepped away.

Giosè came back and the morning went by slowly. Every time I sank to a squat, he told me to stand again so my father could find me.

My father.

Mamma hadn't ever told anyone who my father was.

I imagined him now. He'd have black eyes. His nose would be straight—because mine was straight and Mamma's was crooked, so I must have gotten my nose from him. He'd be able to read. Mamma never would have chosen an uneducated man.

Maybe Giosè was right; maybe my father was here. I stared at each man. None of them looked at me.

After a while I switched to staring at the boys. They came in groups, ranging from six years old up, and most of them were with an uncle.

Giosè whispered, "Those men aren't really uncles. They're hired by the *padroni* to bring the boys over. A *padrone* pays a man's ticket. In return, the man watches over the boys until they get through immigration. Then the 'uncle' goes on his way." Giosè brushed off his hands. "And the boys begin work for the *padrone*. It's illegal, but that doesn't stop anyone."

The boys were barefoot, skinny, and dirty. Their "uncle" barked orders, and they obeyed immediately.

I stared at one boy. Mucus crusted his cheek and there was a colored chalk mark on his shirt. His "uncle" pointed at me. "That one, he's my nephew, too."

Giosè shook his head as though he'd been right all along about me. "Get over there behind your uncle."

"I don't know him," I yelped. "I've never seen him before."

The "uncle" grabbed me by the elbow and flung me behind him.

CHAPTER NINE

Trust

"No!" I screamed. "I don't know him!"

"Shut up," said the "uncle."

"Send me back to Napoli!" I screamed.

The "uncle" smacked me across the jaw with the back of his hand. I fell. He went on answering Giosè's questions.

The other boys turned their backs to us, but one of them hissed out of the side of his mouth. "Stupid. You'll have work in America. And food. Get up."

I wouldn't get up. I'd done what Mamma said. I'd watched and learned and fit in. And none of it mattered, because now this "uncle" had me and I'd be lost and alone for the rest of my life. I lay there and screamed.

The "uncle" kicked me. "Get up, or they'll throw

you in a home with sick boys and you'll die." He turned back to Giosè.

My side hurt. I drew my knees to my chest and hugged them.

"That's where I'm going," said the boy with the colored chalk mark on his shirt, "to the sick home. To die." His eyes were glassy with fever.

"I'm going to Napoli!" I forced out as loud as I could.

The "uncle" kicked me harder.

"What are you doing?" The translator from the first line stepped between us. "Don't kick him again." He pulled me up. I held my side where I'd been kicked and looked at him in surprise. I'd thought he'd forgotten about me. Now he pulled me over beside Giosè. "That isn't his uncle. He just says it because one of his boys is sick and he needs a substitute for the *padrone.*"

"The guy says he's the boy's uncle," said Giosè, "so he is."

"Listen to the way he talks. He's from somewhere in Basilicata, but the boy's from Napoli."

"What, do you think I'm deaf?" said Giosè. "You're German; I'm the Italian. This is my country they come from. I hear how they talk. That doesn't change a thing. The boy needs an uncle."

"He's got shoes. He's going to stand right here till his father comes. He's not going anywhere with some fake uncle."

Giosè looked at the "uncle" with both palms turned upward in apology. "Eh, beh, what can you do?" He pointed to the stairs behind him. "Those are the stairs of separation.

67

The sick boy goes in that hall to the left. If you ever want to see him again, you go with him. Everyone else goes down the stairs to fetch baggage and buy ferry tickets." He held his hand out low, at the side of the podium.

The "uncle" put money in Giosè's hand. Then he pushed the feverish boy toward the hall on the left and barked at the rest of the boys to go with him downstairs. The sick boy left without a word. I was sure he believed what he'd said—he was going to the sick home to die. I wanted to yell to him, "Fight!" Hadn't his mother told him to survive?

I didn't want to stand anywhere near Giosè anymore. But where else could I go? The endless lines kept moving.

After about an hour Giosè unwrapped a skinny loaf of bread stuffed with cheese and meats. Lettuce, tomato, onion, and pepper flopped out the sides. He said, "In America they call this an Italian sandwich." He laughed in a chummy way, as though he hadn't just tried to betray me. "These Americans," he said, "they give only an hour for lunch—not enough to get home and eat in pleasure." He shook his head.

His complaints went on and on. Did he think I cared one bit? Did he think he could win me back so easily? I listened because I had to. Otherwise, he might get mad and pawn me off on the next "uncle."

I was hungry for his food, but Jews don't eat cheese and meat together. Still, it looked good. The people in the line glanced at the sandwich, closed their mouths, and looked away.

Giosè stood chewing over me. "Stay here and stand tall while I go eat. Your father will find you soon."

The minute he was gone, I sat on the floor.

A man pushed a metal cart between the lines, selling boxed lunches of sandwiches, fruit, and pie for a half dollar. People paid in their different monies. A box lunch was big enough to feed five men. You could buy bread for four pennies, a sweet cake for six pennies, sausage for ten. I didn't know what the prices meant, and it didn't matter, because I didn't have pennies. But the smells . . .

Finally, Giosè came back. He didn't tell me to stand up. He got back to work.

The German translator said he was leaving for lunch now, and he handed me a piece of newspaper. I unwrapped it. A corner of a sandwich sat there. "Thank you," I said in amazement.

"Don't mention it," he said.

I took out the meat and ate the rest of the sandwich. The meat was pink; it could have been pig. I looked around for a place to stash it so the translator wouldn't find out that I hadn't eaten it. Mamma always said ingrates were the worst kind of people.

I worked the meat inside a pocket. Then I leaned my head against the inspector's podium and fell asleep.

Tap, tap. Someone was tapping on the top of my head.

I looked up into Giosè's face. "The lines are done," he said. "No one reported a lost son. You were a fool not to go with that 'uncle.' " He straightened his cap. "All right, it's time for us to deal with you. Did you come off that ship called *Città di Napoli?*"

I nodded.

The German translator asked, "You're really alone? Like you said?"

I nodded.

He picked up his pen. "What's your last name?"

Could my name get me in trouble? I shrugged.

"I've got to write something. You came over on *Città di Napoli* . . . so, okay, your last name is Napoli."

"Don't do that," said Giosè. "Call him di Napoli or de Napoli or da Napoli—not just Napoli. Only Jews take city names for their last name."

My breath caught. "Napoli is okay with me," I said.

"So you do want to talk," said the German translator. "Good. But Giosè has a point. You don't want to be taken for a Jew, trust me."

Adversity, that was what he was talking about. Like Uncle Aurelio said. I didn't care what adversity I'd face in America. I wasn't going to be here long anyway. And no matter what, I'd always be loyal to my family. "Put my last name as Napoli," I said firmly, feeling Nonna's approval.

He lifted an eyebrow. "All right, Signor Napoli, don't get upset. Anyway, you can use whatever name you want after you leave here. So, what first name do you want?"

I stood there.

"I have to put a first name, or I can't give you the document you need."

"Dom," I said.

"Domenico," he said, writing on a form.

"No, just Dom," I said.

He hesitated. Then he stuck out his bottom lip and nodded. "All right, Napoli, Dom. Birth date?"

"Twenty-fourth of December."

"A Christmas present, huh?" Both men laughed.

"What year?" When I shrugged, he asked, "How old are you?"

"Nine."

"That would make 1883—no, 1882, because you were born at the end of the year. So, who's waiting for you here in New York?"

I shrugged.

"No one? Oh, boy." He put down his pen. "Here's how it works, Dom. Beyond that door you get a physical inspection . . ."

Giosè cut in, "No one's going to let you onto the streets of New York alone. A boy your age needs a family or a *padrone*."

"*Padroni* are illegal," I said defiantly. I could find a policeman and tell him all about the money Giosè took from the "uncles." I could, if I knew where a policeman was. And if a policeman would listen to me. And if he spoke Napoletano. Suddenly it all felt so hard.

"Lots of things are illegal," said Giosè calmly. "The *padroni* have been running the show for years."

"I don't want a *padrone*."

"I don't blame you," said the German translator. "So that means you need a family."

"Change his name to di Napoli," said Giosè, "like I said. The translator in the third line, the one who knows almost no Italian, wrote in di Napoli for at least four men today whose last names he couldn't spell. The kid can try to find one of them and latch on."

The German translator picked up his pen.

"No," I said. "I'll stay Napoli. Napoli, Dom."

71

"All right, then, kid. It's your life. You'll go it alone. If you act smart, you've got a chance. Others your age have done it." He filled out my form.

"What are you doing?" I asked. "Why are you writing without asking me anything?"

"The whole thing's a lie anyway," said the German translator. "But it's the only way you'll get into Manhattan."

"What's Manhattan?"

"The main part of New York City. Where the big buildings are."

"I don't want to go to New York City," I said. "I want to go to Napoli."

"No one's going to pay your fare back, boy," Giosè said. "It's New York City or an orphanage—your choice."

Orphanages. We had them in Napoli; the nuns ran them. Children who had no one in the world lived there in misery. I saw myself in ragged clothing, covering my ears against Catholic preaching, alone forever. "No."

One of the nurses who had tested me earlier appeared, shaking her head and scolding the men. She grabbed my hand and pulled me away.

Something tugged at the back of my waistband. I felt behind with my hand. Someone had tucked folded sheets of paper into my pants. I quickly jammed them in my pocket.

CHAPTER TEN

Needs

The nurse took me to benches at long tables, where tired people sat. Many had chalk marks on their jackets. She tapped on shoulders, getting everyone to look at me. When no one claimed me, she gestured for me to sit and she marked with chalk on the back of my shirt. I could feel her write a giant O.

Every so often, a nurse came up and led someone down the hall to the left. But mostly, we waited. A man pushed a metal cart between the tables and gave crackers to everyone and warm milk to the children. It tasted funny, but I drank it.

Some of us were herded upstairs to dormitory rooms. Triple-decker beds pushed against each other in pairs. I was put in the room with the women and children. We were told to leave our things and come down in two hours to eat. In the meantime

73

we should line up for washing. Mothers stripped their children.

I wasn't about to undress, so I had to find a way to avoid the washing. And I wanted to look at that paper in my pocket.

I went to the bathroom, but women crowded around it. I headed for the stairs down to the bathroom I'd used during the day.

An Italian woman stood in my path arguing with a woman in uniform. "I paid my passage."

"But you came alone," said the official. "And no man is waiting for you."

"See these hands?" The Italian woman held up red hands. "I did laundry night and day to get here."

"Unescorted women are not allowed off Ellis Island. It doesn't matter how many people you argue with, that's the rule. We'll have to contact an immigrant aid society to come get you."

"No charity home. I take care of myself. I have money."

"Don't say it too loud," said the official, "or you soon won't." She fingered the keys that hung from her waist.

"I paid my passage."

"The women's home is nice, I hear." She jiggled her keys.

"I hear it's a hellhole. I paid my passage."

I sidled past them and went downstairs. The bathroom was locked from the inside. I waited.

An official appeared from around the corner. I looked at my feet and hardly breathed. He walked by.

And still no one came out of the bathroom.

Finally I knocked. "Excuse me?"

The door opened a crack. An eye peeked at me. Then a hand grabbed my shirt and pulled me in, locking the door behind me.

We were pressed against each other in the tiny stall. I looked up into a boy's face.

"What are you doing making noise like that, trying to get me in trouble?" He was clearly from Napoli.

"I just want to use the toilet," I said.

"No one's supposed to use this one after hours." He frowned. "Go on."

I hunched over and did my business.

"Hurry up," he said. "And make sure no one sees you leave."

I reached for the doorknob.

"Hold on." He put his hand on my shoulder. "Did you see if the stairs of separation were empty?"

"Are you trying to sneak out?"

His cheek twitched.

"I want to sneak out, too," I said.

"You? What are you, nine? Ten? I'm fourteen. I can do a man's work. I can earn five dollars a week in a textile mill. Or even more. They won't let me work officially till I'm sixteen, but underage workers make it through all the time. I'm going to make it through."

"You'll look older with a little brother tagging along."

He pressed his lips together. "Get out of here."

I opened the door and peeked out.

The boy shut the door, pulling me inside again. "You should have told me you're an orphan."

"Who says I'm an orphan?"

"The *O* on the back of your shirt. Even if you do sneak

75

through, whoever sees that *O* will turn you in and you'll be thrown into an orphanage. You won't get out till you're sixteen."

I took off my shirt, turned it inside out, and put it on.

"That's too obvious. You need a new shirt. And pants, too. Yours are ripped. Tell you what. I know where you can get other clothes. But you have to promise to bring me back some, too."

"Okay."

"Why should I trust you?"

"Why shouldn't you?"

His forehead furrowed.

"Look," I said. "If I bring back clothes, you're better off. And if I don't, you're no worse off."

He swallowed. "You're too smart for your age."

"I'll bring back clothes," I said. "I owe you for telling me what the *O* meant." And then maybe you'll let me come with you, I thought. But I said, "That way we're even."

"Upstairs there's a room full of used clothes. Get me a coat. And pants and a shirt."

"I can't carry all that. Besides, it's hot out."

"Summer doesn't last forever, kid. It's not like Napoli. It snows here."

Snow? But what did it matter? I'd be home soon. "Where's the room?"

"Somewhere upstairs. Search." He opened the door a crack.

I peeked, then raced up the stairs. I walked near the wall and glanced into open doors.

I came to a closed door. Locked. But the next door opened to reveal piles of clothes. I shut the door behind me. From the window I saw people scurrying about. It would be easy to get lost in that crowd—and then I could figure out what to do next.

Across the water tall buildings rose. A ship docked in the narrows. It looked small from here, a wolf in a canyon. Would I ever see the canyons near Napoli again? Would I ever see Mamma?

Not if they threw me in an orphanage.

I took the papers out of my pocket, finally. They were the documents the German translator had filled out. Somehow they would help me. I changed into a clean short-sleeved shirt and lightweight pants and tucked the papers in my new pocket. Then I grabbed a coat for the boy in the bathroom. I stuffed a shirt for him down one of the coat sleeves and a pair of pants down the other. I took the meat from my old shirt pocket and put it in the coat pocket. The boy could eat it later.

I walked back along the balcony. A hand caught my shoulder, and a woman yanked on the coat. I pulled away and ran. When I snuck a glance back at her, she was watching me.

The boy in the bathroom was waiting. He'd make a dash for it soon. Then I'd be alone again. And someone would write another O on my back. And I'd never make it onto a boat. Never get home to Mamma.

I needed something to catch that woman's attention so I could get to the bathroom. Anything.

I took the meat out of the coat pocket and tapped on the shoulder of a man. He looked at me. I pointed at the woman and handed him the meat. The man frowned. He stood up and walked toward her. I forced my way past the rest of the men and ran down the stairs. I tapped on the bathroom door.

The door opened. The boy snatched the coat and shut the door in my face.

Panicked, I dashed down a hall and opened a door.

Men stood with their shirts in their hands, waiting to be inspected. A young girl carried a coffee cup to a doctor. She left through a side door.

A few of the other doctors had cups on the tables near them.

I picked up two empty cups. One in each hand, I walked out the door the girl had used.

I was in a kitchen.

A woman tilted her head at me and said something.

I forced a smile and put the cups on the counter. Then I walked through the kitchen and out another door and, sure enough, there were stairs. I went down and out onto the street.

CHAPTER ELEVEN

Manhattan

I broke out running. I wove in and out of the people, checking over my shoulder. No one had followed me.

Ellis Island was easy to figure out. Ships docked on one side to drop off people. Smaller boats docked on the other to take them away. Immigrants stood in little groups and wrinkled their brows, carefully counting American money. Some were met by the joyous shouts of relatives. Others milled around in the early evening heat with paper pinned to their shirts. They looked hopefully at everyone who passed. A tall man went from person to person, reading their names off those papers. He gathered some together. One man said, "Ah, so you're my *padrone.*" After that, anytime I saw someone reading name tags, I hurried the other way.

Women in white uniforms with red crosses on the sleeve gave out doughnuts and apples. They didn't offer me any, so I took two doughnuts off a pile. They weren't nearly so good as *zeppole* back home, but okay. People ate sandwiches the women had given them, but there weren't any left. When I finished the doughnuts, I took an apple. Other women not in uniform but all wearing the same little hats helped people find lost baggage or relatives. America was full of women who wanted to help strangers.

Many spoke languages I understood more or less—Italian dialects, I heard a woman call them. I followed her around for a while, until I heard her explain she was sent by a society to help protect Italian immigrants. I would have asked her what we needed protection against, but I didn't want her to notice me.

A man clutched a scrap of paper and showed it to another man in uniform, who pointed. "That's the boat to Mulberry Street."

Mulberry Street. Napoletani. Maybe Tonino, Mamma's friend. I'd try to get on a ship back to Napoli first, but if I needed help, I'd look for Tonino.

At the boat I walked past the ticket-taker, ready to show the documents in my waistband. But he didn't ask for anything. In Italy, I'd have gotten nabbed by the collar. Here, I was almost invisible. Good. That would make it easy to stow away on a ship back to Napoli when I reached the Manhattan docks.

The ferry left Ellis Island. Seagulls flew alongside. The evening sun seemed to sink into their white feathers and get lost entirely, turning them into flying balls of light. It was the strangest thing, but those seagulls made me happy.

I remembered my last full day in Napoli—how a seagull had watched what the *scugnizzi* were doing, how it had probably been waiting for its chance to steal. It felt like years ago.

We docked at a pier and got off. The press of people during the ferry ride gave way to nothing but a sea breeze at my back. Night was coming, and how I wished I could wrap up in Mamma's shawl. But I'd find a ship to hide on; everything would be okay.

Horses pulled wagons and people pushed carts of all kinds. A fish market was closing, and a man threw buckets of seawater over the wooden planks outside the shop. He scooped a few fish out of a tub of melting ice, the remains of the day, and laid them in a row on the pier. Then he dumped the icy water into the harbor. He went back inside the shop as boys ran up, grabbed the fish, and disappeared down a street. They were naked, but for two in short pants. They'd been swimming. The fishmonger came out, locked his shop, and walked away. He didn't even glance at the pier.

Laying the fish side by side like that, so neat and clean, had been a gift to the poor. And women gave out apples and doughnuts on Ellis Island, even if the doughnuts tasted pretty bad. Maybe everyone in America took care of the poor.

A lamplighter worked his way along the road. People left the wharf area and seeped back into the innards of the city. I ducked into a side street. A man turned the corner up ahead and walked toward me with a dog. I darted down an alley.

There was excrement everywhere, from dogs and cats

81

and horses. And from people. The walls stank of urine. A rat shrieked and ran by with another one chasing it.

I ran out onto the next street. Stay out of alleys! And there was the man from the ferry, the one who wanted Mulberry Street. I followed him. I could wait till morning to find a ship. For now I needed a place to sleep.

A coach rolled past, pulled by two horses. Men with an air of importance sat tall on its benches, wearing black hats. They knew exactly where they were going, where they belonged.

I held the hem of my shirt in my fists and squeezed tight. I wanted to stop and lie down. Exhaustion washed over me.

The man I was following stopped, asked directions, and got pointed along. Cafe tables and chairs cluttered the sidewalks, where people ate and talked under round lanterns. Spicy aromas circled them.

A woman passed with a cloth sack over her shoulder and a pig at her heels. She stooped to pick up a bottle and slide it into the sack as the pig trotted to a garbage can. Together they sorted through the stinking waste.

I hurried to keep within sight of the man. He turned right, went a few blocks, then turned left. He knocked on a door and people rushed out to surround him. A smell came with them—porcini mushrooms and garlic and rosemary and tomatoes. They all talked at once: "Giorgio was supposed to go meet you, but he got the day wrong." "Sorry, sorry." "Now you're here and everything will be good." They rushed him inside.

The door closed. The dinner smell faded.

I stood there. On Mulberry Street. My bottom lip trembled.

A rock hit me on the shoulder. I went to grab it and throw it back, but it was a rock-hard dog turd. I almost fell on it, I was so surprised.

A boy a few years older than me stood at the opening of an alley. "Get out of here."

I walked up the sidewalk fast, checking over my shoulder for him. I crossed a street and a man pushing a cart had to swerve around me, cursing. Things fell off his cart. I stooped to help pick them up, but he shouted at me, "Thief!"

A woman yelled, "For shame! Think of your mother. Think how humiliated she'd be."

I ran to her. "Do you know Tonino?"

"Which Tonino?"

"The widower. He left his children in Napoli."

"Go home," she said over her shoulder as she walked off.

It was dark by then and I wanted to run away. I turned around and went back to the alley where the boy had stood. After all, that boy looked just as alone as me.

He was gone.

"Where are you?" I tried not to step in anything putrid, calling, calling. I crossed a street and went up the next alley. It was slow going because of all the garbage. And it wasn't just garbage. The carcass of a big dog lay to one side. The smell was awful. I remembered the body in the grotto back home and cleansing myself of that stench in the lake on Vesuvio. Nowhere to wash here.

Then I saw the boy up ahead. I walked more quickly. So did a man in uniform. He blew a whistle. The boy ran and the policeman ran after him.

Nothing was going right. I had no new plans—me, the boy full of plans. I went back to the alley with the dead dog. I threw pieces of a crushed wooden box into a half-empty barrel to make a clean layer on top of whatever was inside. Then I climbed in. I looked up to say good night to the stars, but I couldn't see any. At home, no stars meant rain was on the way.

I checked to make sure the documents were safe in my pocket. Then I recited every one of Nonna's charms I could remember—charms to keep evil at bay.

That was where I spent my first night in America, grateful for the exhaustion that let me sleep. If there was one lesson I'd learned since I left Mamma, it was to sleep: sleep puts aside cares.

CHAPTER TWELVE

Sharks and Mooks

I woke to the noise of horses on cobblestone streets.

My neck hurt from being bent over my knees for hours. I stood and picked a chicken bone off my pants. It had jabbed my thigh all night, but I'd been too afraid of what it might be to touch it.

Rain started, turning the gray alley stones to black. It was just a drizzle and it felt good. I climbed out onto a log that rolled out from under me. I fell onto my bottom with a smack.

I brushed off everywhere and rubbed my shoes with the underside of the front of my shirt. Then I raised my face to the rain, mouth open. The fat, slow drops soothed my cheeks and throat. A high-pitched tinkling came, so delicate I thought I was still dreaming. I followed it.

A bony boy walked down the sidewalk beating a

metal triangle with a rod. Other people were out on the sidewalk already, too, heads bowed under kerchiefs and hats. Some carried umbrellas. Whenever the boy passed someone, he beat the triangle louder, then put out his hand. A man gave him a coin.

He was nothing but a beggar.

The beggar boy went slowly, so I had a chance to look around. Windows were open everywhere. People lived crowded together as in Napoli—filling basements and garrets, as well as all the floors between. A man came out of an outhouse, and the way he stretched, I knew he'd spent the night there.

I gritted my teeth. I wouldn't sleep in a barrel again. I wasn't a *scugnizzo*.

By the time the beggar boy finally stopped on a corner, the rain had let up. Early sun glinted off the wet stones. Too bad I hadn't stood in one spot and drunk the rain while it was still coming down. My throat was dry.

The beggar boy took a tin cup out of his pocket, put it on the ground, and played his triangle. Then he whistled a tune. Men dressed in fancy suits dropped in coins.

"Hey," I said to him.

He turned his back to me. He was pretty tall, but I bet he was only a year older than me.

"Hey, can you tell me which way to the boats to Napoli?"

"Bolivia," said the beggar boy. He pointed.

Soon I was out on the wharves again, where a huge passenger ship was docked. Officials on the steerage deck processed the first- and second-class passengers.

I walked around until I found two men talking Napoletano while they laid bricks in a sidewalk.

"Excuse me. Do you know about the *Bolivia*?"

The younger man jerked his chin toward the dock. "That ship?"

"Is it going to Napoli?"

"It just came from there," said the other man. "No one cares where it's going next."

"I do," the younger man said. "In Italy the air is *bell' e fresca*—clear and cool. I'm going back as soon as I make enough money."

"Yeah?" said the other man. "You'll take one whiff and you'll be on the next boat back to America, like every other fool who forgot what Italy's really like."

"I'm going back to Italy," I said.

The man wiped his mustache. "Get a load of this kid," he said to the younger man. "Talks like a big shot."

"It's true," I said.

"Don't let your mother hear you say that," said the younger man. "You'll break her heart."

"My mother's in Italy."

"Where's your father?" said the other man.

I didn't answer.

"You alone?"

"Not for long," I said. "I'm going to sneak onto that ship."

"You'll never make it," said the man. "See the guards?"

"And if you get caught trying," said the younger man, "you'll wind up in an orphanage."

"Orphanages aren't as bad as the streets," said the other man.

"Remember that one that burned down? Half a dozen kids died."

A shopkeeper came outside and said something to the men in English. They got back to work.

If my experience on the last passenger ship was typical, it would be a long time before the *Bolivia* was empty and I could sneak on. Days, probably. So I walked along the wharf toward the Statue of Liberty.

A ferry crossed from Ellis Island. My eyes fixed on it. There was no one aboard I could know, no long-lost cousin. But I stood watching anyway.

A man got off and went up to a policeman and asked him something. The policeman answered in English. The man got so flustered, he pulled a piece of cigar from his pocket and fiddled with it. The policeman took out a match and lit the man's cigar. The man's face widened in a huge smile of surprise. I was smiling, too. For this moment it didn't matter that no one understood anyone else.

A group of men came up to the policeman now. They said the same words over and over, till I found myself whispering them, too—the English words: "Which way Lester Brothers?" The policeman turned to other passing men, and more people got consulted, and soon there was a crowd.

An Italian said to another man, "Ignorant Irish. They want to make shoes at the Lester Brothers factory, and they don't even know it's way out in Binghamton. Days away."

"Someone ought to tell them to go over to Chatham Square to earn the travel money to get to Binghamton," said the other man.

"You going to tell them? You going to help the Irish?"

They laughed and went on.

And just like that I had my next plan. I'd work in

Chatham Square till the *Bolivia* was empty and I could sneak on. But first I had to get breakfast. Where were the American ladies who liked to help strangers? No one handed out food on this wharf.

I went back up the street. It was busier now; skinny children in rags hawked their wares. Their dirty hair was blond or light brown, their faces red and snot-streaked. They had scabs and open sores on their elbows and knees.

The beggar boy with the triangle stood on the same corner. "Have you got anything to eat?" I asked him.

He turned away and whistled again, the same tune as before. Someone dropped a coin into his tin cup.

What a stupid question. Maybe a night in a barrel had softened my brains.

Okay, so there was no food sitting around for the taking. That meant a job came first, then breakfast. "Which way Chatham Square?" I asked him, using the English I'd heard from the men who came off the ferry—my very first attempt.

He spat on the ground in front of me.

"Come on," I pleaded in Napoletano. "I need to get to Chatham Square."

"So what," he said in English. I didn't understand, of course, and he knew that. After a bit, he said in Napoletano, "Why?"

"I need money."

"You, begging? With those fancy shoes?" He spat again. "Forget it. That area's taken. And the *padrone* in charge of those boys will whip you bloody if you move in."

"I'm going to work, not beg," I said.

"So what," he said again in English. Then he shook his

head. "You think I don't work? I stand here all day long. I have to bring in eighty cents or my *padrone* will beat me."

"Why don't you run away?"

"He binds our wrists to the bedpost at night."

I looked around. No one was watching this boy, so far as I could see. "Why don't you run away right now?"

"Think you're so smart, do you? Where would I go? Anyway, I owe him money. And this is work. Decent work. There's no crime in being poor."

"That's the truth." Everyone I'd ever known was poor. "But begging . . ." I didn't finish.

"I make music. It's not the same as begging. I give people what they want to hear. What's the matter with you? You don't recognize 'Daisy Bell'? The new song about the bicycle built for two?" He whistled the tune again. Someone dropped a coin in his cup. He whistled another tune. Another person dropped in a coin. He gave me a self-satisfied look. "That was 'After the Ball Is Over.' You don't know that one, either, do you? It's the most popular song from Tin Pan Alley." His last three words were in English.

"What's Tin Pan Alley?"

"Twenty-eighth Street. Where they write the songs."

I shrugged. "I've never been there."

"So what," he said in English. His mouth twitched. "I've never been there, either. But everyone knows the songs."

I shrugged again.

He pressed his lips together. "It's okay. I wouldn't actually know about them myself if the woman downstairs didn't sing them half the night. You need money, huh? Tell you what. Give me those shoes to hold for you, and you can take my corner and play this triangle. As soon as you've got a dollar, I'll split the extra twenty cents with you, half and half."

That was how I learned that a dollar was one hundred cents. "No," I said.

"That's ten cents each."

"I can count."

"You'd get the money fast. They always give more to smaller boys. And you're clean. You'd be done by afternoon."

Me, clean? Nonna would be appalled at how filthy I'd gotten. "I won't take off my shoes."

"Then they won't give you nothing. You got to look poor."

"There's no way I'll beg."

His cheeks flushed. "You don't listen good." He spat. "So what," he said in English. "No one cares what you think."

"Which way Chatham Square?" I said jokingly, trying to make up.

"Get out of here. You'd only get me in trouble with my *padrone* anyway." He pointed. "Turn right at Park." And he went back to playing his triangle.

"Thanks," I said.

He turned his back on me and whistled that second tune.

I walked the way he'd pointed. At every corner I asked, "Park?" After several blocks someone finally nodded yes. I looked at the street sign. *P-A-R-K.* That was how you spelled *park.* It was almost the same as how I'd have spelled those sounds in Italian. In the top right corner of the sign were the letters *S-T.* Could that be a word?

91

I turned right. It wasn't long before I was passing all kinds of factories. They made silverware, jewelry, billiard tables. They made umbrellas, lightning rods, false teeth, paper, medicines, guns. I passed a piano factory and a carriage factory and one for ship propellers. I stood outside the windows and watched and listened. I heard so many languages, even one that sounded sort of like singing, out of the mouths of gaunt men wearing funny quilted jackets in a cigar factory. But no one spoke Italian.

It didn't seem possible. I knew where Chatham Square was—I'd passed Mulberry Street to get here, so it was right at the bottom of the street where all the Italians lived. Where were the Italian workers?

A boy stood on a corner with a tin cup on the ground. He played a small harp. I went up to him. "Where are the factories that Italians work in?"

He turned his back to me. Red welts showed under the collar of his shirt. I stepped away in a hurry, praying his *padrone* hadn't seen me, that I hadn't gotten him in trouble.

I hurried to Mulberry Street and went up the block, past the hanging sides of beef and pork in front of the butcher's, past the pharmacy, past the ratcatcher who stood by a wall, holding out a string with dead rats attached by the tail. He was good! I hurried along listening for someone I could talk to, anyone who could explain how I could earn money.

And he appeared, the boy who had thrown the dog turd at me the night before. He stepped out of an alley into my path, legs planted. "I told you to get out of here."

"I'm glad the policeman didn't catch you," I said.

"How'd you know about the policeman?"

I shrugged. "I need to find a factory with Italian workers so I can earn money."

"That why you were in Chatham Square?"

"How'd you know I was there?"

He crossed his arms on his chest. "Even if you weren't a little squirt, you couldn't get a job there. Chatham Square factory managers don't hire from this neighborhood. They think they're too good for Five Points people. Italians can only work laying bricks or breaking stones or digging ditches."

"What are you talking about?"

"You don't know anything, do you?" The tough guy walked around me. "Where'd you get those shoes?"

"My mother bought them for me."

"Where's your mother?"

"At home."

"Where's home?"

I shrugged.

"I bet you live in Brooklyn, and you got lost in the city, right? So now you want to do some piddling errand so you can make enough money to take the streetcar home. Or, no, you live in the Bronx, that's it, right? The Italians in the Bronx make good. That's how your mamma got money for those shoes." He smirked. "That, or she works at home."

"Of course she works at home," I said. "She helps Aunt Sara with laundry and mending."

He laughed. "You really know nothing. That's not what 'working at home' means. You want to know how to get a job?" He leaned toward me and beckoned with a curled finger.

93

I stepped forward.

"Turn Irish," he whispered.

"Irish? How?"

He laughed again. "You don't. You can't turn white just by wishing. Irish boys get all the bootblack jobs. They deliver all the newspapers. There's no way an Italian boy like you can get a penny without begging or stealing. And if you beg around here, the *padroni* will beat you to a pulp. They own every street corner worth begging on. And if you steal, you have to give half of everything to me."

"I don't steal. And I'd never beg. And why would I have to give you half, anyway?"

"So I wouldn't turn you in. That's how it works."

My stomach hurt. "I'm hungry."

"Who isn't? Give me your shoes and I'll give you fare for the streetcar."

I knew what a streetcar was. They were building one in Milano, up in the north of Italy. Uncle Aurelio had talked about it.

"My shoes wouldn't fit you," I said.

"You think I'd want to wear them? I'd sell them in a second."

"If I wanted to ride a streetcar, I'd sell them myself," I said.

"You don't know who to sell them to," said the boy.

"I do."

I walked around him. I passed a shoemaker and a barbershop and a candy maker, and from each of their doorways I heard Italian. So that boy was wrong. Italians could get jobs—at least on Mulberry Street.

A produce vendor was taking oranges from a bushel

basket and arranging them in piles on a low table outside his shop. "Want me to do that for you?" I asked.

He glanced at me. "Go home."

I stepped closer. "It'll only cost you an orange."

"Didn't you hear me? Don't bother me. Don't bother my customers." He didn't speak Napoletano, but I could understand him pretty well. And his tone wasn't mean, just wary.

"You've got better things to do," I said. "And I can do it perfect."

"Perfect?" He looked at me again, amused.

I made a circle of my thumb and index finger and drew my hand across the air in front of my chest in the gesture that meant *perfect.*

Was he almost smiling?

I lifted my chin and looked straight into his eyes, hopeful.

"What do you know about stacking fruit, a little kid like you?"

"If you don't like the job I do, you don't pay me."

"If I turn around and you run off with an orange in each hand, I'll come after you and make you sorry you were ever born."

"I don't steal."

He pushed the bushel of oranges toward me. "You get a tomato, not an orange," he said.

So I stacked the oranges, the way I stacked Nonna's yarn balls at home. I was careful; not a single orange rolled away. I imagined Nonna watching me, saying some proverb—maybe the one about how the eye had to have its part in everything. That was why it was worth it to make even the smallest thing beautiful, even a plate of food that would be eaten in an instant. I stacked the oranges for Nonna's sake.

The man was standing behind me when I finished. "Do these tomatoes and the zucchini and the onions, and I'll give you two tomatoes."

Amazed, I stacked them just right. "Can I come back tomorrow?"

"Sure, but it's Sunday. I'll be closed. Here." He handed me a bruised orange, as well as two tomatoes.

"I wonder, do you know a widower named Tonino?"

The man shook his head.

I put the food in my pocket and walked back to the mouth of the alley. I knew the tough guy would show up sooner or later.

It was sooner.

Before he could speak, I handed him a tomato—a tomato my own mouth was watering to eat.

"That's right," he said. "Half of everything."

"I didn't steal them," I said. "And I didn't give you one because you said I should. I gave you one 'cause I wanted to."

He looked me up and down. Then he leaned over and bit his tomato. Juice squirted out and landed on my shoe.

"Watch it!" I pushed him away, squatted, and wiped off the mess with the hem of my shirt.

When I stood again, he stuffed the rest of the tomato in his mouth and grinned as he chewed. "I knew it. You wouldn't sell those shoes no matter what. What were they, a birthday present?"

I ate my tomato.

"So why'd you want to give me a tomato, then?"

I thought of how Nonna had made me bring the bowl of meatballs to the Rossi family next door the night before I left home. "You get, you give."

"*Magari*. What gave you such an idea? Look at you: the king of Mulberry Street, just giving things out right and left. Well, listen good. In this neighborhood it's everybody for himself."

Magari. I had to shut my eyes hard against the surge of longing; I could see Nonna sitting at the kitchen table sighing, "*Magari*." I could smell her garlic hands, see the thick knobs of her knuckles. And now I realized I'd given this guy the tomato for another reason, too. Mamma said survive. This guy could be an ally. As Nonna's proverb went: *"A chi me dà pane io 'o chiamme pate"*—Anyone who feeds me is like a father to me.

I took out the orange and peeled it. It smelled like flowers. The boy watched me closely. Before I had a chance to think, I gave him half and ate a section of my half. It tasted wonderful. Juicy.

He ate his orange fast. "So you think you're a big guy 'cause some jerk from Calabria paid you, huh? Big deal, tomatoes cost next to nothing. And that orange was too bruised to sell. You still don't have your streetcar fare."

I finished my part of the orange and licked my fingers. This guy was older than me, but he wasn't that tough. The way he devoured the food told me that. Really tough guys were never that hungry—not in Napoli. A bad guy would have simply knocked me down and stolen my shoes. "I don't want money. I just want enough food to last me two days."

"Two days. I'm supposed to put up with you for two days?"

My heart banged; I could stay with him. "Yeah. Where do you sleep?"

"Whoa. You're not sleeping anywhere near me. And don't ask where I sleep. Look. I like being alone. There are gangs of boys around here—but they're always noticed, so they're always getting in trouble. I stay alone, and I don't stay in one place too long, so no one hassles me. The most I'll do is look out for you. But if you want my protection, you're going to have to show you're worth it."

"How?" I said.

"In the next block Pasquale Cuneo runs a salami shop. Go do a chore for him, and bring me back prosciutto—the raw kind."

Prosciutto was pig meat. "No."

"Don't make me mad, kid."

That was the last thing I wanted to do. "What's your name?" I asked.

"What's yours?"

"Dom."

"Mine's Gaetano."

"I can do lots of work, Gaetano. But not in a shop that sells pig meat."

"Why not?"

I shrugged.

"If you don't do what I say, you'll be alone. You can't make it alone. Not in Five Points."

I was sick of being alone. It couldn't be that bad to be around pig meat, so long as I didn't eat it. "I'll do it."

"You bet you will. You're lucky it's a slow day, or I wouldn't pay any attention to you at all. Understand?"

"Yeah."

Gaetano rubbed his mouth in thought. "Okay. I got a better idea. On Park Street there's a big store run by Luigi Pierano. He's got every kind of Italian food." He slapped me on the back. "Go work for him and bring me four pennies."

I wanted to ask him to show me a penny, so I'd be sure to bring him what he wanted. But then he'd know I wasn't from that place he said—the Bronx. I felt safer having him think I had a mother close by who might show up on a streetcar at any minute.

I turned around and went back to Park Street. There were lots of stores with writing on the windows. None of them had the name Luigi Pierano. But one was bigger than most. I went in.

Rows of shelves from floor to ceiling brimmed over with food. A line of bins held spices. I stood over the one with the seeds I knew so well—anise—and breathed deeply. Mamma's scent. For an instant the room swirled and my head went light.

A woman clamped a hand around my upper arm and steadied me. She said something in English, then in some Italian dialect, "Are you ill?" I smiled to reassure her. She walked on.

A man behind the counter was making gigantic sandwiches. A card taped to the front of the counter read *25¢*. Twenty-five cents? Was it a lot?

"Can I do a chore for you?" I asked the sandwich maker.

99

"Get out of here." He didn't even look at me. His tone was final.

I went outside. A crowd had gathered at the foot of the next street. I crossed Park and worked my way between the adults to the inside of the circle. An organ grinder played music and a monkey on a chain took off his cap to people in the crowds.

The woman beside me put a coin in the monkey's cap. The monkey's tiny, long fingers clasped around her thumb for a shake. She gasped. The monkey chattered, showing sharp teeth. His eyes darted around with a quick intelligence that made my stomach sick. He knew he was a prisoner and he hated all these people; I could have sworn it.

Everyone took out coins; they all wanted to shake the monkey's hand.

I pushed my way back through the people, bursting free onto the street, and ran the path I'd already traveled twice that day, back toward the boy with the triangle. He was still on the corner. "How much have you gotten?" I asked.

He turned his back to me.

I moved around in front of him. "I asked how much you've gotten."

"So what."

"Listen, Tin Pan Alley, I'll do it. I'll play the triangle."

Tin Pan Alley put his hand in his pocket and counted the coins. "Thirty-two cents," he said. "You have to make sixty-eight more. Then we split the last twenty. Promise?"

"I promise." I took off my shoes; then I suddenly clutched them to my chest. "If you run off with my shoes, I'll catch you," I said. "I'm fast."

"If you run off with my triangle," he said, "my *padrone* will catch you. You can't hide from him."

"I don't steal," I said for the third time that morning.

"You think I do?" Tin Pan Alley stiffened.

I shook my head. He was too proud to steal. I handed him my shoes.

He handed me the triangle. "You smell like oranges." His face looked wistful for a moment. "Play."

I tapped the little metal rod against the triangle. Most people walked by quickly, not looking at me. But whenever someone looked, I smiled big, and, more often than not, they dropped a coin in the tin cup.

Tin Pan Alley sat with his back against the nearest lamppost and kept an eye out. If he saw his *padrone* coming, he was going to jump up, throw me my shoes, and grab the triangle. I was supposed to run as fast as I could. And if the *padrone* caught me, I was supposed to tell him I worked for someone else; no *padrone* would beat a boy who belonged to another. Instead, he'd take whatever I had and send me on my way with a warning.

The very idea of his *padrone* made me queasy. But I didn't want to be alone again that night, and I didn't see any other way of getting four pennies for Gaetano.

Every so often Tin Pan Alley came over and emptied the tin cup. It had to stay close to empty or no one would give.

People ate as they walked along—ugly meat sticks that Tin Pan Alley called wienerwursts—German food. Sometimes the meat was covered in a stinking rotten cabbage. And they ate sandwiches, much smaller than the ones back in the store on Park Street.

The tomato and the orange half had made me hungrier. The sun was hot. The rumble of horses and carts hammered in my head. I felt woozy and smiled weakly at everyone, whether they looked at me or not.

Tin Pan Alley jiggled his cup in my face. "Ninety-eight cents already. You're good at this, and you don't even whistle. Usually it's slow on Saturdays."

Saturday. It was Saturday. The Sabbath. Jews didn't work on the Sabbath.

But I'd already arranged the fruit. That was work, because the man had paid me.

In fruit, not money. That's not really pay—that's not really work.

And playing music, that wasn't really work, either. It was entertainment. So long as I didn't pocket any of the money. "I'm stopping," I said.

"You look sick." Tin Pan Alley counted out nine coins. "Here's your nine cents."

I shook my head.

"That's half of eighteen," said Tin Pan Alley, "which is what's left over after I pay my *padrone*. I'm not cheating you. You'd have had to get a whole dollar to earn ten cents."

"I told you, I can count," I said.

"So you're trying to cheat me now, is that it? And I thought you were okay. Well, you can't have ten cents. You can't cheat me."

"I'd never cheat you," I said. "I keep a promise. Look, how about you do me a four-cent favor."

"What's that mean?" asked Tin Pan Alley.

"Come with me to Mulberry Street to give a boy four cents."

"Why don't you give him four cents yourself?"

"I can't."

"Why not?"

"I don't want to tell you."

Tin Pan Alley looked at me with troubled eyes.

"Come on, Tin Pan Alley. If you do this, you get to keep my other five cents."

Tin Pan Alley put the coins back in his pocket. "Let's hurry. If my *padrone* passes and finds I'm missing, he'll be mad."

I thought of the welts on the neck of the boy who played the harp in Chatham Square. "How often does he come by?"

"Most days not at all. Other days he'll come a few times. But never early in the morning. Besides that, you can't predict. That way he keeps us honest."

"Mulberry isn't that close," I said. "It'll take time."

"I know where Mulberry is."

"Look, let's not risk trouble with your *padrone*. Just keep the money."

"What, are you feeling sorry for me? Don't waste your time. I'm going to earn back what my *padrone* paid for my passage over and then I'll find a regular job and I'll send to Italy for my aunt and my cousins on Vico Sedil Capuano. We'll all have the good life." He started up the road.

Vico Sedil Capuano. I knew that street. Tin Pan Alley's family was practically my neighbor. What had happened to his parents?

"Come on," he called to me. "A deal's a deal. You think you're the only person in the world who can keep a promise?"

We went to Mulberry Street, to the alley where Gaetano had shown up before, and waited.

"You got the four cents?"

I turned around. Gaetano stood there. Tin Pan Alley put four cents in Gaetano's hand.

"Wait a minute," said Gaetano. "I've got a treat in mind, and it's four cents just for the two of us. I'm not paying for this mook."

"I don't take nothing from no shark," said Tin Pan Alley.

I didn't know what a mook or a shark was, but I could tell they were insults. "Tin Pan Alley," I said quickly, "meet Gaetano. He's my friend. Gaetano, meet Tin Pan Alley. He keeps his promise."

"Oh, another good boy, like you," said Gaetano. "A beggar, huh?"

Tin Pan Alley spat on the ground.

I moved between them. "He's a musician."

"A musician? Not a beggar, just a really skinny musician." Gaetano blew through his lips, making a horse noise. "Well, come on, then." He walked and talked, pointing as we went. "This is Baxter Street. Lots of people from Napoli live here. Like on Mulberry and Mott Streets. But the people from Genova live here, too. And the best ice cream vendor in all of Five Points is here." He led us past grocery stores with wooden barrels of dried fish—delicious *baccalà*—and up to the ice cream vendor. He put the four pennies in the man's hand.

"It's a penny a serving," the man said in his dialect. "You want three extra-large servings for four cents?"

"No. Two doubles," said Gaetano, talking in the same

dialect the ice cream vendor used, "for me and the little squirt." He jerked his elbow toward me. "Nothing for the mook."

"One double," I said. "And two regulars."

The ice cream vendor raised his eyebrows at Gaetano. Gaetano gave me a look of disgust. "I had a big lunch, but I guess I can stuff down a triple serving," he said to the man. "Give the squirt one regular serving, then."

The man took out a bit of brown paper and put a dab of ice cream on it and handed it to me. He gave three dabs to Gaetano.

What Gaetano had done was lousy.

I ate half the ice cream as slowly as I could. It was creamy and cold and not nearly enough. "You could buy a serving," I said to Tin Pan Alley. He had fourteen extra pennies in his pocket, after all—his nine and my five.

"It's not your business what I buy or don't buy," said Tin Pan Alley.

There must have been days when he didn't take in eighty cents. When extra money saved from a good day could spare him a beating.

I handed the paper to Tin Pan Alley.

He ate the rest of the ice cream in one bite and licked the paper clean. Then he turned and walked down Baxter toward Park.

"Bye," I called.

In answer, he looked back over his shoulder at me.

"Where'd you pick him up?" asked Gaetano.

I shrugged. "What's a mook?"

"An idiot."

"He's not an idiot."

"He's got a *padrone,* doesn't he?" asked Gaetano. "Any kid who's owned by a *padrone* is an idiot. If you weren't one to start, you become one fast."

"What's a shark?"

"A boss."

"It can't mean just that," I said. "A boss isn't something bad, but a shark is."

"Depends on how you look at it. A shark sees what there is for the taking and takes it. Sharks are smart." Gaetano pointed at the doors we passed. "That watchmaker, he's a banker on the side. He takes in Italians' money and saves it for them until they've got enough to send for relatives back home. Or, for the really stupid ones, until they think they've made their fortune and decide to go back to Italy. But in the meantime, he gives them nothing—not a cent—and he has their money to use however he wants. He can spend it to start a business of his own. Or he can lend it to immigrants who want to start businesses. None of the real banks will lend them money. But a shark will. He does nothing—he just sits there and makes money off the hard work of the people he lends to. And he makes money off the savings of other people, see? That's a smart shark." He pointed. "That wine store, it's the Banca Italiana. It has no license, nothing. The owner did nothing but say he was running a bank, and people gave him their money. That's what I'm going to do when I get it all together. I'll open a bank."

"And who's going to trust you with their money?" I said.

"You. And mooks like you."

"I'm not a mook."

"Oh, right, you're a king, the way you gave Tin Pan

106

Alley the rest of your ice cream. Listen, mook. Half-wits like you can't protect yourselves. It's either give me your money or get robbed on the street." Gaetano tilted his head at me. "You keep surprising me, Dom. You know less than the Baxter monkeys."

"I saw a monkey today," I said.

"You like monkeys? That figures. Come on." Gaetano swaggered up the street like a big man—a shark—and I followed like a mook. He stopped midblock. "Here it is. The most famous monkey-training school in the city. A smart monkey goes for thirty dollars." He grinned at me. "You'd go for maybe twenty."

There were curtains over the windows, so I couldn't see inside, thankfully. But I could hear monkey chatter from within. And I heard something else, too. Snaps. A whip?

It was right then that my stomach cramped. I doubled over.

Gaetano laughed. "The price of ice cream," he said. "The Genovesi are pigs. They use dirty ingredients and dirty mixing bowls and they make dirty ice cream. But it tastes the best. If you stick around long enough, your guts'll get used to it."

CHAPTER THIRTEEN

Church

I knew Gaetano was following me. And he knew I knew. He didn't even try to hide. Every time I'd look back over my shoulder, he'd be there, a half block behind.

I didn't go to him, though, no matter how much I wanted company. The ice cream had taught me a lesson. Anyone who would let me get that sick couldn't be trusted. Mamma was right—Eduardo was right—no one could be trusted.

Except maybe Tin Pan Alley; Tin Pan Alley was a stand-up kind of guy. But he was off somewhere with his *padrone*.

So I walked up and down alleys, relieving myself whenever the cramps from the ice cream were too great, never stopping for longer than that, trying to lose Gaetano.

After a while, I stumbled the two blocks east to Elizabeth Street, where Gaetano told me the Siciliani lived. He followed. But when I went beyond that, he stopped and turned around.

I got scared: was something awful east of Elizabeth Street? After all, Gaetano seemed to know everything. I turned back.

And there he was, waiting for me. He followed. Four blocks west of Baxter he stopped again. So I turned back.

Then I went south. Gaetano didn't cross Park. But I knew there was nothing dangerous south of Park, because I'd gone all the way to the wharves.

That meant Gaetano was like the stray dogs back in Napoli. He had a territory. If I slept outside his territory, he couldn't bother me.

But the only place I knew to sleep in was my barrel. I wandered south of Park, until I felt sure he'd given up. Then I snuck back to my barrel.

Sunday morning announced itself with church bells. For a moment I thought I was home in Napoli. Those could have been the bells of San Domenico Maggiore or Cappella San Severo or the Duomo itself.

I thought of that last morning in Napoli. Mamma's black hair, spread across my arm. The smell of meatballs and citronella candles. Sneaking out. I remembered other mornings, too. Her constant singing. Her hand on my cheek. How she lifted me to touch the *mezuzah*.

I didn't cry, though. I didn't make any noise at all,

nothing to let anyone know where I was. Napoli was a dreamworld. I was here. In America. In my barrel.

I had to make sure Gaetano didn't see me getting out of the barrel. I peeked over the edge. An old woman with a sack thrown across her back rummaged at the opening of the alley, putting bones in the sack. When she saw me, she ran off.

This area was filled with ragpickers. Most were women or boys who worked for a *padrone,* picking up junk. I'd seen them the day before.

I jumped out of the barrel and ran all the way to the wharf.

The top deck of the *Bolivia* was empty. The third-class passengers must have been taken to Ellis Island fast. Or maybe the *Bolivia* only had first and second class.

I ran to the plank.

A man came down, addressing me in English.

"I need a job on your ship," I said. "I can do anything and everything. I'll be the errand boy. Everyone's job will be easier with me around."

"Italian?" he said in English. Then he tried to shoo me away.

I stood my ground.

He said more things. Louder.

I wouldn't leave.

He waved over someone from across the street. A policeman.

Okay, keep calm, I told myself. Walk, don't run. Like when a dog's coming at you. I walked along the wharf road without looking back.

I crossed the road and went back up to the neighborhood Gaetano called Five Points.

Gaetano appeared in my path almost immediately. I knew he would. He looked cleaner than usual. His hair was slicked down and the crust he'd had on his chin the day before was gone. "I've been looking for you. It's time to go to church."

"I don't go to church."

"Don't say that." Gaetano hit me on the ear. "Don't ever say that." He walked ahead up Mulberry Street. "Come on."

I didn't move.

"Come on," he said. "There's food."

"Why would you care if I get food?"

"I'll get more if you're with me. Come on, don't be a mook."

I caught up to him.

Gaetano looked down his nose at me. "Yesterday you told that mook we were friends. So are you my friend or not?"

We walked.

"Speak up. Are you my friend or my enemy?"

"I'm not your enemy," I said.

He grinned. Gaetano was the biggest grinner I'd ever met. "Then when I say 'Come,' you come. *Chi me vô bene appriesso me vene.*"

I knew that proverb—If you like me, you follow me. It seemed strange that someone as young as Gaetano would recite proverbs. He was trying to make himself seem important again. "How come you never leave this area?" I asked.

He smirked. "You think you're smart. You think you're smarter than people who are a lot older than you."

I shrugged.

"Like I said, you know nothing. You want to get sick on meat from a Polish butcher, huh? Or fish from a Yiddish fish peddler?"

"What do *Polish* and *Yiddish* mean?"

"Dirty. Polish people come from Poland. Yiddish people come from Germany and other places. Some of the Poles are Jews and all of the Yids are. If you go outside Five Points, who knows what they'll feed you. You'll get sick as a dog."

Jews, dirty? Never. "Sick as I got from that Italian ice cream?"

"Don't be disloyal to Italians," said Gaetano.

That stung. Nonna had always prized loyalty. She said the worst thing you could do was leave someone you loved hanging in the wind.

But I didn't want to give Gaetano the satisfaction of agreeing with him. "Yesterday you said the Genovesi were pigs."

"Between you and me, sure. Among the Napoletani, you can criticize the people from Genova all you want. But don't ever criticize them to people who aren't Italian. Loyalty is more important than anything else."

There was something about his voice that made him seem younger than he was. I felt bolder. "So you stay within Five Points so you won't get sick from Jewish food?" I said. "I don't believe you. I think you're afraid. You're a rabbit."

"Me, a rabbit? It has nothing to do with being afraid. Have you talked to anyone out there?"

"I talked to a ship captain just this morning." Maybe the man I talked to wasn't the captain, but it sounded good.

"In Napoletano?"

"Well, sure. I spoke Napoletano."

"What did he speak?"

"English."

"How's your English?" asked Gaetano.

"Which way Chatham Square?" I said in English. I expected him to laugh.

He looked stricken. "Where'd you learn that? You go to school, huh? All the Italian kids in the Bronx go to school?"

"Those are the only English words I know."

"You swear?"

What was he all worked up about? "Of course."

"You better not be making fun of me."

"I'm not."

"Don't make fun of me ever." Gaetano threw back his shoulders.

"I don't make fun of anyone," I said quietly.

"If you're my friend, you don't make fun of me. Ever."

"I won't. Ever."

He looked around; then he turned back to me. "So that's all the English you know?"

"That's it."

"Well, once you try to say other things, you'll see. Go outside Five Points and people laugh at how you talk."

"How do you know? You don't go outside."

"I hear the Five Points men complaining," he said. "That's why they only work for other Italians."

"They can't work in Chatham Square because they don't learn English?"

"That, and other things. Italians belong together anyway. Especially southern Italians."

I scratched dirt off my arm. "Let me get this straight. Immigrants who aren't Italian, they learn English?"

"Yeah. You should hear the big, dumb Swedes speaking English in the factories in Chatham Square."

"Dumb like a fox," I said. "The Italians are the dumb ones. It's better to learn English and get any job you want."

"What'd I tell you about being loyal?" said Gaetano. "Especially here, right now."

"Why especially here?" I asked.

"Because of the Irish. Shut up, okay?" Gaetano stopped. "See that big building across Prince Street? That's Saint Patrick's Cathedral."

The bells rang as we stood there. People came from the north and went through the central front door with the pointed arch over it. People came from behind us on Mulberry Street and went around to the side. Gaetano walked toward the side entrance.

"Why don't we go in the front door?" I asked.

"Because we're not Irish. Shut up. I mean it."

We went down to the basement. Everyone crowded onto benches. I stared straight ahead at the neck of the woman in front of me. She reached a hand up under her black mantilla and a curl tumbled down. Her hair wasn't as dark as Mamma's. But that curl made my face prickle with pins and needles. She tucked it back under. It fell again.

A priest came in. Everyone stood. For the next hour the priest spoke in an Italian that I could mostly understand and a Latin that I loved listening to. We stood and sat and kneeled and recited Latin. They passed around a basket. People put in coins. Not Gaetano.

The priest read a part of the Bible about Saint Paul working hard. Then he talked about the virtue of persisting against the odds. He talked about the opportunities that lay within reach for hard workers. He said Italians could never be faulted for not working hard. The people murmured agreement. He said the possibilities were endless for us—for every last one of us. I thought of Uncle Aurelio and his lectures on *le possibilità*, Uncle Aurelio, who would be aghast to see me at a Catholic mass. My whole family would. I was.

I stood up to leave, but Gaetano yanked me back into my seat. "Stay still," he hissed. "The gospel is the most important part."

I looked at my hands and tried to close my ears to what was going on outside my head. It was my body in this church, not my heart and soul.

Afterward, I asked Gaetano, "Why go to this church if the Irish make you sit in the basement? Aren't there Italian churches?"

"Sure there are. But they're outside Five Points. Here there're only Irish churches—the Most Precious Blood Church and the Church of the Transfiguration and this one—Saint Patrick's. But Italians have to sit in the basement at the other churches, too. And the Transfiguration is on Mott Street; I hate Mott Street. Anyway, it's better than it used to be—they used to forbid the priests from using Italian."

He pulled me into a building a block away. Adults

drank coffee and ate pastries. Kids ran around knocking into things. Gaetano stuffed a pastry in his mouth and filled a cup with coffee. I did the same. I didn't usually like coffee, but it was delicious at that moment. I hadn't had anything to eat since the ice cream Saturday afternoon.

"I've seen you here before," said a woman in an Italian dialect as she approached Gaetano. "But without your little brother. Where's your mother?"

"She's sick," said Gaetano, speaking her dialect—just like he'd spoken the ice cream vendor's Genovese the day before.

"That's too bad." She looked doubtful. "What's her name?"

Gaetano backed toward the door.

"Don't run off," said the woman. She picked up two more pastries and handed us each one. "If your family joins, then when someone gets sick, we'll help out. And when someone dies, we'll pay the funeral costs. Tell your mother that."

"I will," said Gaetano.

"Or, better, let me tell her." A little girl yanked on the woman's skirt. The woman picked her up without turning her eyes from us. "Where do you live?" One hand caressed the little girl's head. Mamma used to do that to me all the time. "I can bring your mother soup," said the woman, her hand on the child's cheek.

"We have to go." Gaetano put down his cup and took my hand. "We're late."

"See you next week," said the woman.

Gaetano pulled me outside and we ate our pastries. "Next week I'll go to a different one."

"A different what?" I asked, forcing away the picture of the woman's hand on the child's cheek. "Are there always parties after church?"

"It's not a party—it's a meeting of a mutual aid society. There are lots of them around here. Don't they have them in the Bronx?"

I shrugged. "What dialect were you talking with her?"

"Milanese. It's from the north of Italy."

"Do you speak every Italian dialect?" I asked.

"Nah. Only the useful ones. To tell the truth, I hardly speak Milanese at all. Just enough to keep out of trouble for sneaking in."

"Why don't you go to a mutual aid society for people from Napoli?"

Gaetano laughed. "There aren't any. It costs fifty cents a month to be a member. None of the southern Italians can afford that. And the northerners wouldn't let us join theirs anyway, even if we had the money."

"Why not?"

"They look down on us. And we don't care. Who needs them? Look. It's like this, Dom. You're Napoletano. I'm Napoletano. We're our own group. We stick together. But the next best guy is someone from the south—except for Sicilia. Don't ever trust a Siciliano. But the Calabresi aren't too bad. There's lots of them on Mulberry Street. And the ones from Basilicata—they're dirt poor and they know nothing, but they're okay. And then, after that, there's northern Italians. The Piemontesi and Lombardi. They live west of Broadway."

"Then who?"

"No one. After the Italians, there's no one you can trust."

117

"What else do these societies do beside help with funerals and take care of the sick?"

"Sometimes they get jobs for people. And if they can't find anything in New York, they'll pay your fare to the coal mines in Pennsylvania or West Virginia. Or, if you want to go farther, Colorado, or Wyoming, or Montana. But then you have to work with Slavs and Welshmen. Still, the mines will always hire Italians first."

Tonino had a job in a coal mine. He must be off in one of those places. "That's what you should do when you're older, Gaetano, start a mutual aid society for southern Italians, not some stupid bank."

"People who run mutual aid societies don't get rich. Bankers get rich."

Everything he said came out like the gospel of that priest—like a truth no one could argue with. "How do you know everything, Gaetano?"

"I pay attention."

"No one pays attention that well," I said.

He grinned. "They would if they got paid for it."

"You get paid for paying attention?"

"I see something someone would want to know—I hear something someone would want to know—and I sell the information." Gaetano sat down on the steps of a building and stretched his legs in front of him, crossed at the ankles. He leaned his elbows back on a higher step.

"How can you figure out what someone would want to know?"

"People need information. All kinds of information. They pay me for the craziest things. You wouldn't believe it. And don't get any ideas about sticking around here and

118

stealing my job. You'd never survive. You don't understand anything you see."

"Sticking around here is the last thing I want to do." I sat beside him. Gaetano really did understand everything he saw. People wouldn't pay him for information if he couldn't be trusted. "Want another job, Gaetano?"

"Who's offering? You? You've got nothing to pay with."

It killed me to say it—but what else did I have? "My shoes."

Gaetano sat up. "What's the job?"

"Get me onto the ship that's down at the wharves. The *Bolivia*."

"You want to go on a ship? Where?"

"Napoli."

Gaetano stared at me. Then he gasped. "You're not from the Bronx at all. You're fresh off the boat, aren't you? You're really lost." He slapped one fist into the other palm. "I should have known it."

"Why? How could you have known?"

He flushed. "If you had a mother, she'd have come storming down here by now." His temples pulsed. His jaw tightened.

"Is your mother really sick, like you told that woman?"

"That's none of your business."

"Do you have a mother?" I asked.

"Shut up. I mean it. Don't ever ask about my family."

I raised my hands in surrender, to calm him down. Then I leaned toward him. "Get me onto that ship and these shoes are yours."

"I don't go down to the wharves. You know that." Gaetano shook his head at me now. "You're alone. You don't even have a *padrone*. Now I get it. The way you act so much older than you are. That's all it takes—a few days alone, and you grow up just like that. What else could you do? I've seen it before. Kids like you, acting so big."

"You don't have to talk to anyone in English out there," I said. "Just come with me to the wharves—come and listen and watch. Figure out a way to get me on the ship. Please. I want to go home."

Gaetano looked away. I knew by now that that was what he did when he was trying to make up his mind. I squeezed my hands together.

He turned back to me. "I'm not promising a thing. But I'll see what I can find out. When's this ship sailing?"

"I don't know, but it's got to be soon."

"Meet you back here at suppertime." He got up and walked down Mulberry. "And don't follow me," he called over his shoulder.

So I went the other way, up Mulberry. No one talked to me. No one looked at me.

Mulberry ran into another street at an angle. If I kept going in the same general direction, there was no way I could get lost. The only thing I needed to know was where to angle off on the way back. I counted the number of streets I crossed. At the fifth corner, my street angled again. Well, okay, I could keep track of that. At the fifth corner, this street angled, too. That was easy to remember—five and five. I was at the edge of a park.

The street sign said PARK, with the little letters *A-V-E* in the upper right corner. I knew *park*. It was the one word of English I could read. And suddenly I made the connection—the Italian word *parco* and the English word *park*—they must mean the same thing. English wasn't such a hard language, after all.

Could this possibly be the same Park Street that ran into Chatham Square? Just in case it wasn't, I counted blocks again. I walked along looking around at the tall buildings, the passing carriages, the people. Stores were closed and shuttered, but I looked at the carvings in the stone over doorways and the huge, feathered hats that the ladies wore. Most of the women held on to the arm of a man. One woman strode by me with a frilly white blouse and a skirt with a wide waistband. Two rows of buttons ran down the front of her blouse. She wasn't pretty, but she caught the eye. Mamma would have been beautiful in those clothes.

I lost count of the blocks somewhere after twenty, because I looked up and my breath was taken away. A giant building loomed ahead. There were three levels of windows. I walked along one side counting the cupolas. Behind the building was a large train shed. Oh, it was a railway station.

I went inside. Men in white straw hats with black bands around the center and broad brims stood in groups. Some carried canes, though they weren't old. They wore ties and vests under their jackets and spoke English.

But then I saw men with curly black hair and mustaches and bow ties. They spoke Napoletano and they bought tickets to Bronxville. Eight cents for a twenty-minute ride. They complained about the high fare, but that was what it cost to visit the relatives on Sunday.

I went out to the train platforms. A gleaming steam engine pulled in. I watched people and trains for hours. When I got too hungry to stay still, I left, passing an area where they kept baggage. A penny to check your belongings overnight.

A penny for this, a penny for that. Life in New York was measured out in pennies.

It was hours yet till suppertime. So I let myself wander. After all, I could say "park" and anyone could point me back to the right road.

Within a couple of blocks I wound up on a broad street. I followed it a long way and came to the countryside. Look at that. Manhattan wasn't such a big place after all. I'd walked the whole length of it. Where there was country, there were farms—and where there were farms, there was food.

A family sprawled on tablecloths spread out on the grass, finishing a meal. The smell of strange spices hung in the air. Fancy food. And these people looked fancy—not at all like farmers. They wore their Sunday best.

I hid behind a tree and watched. A few children took handfuls of leftovers and ran toward a pond. Three huge waterbirds, white things with long necks, swam at the edge. They looked toward the children expectantly. One of them got out of the water and waddled up.

The children screamed and laughed and threw food at the birds. Perfectly good food.

I ran out and grabbed a handful. It looked like a pastry with something green in the middle. Spinach?

Honk! A big bird charged me, flapping giant wings. *Honk honk honk!* I clutched the food and ran. The bird ran faster. It bit the back of my pant leg, its huge bill clamping onto my flesh. I threw the pastry at it. The bird let go and swallowed it whole, then honked at me. But I was already running again. The bird went back to the water.

I watched from a safe distance. How could such beautiful birds be so nasty? I was sure they weren't as hungry as I was. They looked sleek and clean.

I was so dirty. And thirsty. That water looked pretty good. I circled the pond and went down to its edge farther up, far from the dangerous birds.

I drank and washed my face. Then I rolled up my pant legs and waded in. The bird had left two red marks on the back of my calf, but the skin wasn't broken.

My hair was clumped with filth, so I leaned forward and dunked my head and rubbed at my hair. It felt so good.

When I turned, a woman stood on the shore. She was from the family whose children had fed those birds. She waved and put a piece of paper on the ground with food on it. Then she walked away.

I waded out and grabbed the paper. I wolfed down a pastry: spinach with a sour white cheese. And there was eggplant with beef and a sauce. The sauce was white—oh, no. I licked it. It didn't taste like milk or cheese, so maybe it was white from flour. If that was so, the dish was kosher—no mixing of milk and meat. Should I risk it?

Chi nun risica nun roseca—He who doesn't risk, doesn't gain. One of Nonna's proverbs. But I'd never heard her say it about risking breaking kosher laws. Still . . .

I nibbled. It was good. I ate all of it. Then there was a corner of sweet pastry with nuts and honey. What a feast. Not Italian food, but good food.

I wandered off to view the farms I expected to find past

the next set of trees. There were only more trees, though, and more paths with more people. I came upon a throng of people. Out for a Sunday stroll in the sun. And here was a wide set of stairs with a big fountain and another pond. People took rides on little boats with awning tops. This wasn't the countryside at all. It was a colossal park. The atmosphere was like that at a saint festival; everyone was happy and talking and calling to their children. The women had parasols with lace at the edges. In Napoli rich women held them to keep the sun off their faces.

I could pick out English easily. But there were many other languages, too.

Bicyclists went past with white caps and numbers on their shirts. On another path, people rode by on horseback. How big was this park, anyway?

I went in a straight line until I hit a road on one side. Then I went in a straight line in the opposite direction until I hit a road on the other side. It was as far across this park as it was from my home in Napoli to the bottom of Via Toledo.

Now I walked along one edge to find out how long the park was north to south. But it was getting late and people were leaving, so I had to start back. I walked and walked and walked. It took more than an hour to get to the south end of the park. I ran. Stupid me. Gaetano would be waiting on the steps by now.

The street was empty of walkers and only the occasional carriage passed. I tried to flag one down. The driver yelled at me and sped up. The next one did the same.

I ran faster. I heard a train to my left. Good, that was where the depot was supposed to be. I ran a long way.

Then I turned and went two streets over. The streetlamps were lit now, and the sign said PARK. Everything was exactly how it was supposed to be, except that I was late. I couldn't run anymore. I was out of breath. And I got spooked by every shadow. The buildings were too tall here. Who knew what could jump out from between them, or fall from a window high up?

I walked in the street, at the edge so carriages wouldn't hit me. Finally, I came to the medium-size park and I ran by the steps of Saint Patrick's Cathedral to the mutual aid society.

It was night by now; what a fool I'd been to stay in the park so long.

No Gaetano.

I went to my barrel and slept.

CHAPTER FOURTEEN

Sandwiches

On Monday the alley came alive with loud bangs long before dawn. I leapt out of my barrel and ran to the next street before I dared to look back. It was street cleaners, lugging trash out to a wagon and shouting in English. They took away the dead dog, and with it the stench that meant no one would come near my barrel.

Who cared, anyway? I was leaving on the *Bolivia* soon. Maybe that day.

Girls who were almost young ladies walked along the block toward me, arm in arm. They wore black skirts down to their ankles and white aprons and blouses with black bows at the neck. They had on black boots. I flattened myself against the wall as they passed, talking of someone named Maria Luisa, who had the good fortune to be getting married. She

wouldn't have to work anymore. Their voices were as-
toundingly loud.

I looked around. No Gaetano. I might as well head for
the wharf.

I got there in record time, running so hard I had to
bend to wheeze on the last corner.

The *Bolivia* was gone.

Noooo. I ran into the nearest cafe. "What happened to
the ship?" I asked.

The man making coffee said something in English.

"*Bolivia,*" I said. "*Bolivia.*" I pointed to the wharf.

The man said something else in English, then went and
served his customers.

This wasn't possible.

A policeman passed the window. I ran outside to him.
"*Bolivia,*" I said.

He looked down at me with fat, ruddy cheeks and said
something in English.

I pointed to where the ship had been. "*Bolivia.*"

The policeman shooed me away.

It couldn't have left. It must have just moved to another
dock. Someone had to know.

I looked around for the Italian bricklayers. But the
sidewalk in front of the shop was perfect; they'd finished
the job. Well, maybe they'd be back. I leaned against the
shop window and sank to my bottom, my knees pressed
against my chest.

The shopkeeper showed up to unlock.

"*Bolivia?*" I said.

He got out a broom and shook it at me.

I ran along the waterfront. I ran and ran. But who was

I kidding? If there was a ship docked anywhere along here, everyone could have seen it from far away.

The *Bolivia* was gone.

I kept running, without thinking, back and forth along the wharf, back and forth, back and forth. Tears blurred my vision.

Traffic had picked up; the day was really started. Another day here. In New York, in America, an ocean away from home.

I stopped and leaned my forehead against a pole and waited for my eyes to clear. Then I walked back up the road.

"Who died?" It was Tin Pan Alley, standing on his corner, the tin cup at his feet, the triangle in his hand.

"The ship left. The *Bolivia*. I was supposed to go on it. But it left without me."

"That's bad." He tapped his triangle and whistled the tune about the bicycle built for two.

I stood there, too sad to move.

Tin Pan Alley reached in his pocket and took out a small brown rock. He threw it on the sidewalk. It split into shards. He scooped some back into his pocket and he put the rest in my hand.

I looked at them.

"Rock candy," he said. "An old Chinese man gave it to me."

I looked at it. "I can't take that. I bet you almost never get candy."

"How often do you get ice cream? You're not the only one who can share." He tapped his triangle again. "I have to work hard now. The early crowd is good on Monday. Come back in a couple of hours."

"Why?" I said.

"You got something better to do?" He whistled.

I put my hands in my pockets and watched the people go by. The ship had left. Without me. But . . . another had to be coming soon. This was a delay—that was all. The job now was to get ready for the next ship. That was what Uncle Aurelio would have said.

I sucked on the rock candy. The sweetness made my mouth water—and now all I wanted was real food. I went back to the produce vendor on Mulberry Street, who was polishing fruit with a towel and arranging it in piles.

"Tomatoes should go in front," I said.

He turned around. "So you're back."

"They'll catch the eye better. Red does that. Then the green zucchini should go at the back. And the onions can stay in the baskets on the ground in front of the table. All they really need is for the ones on top to be brushed off a little."

"All right, all right, you've convinced me. Go to work."

"But I need three oranges today."

"Oranges get trucked up from Florida, in the south. They don't grow around here. It's not like the south of Italy. They cost."

"I'll work as long as it takes to earn them. I'm good at sweeping, too."

He threw his towel over his shoulder. "Arrange the produce. Then we'll talk."

I worked for an hour. I put everything in its perfect place.

"Beautiful," the vendor said. "What's your name, kid?"

"Dom."

"I'm Grandinetti. Francesco Grandinetti. Can I trust you, Dom?"

"Yes."

"Let's find out. Here's a penny. Go to the corner and pick me up an Italian paper."

"Do they speak Italian at the newsstand?"

"Yes."

I bought the newspaper. Then I ran back to Grandinetti's.

He spread out the paper on the weighing counter inside and pointed. "What can you make of that?"

The paper was full of drawings of people with words printed in little clouds over their heads. One guy was saying he needed to use the bathroom. The other was talking about money. It didn't make much sense to me. I glanced up at Grandinetti.

"Don't worry about the words," he said. "You don't have to be able to read to get it."

"I can read," I said.

He smiled like he didn't believe me. "Most people lie and say they can read. That's why there's lots of illustrations. See? I got a customer. You look at the paper."

I turned the page. These illustrations were of people working in factories. A man yelled at them and brandished a whip. The people were small and scrawny and dark-skinned. The boss was tall and fat and light-skinned.

Grandinetti came back in and weighed carrots and lettuce and tomatoes and onions for a woman in a bright flowered dress. Her face was powdered so white she looked

130

sick. She watched every move he made, as though afraid he'd cheat her. She left in a haze of strong perfume.

"She watched you weigh everything," I said.

"She's a widow." Grandinetti tsked. "She's got it as hard as anyone. Most people would cheat her if they could."

"Not you."

"No. But you don't know me well enough to say that yet. Did you read the paper?"

I pointed. "Are the workers Italian?"

"Yes."

"And is the boss Irish?"

Grandinetti smiled. "You've got it all figured out."

"At church yesterday, the Italians went into the basement, while the Irish went upstairs."

"The church belonged to the Irish first. This used to be their neighborhood."

"Doesn't a church belong to whoever goes to it?" I asked.

"Spoken like an Italian, my boy. Look, the Irish fill the offering basket with money. They pay for the church. The Italians have close to nothing to give, but even if they had it, they wouldn't pay the same way. To us, the priest is like a friend. We offer him produce or a pie. We have him over to supper. So . . . that's how it is . . . the Irish get the upstairs."

"And they get all the jobs. So why stay here? Why not get on the next ship back to Italy?"

"Is that what your father says? Listen here, Dom. Lots of us had it rough at first. America's not perfect, God knows. In Calabria I farmed—and after living an outdoor life like that, being in the city is like being in a cage.

131

Sometimes I can hardly stand it. But in Italy my family was always struggling. Here, we're doing better."

I tapped the illustration. "That's 'cause you're not working in a factory."

"In Italy workers get paid whenever the boss feels like it—here they get paid every week. In Italy men have to work till the job's finished, no matter how long it takes—here they work till quitting time. It's better here. Your father will get used to it. An Irish boss who pays on time is better than an Italian boss who doesn't." He waved to someone out on the sidewalk. "A customer. There's a bushel of new potatoes in the storeroom. Go through them and set the biggest ones on the floor."

I had sorted the potatoes by the time Grandinetti finished with his customer. He put the small potatoes aside and wrapped the big ones in newspaper. "The Cassone family lives on Mott, at the corner of Canal Street, left-hand side. There's a high tenement there. They're two flights up. Bring these to them, okay?"

"Yes, sir."

He handed me three oranges. "Valencias. Juicy. See you tomorrow?"

"Yes, sir."

I put an orange in each pocket and kept the third in my hand.

Sure enough, Gaetano was by my side within a half block, and his eyes went immediately to the orange in my hand.

"The ship's gone," I said.

"I know. It left last night."

132

I knew he'd know. "I'm a mook. I took a walk way up by this huge railway station. . . ."

"Grand Central Depot? You saw Grand Central Depot? What's it like?"

"It's huge. And then I went to a giant park with ponds and people on boats. . . ."

"Central Park. I can't believe you went all the way to Central Park. Did you see the swans? Did you play in the fountain?"

"And by the time I got back here it was night. I'm the biggest mook there is."

"You're not a mook," said Gaetano.

"You don't have to be nice to me," I said. "I'm going to give you this orange anyway. You earned it by finding out how to get me on the *Bolivia,* whether I ruined everything or not."

"I couldn't get you on that ship. The security is tight. Everyone told me it's impossible. The only way on that ship is with a ticket. So it doesn't matter whether you were late last night or not. Keep the orange."

"It's for you." I handed it to him. He tried to hand it back. "Eat it," I said. "We're friends."

"Friends." He tossed the orange from hand to hand. "This is just 'cause we're friends?"

I smiled. "Well, it's for helping me get on the next ship, too."

"Oh. Look," said Gaetano softly. "There's something else."

"What?"

"Maybe with a lot of bribing you could have gotten on

133

that ship without a ticket—or if not that ship, another one. I don't know. It's not likely."

"What do you mean, it's not likely? Another ship will be different," I said. "They can't all be so hard."

"I don't know, Dom. Maybe bribing would work. Only . . ."

"Only what?"

"The guy I talked to said you needed documents to get on a ship—any ship—because if you get caught, the crew member gets in trouble. And the penalty for letting someone sneak on is worse if the stowaway doesn't have documents."

I practically laughed in relief. "I've got documents."

"No, you don't."

I reached into my pocket. But the folded papers the translator on Ellis Island had given me were gone. I stopped and stared at Gaetano. He looked down. His temples pulsed. "You knew they were gone. You stole them!"

"Don't talk so loud." Gaetano took me by the arm.

I pulled free. "Give them back."

"I can't."

"Give them back!" I shouted.

"I sold them."

"Then just go unsell them! Right now!"

"Be quiet, will you?" Gaetano looked around, then took a step toward me. "I can't," he said in a loud whisper. "I sold them Saturday. I tried to get them back yesterday, but the guy had already sold them to someone else."

"No. That's not possible."

Gaetano bounced the orange against his chest and stared at the ground.

I couldn't believe what an idiot I was. Here I'd been worried about guarding my shoes, when those papers were so much more important, and I hadn't even checked on them since Friday night. If I had checked on Saturday, I would have guessed that Gaetano had taken them. I could have gone to him and made him get them back before the other guy sold them. What a brainless mook. I hadn't even noticed that they were gone when I washed off in the park. Or when I put the oranges in my pockets. I should have, I should have, I should have. I stamped my feet and turned in a circle.

Now I couldn't get on any ship. Ever. "You're a thief. You're a dirty thief after all." I ran along the sidewalk, clutching the package with the potatoes.

Gaetano ran beside me.

I wanted to hurl the potatoes at him—knock him into the street. Maybe a carriage would run him over. I turned and swung the package hard.

Gaetano pinned me against a wall.

"Help!" I screamed. "Thief!"

"Shut up a second." He panted in my face. "Look, I thought you were some rich kid from the Bronx. I didn't even know what the papers were. Not till the guy who bought them told me. I'd never seen documents before. They're hard to come by. I didn't know you were alone. I wouldn't have done it otherwise. I swear."

"Thief."

"We weren't friends yet."

"We aren't friends."

"Yes, we are," said Gaetano.

"You don't know what a friend is."

Gaetano jerked his head back as though I'd punched him. He put the orange in my free hand. "I didn't have to tell you," he said. "I didn't have to say anything about the documents. You'd have thought you lost them in that barrel you sleep in every night." He turned and walked off slowly.

I wanted to throw the orange at his head. He couldn't make me feel sorry for what I'd said just because he'd told the truth. And because he knew where I slept and he hadn't stolen my shoes. He was the one who had done something rotten, not me. And I was the one who was stuck here. "Give me the money you got from selling them," I called.

Gaetano stopped and stood there, his back to me.

I had no choice but to catch up.

"I spent it." He turned to face me. "On a steak lunch."

"So I'm stuck here now. I'm stuck here and it's your fault."

Gaetano spread his hands, palms up. His eyes were solemn. "I'll let people know I want documents. Maybe someone will sell me some soon."

"They're hard to come by," I said. "Guess who told me?"

Gaetano's temples pulsed. "I'm your friend. I'll never do anything bad to you again."

What was left for him to do to me? Nothing would seem bad in comparison. All at once, I was too tired to argue.

He fell into step beside me. "Look."

I dragged my feet. I wasn't even hungry anymore.

He cleared his throat. "I'm sorry, Dom."

His apology caught me. I didn't want it to. I wanted to hate him. It wasn't fair, what he had done.

But what was?

Napoletano boys didn't apologize. That sorry cost Gaetano. He wanted my friendship a lot.

How come? What was his story, anyway? The other day he'd said he stayed alone, but he'd told me not to ask where he slept. And later, when I wondered if he had a mother, he'd told me never to ask about his family. He'd said it as though it was a sacred rule: don't ask. How did he get here? What happened to his parents? Why didn't he have a *padrone*, at least? Don't ask, don't ask.

I stopped and looked around. I was either with Gaetano or totally alone. "Do you really think you could buy more documents?"

"I can try," said Gaetano. "It'd probably cost a lot."

At least he was telling the truth now. I tossed him the orange. He caught it.

We walked up the street in silence.

When we got to the corner of Mott, Gaetano asked, "Where are you going? I hate this street."

"Then don't come. I didn't ask you to."

"Wherever you're going, I'm going," said Gaetano. "You're only nine."

"How'd you find that out? From my documents? Don't do me any favors. I'm fine on my own."

"Then I'm coming because we're friends."

"Suit yourself," I said.

We turned onto Mott Street.

"You shouldn't go here," said Gaetano. "The Chinese have been moving in."

"What's wrong with the Chinese?"

"They're tricky. You should see. They get jobs all over

the place rolling cigars. I've heard they make as much as twenty-five dollars a week. An Italian laborer gets a dollar a day. The lowest of anyone."

"What do you mean, the lowest of anyone?"

"Whites get a dollar and twenty-five cents a day. Negroes get a dollar and fifteen cents a day. Italians get a dollar."

"For the same work?"

"Yeah."

"What do the Chinese get for a day's labor?"

"No one hires them for day work. They're too skinny. But Italians are strong and still they get paid bad. And if there's any difference in the types of jobs, Italians are allowed only at the worst ones. They can't collect the piles of garbage, they can only shovel it off barges into the sea."

"So you're jealous of the Chinese."

"I'm not jealous," said Gaetano. "That's ridiculous. You should hear the Chinese talk English. They're horrible. Everyone makes fun of them."

"Yeah, you're jealous," I said. "Here we are." We went into the tenement and up two flights. There were three doors. "Which one do I knock on?"

"Who are you looking for?"

"The Cassone family."

A little girl was coming down the stairs. She pointed. "At the front."

"I could have told you," said Gaetano. "They hang out the window at night and watch the action on Canal Street. I told you. I know all of Five Points."

I knocked.

The door opened. A woman with puffy lips and white

hair pulled back tight into a bun looked at us in a daze. A younger man gently moved her aside. He glared. "What do you want?" His breath was rancid.

I handed him the potatoes. "Grandinetti told me to bring you these."

The old woman took the package from the man. "I'll make potato and fried egg sandwiches for breakfast," she said. "Your favorite."

The man said, "Thanks," and shut the door.

We went downstairs. The smell of potatoes sizzling in oil already wafted past our noses. And rosemary. And pepper. It was heavenly. Gaetano rolled that orange in his hands. I bet he hadn't had any breakfast, either.

But he'd had a steak lunch two days before. On me.

Still, hunger came every day.

"Go ahead and eat the orange," I said. "I've got two more. One for me and one for Tin Pan Alley. I'm going to the corner where he works." I looked at him with a dare in my eyes. "Come if you want."

"Nah, I'll see you later."

"What about all that stuff you said before—all that stuff about coming because you're my friend?"

"You know the way," said Gaetano. "Besides, I don't like that mook."

"You're the mook, you know that, Gaetano?"

"Hey, I said I was sorry about the documents."

"That's not what I'm talking about. You speak every dialect of Italian, and then you're afraid of English. So you live your whole life in just these few blocks. I've seen more of this city than you have. What a stupid way to live. You're the biggest rabbit I've ever known."

"I'm no rabbit. I'm afraid of nothing."

"You're afraid to go with me to see Tin Pan Alley."

"No, I'm not."

"Prove it."

We walked fast all the way to Tin Pan Alley's corner, eating our oranges.

"Hey," I said, and handed Tin Pan Alley the orange.

"What's this?" he said.

"What do you think?" I said. "Eat it."

"Are you kidding?"

"I can't believe it's so hard to give away oranges. What's with you two?"

"Don't throw me in the same category as this mook," said Gaetano. "I had a reason for not taking mine. He's just dumb."

"I have a reason," said Tin Pan Alley. "If this is really mine, I'm selling it. This is Wall Street. The people who work down here don't know the value of money. They get big salaries. I can get five cents for this orange. You don't believe me, but it's true. The big guys spend as much as fifty cents for a sandwich here, and it's small."

"Fifty cents? That's a fortune," said Gaetano. "How do you know?"

"I heard someone say it."

"In English?" asked Gaetano. "Maybe you didn't understand right."

Tin Pan Alley smirked. "I understood."

"It's not your orange," I said. I took it back.

Tin Pan Alley didn't look surprised. "So what," he said, and turned his back to me. He wasn't going to fight. I wanted to shake him. I knew how to fight back better than him when I was five years old.

I peeled the orange and broke it into sections. Then I walked around to the front of him. "You can't sell it now. So you might as well eat it."

"That was dumb," said Tin Pan Alley. But even as he spoke, his hand reached out. He put an orange section in his mouth. His eyelids half closed as he chewed.

So far that day I'd eaten only rock candy and one orange. I couldn't risk looking at the orange sections in my hand, or I might gobble them up.

Tin Pan Alley smiled. "Now and then dumb makes sense." He ate another section. "Five cents lost. But, oh . . ." He ate another and another.

"Five cents is nothing compared to fifty," I said.

"Fifty?" Tin Pan Alley's eyes sharpened. His cheeks pinched, as though he was sure I was about to pull a fast one on him.

"You're going to be eating a lot of oranges from now on." I put the rest of the orange in his hand.

"What are you talking about?"

"I've got an idea." And it was a beauty, all right. I could hear Mamma in my head, telling me to be my own boss. "Come on, Gaetano, hurry."

Gaetano had been watching me this whole time as though he couldn't figure me out. But now he flinched to attention. "Why?"

I was already racing toward Five Points. "Can you get your hands on some clean paper?"

"What for?"

"That brown paper the ice cream man uses—that would do."

"Yeah. I can get some. What for?"

"And can you get a knife?"

"A knife? Whoa. Tell me what for or I don't want any part of it."

"Forget the knife. I bet Grandinetti has a knife I can use. Just get the paper."

By this time, we were at the corner of Park Street. Gaetano grabbed my arm. "What's going on?"

"I'm going to make money, Gaetano. Lots. And Tin Pan Alley is going to help me. You can be part of it, unless you're too much of a rabbit."

"You think I'm stupid enough to do something just because you call me names?" he said. "I do what I want to do. And I don't hurt anyone. No knives."

"We won't hurt a soul. I'm going to earn enough money for a ticket home and new documents. You want something, that's for sure. You're always hungry. Except when you're eating steak. So are you in?"

"All I have to do is get brown paper?"

"Yeah. Four big pieces."

"What about that knife?" he said.

"Just get the paper and meet me at Grandinetti's."

"Where?"

"The produce store. And if I'm not there, wait for me, 'cause I'll be coming."

I ran to Grandinetti's. He was standing behind the weighing counter, reading the paper. "Please," I said.

Grandinetti looked over the edge of the paper at me. "Please what?"

The words burst out of me. "I need to borrow twenty-five cents. Only for a couple of hours."

"I'm not a bank." He clapped his hands together in front of his chest as though he was praying and shook them at me. "Small as you are, you're a good worker. You keep it up and I'll be square with you. But I'm no chump."

"Here." I took off my shoes. "You can keep them if I don't pay you back by the end of the day."

Grandinetti frowned. "Your folks will be angry if you come home without your shoes."

"I'll have my shoes at the end of the day—and you'll have your twenty-five cents. Please."

"I don't want to face your angry father."

"I don't have a father."

Grandinetti blinked. "Your shoes are worth more than twenty-five cents—but twenty-five cents is all I'll lend you."

"That's all I'm asking for."

"All right."

"And do you have a knife I can use?"

"What's this all about?"

"I'm just going to cut a sandwich with it."

"Bring the sandwich in here," he said. "I'll cut it."

I took the twenty-five cents and ran barefoot to Luigi Pierano's store on Park Street. I bought a long sandwich stuffed with salami and provolone and hot peppers and onions and tomatoes and lettuce, nodding my head yes to everything he offered.

At Grandinetti's, Gaetano was waiting with the brown paper.

Grandinetti shook his head. "Exactly how do you expect to get your shoes back?"

"I'll bring you money, I swear. Just cut the sandwich into four equal sections. Please."

"His shoes, for a picnic," said Grandinetti under his breath as he cut the sandwich.

Gaetano and I wrapped the four pieces. Then we ran back to Wall Street. We didn't have to talk; Gaetano knew what was up.

"Here." I held out the cut sandwiches to Tin Pan Alley. "Sell them. Fifty cents."

"Sandwiches?" He looked around. "I'm not a vendor. I just make music."

"You were going to sell the orange," said Gaetano.

"One orange. That's easy. But I can't sell four sandwiches. Who would buy them from me? People have to trust food vendors."

"Try," I said.

One side of Tin Pan Alley's mouth rose nervously. He held out a sandwich to a passing man. "Sandwich?" he said in English.

The man looked at the sandwich. Then he looked at me, standing behind Tin Pan Alley with three more sandwiches. I smiled at him and tried to look trustworthy. He looked at Gaetano. Gaetano smiled at him. He said something in English to Tin Pan Alley.

"Chicken," said Tin Pan Alley in English.

The man said something else in English. Then he handed Tin Pan Alley a coin, took the sandwich, and walked away.

"A quarter," said Gaetano.

"How much is a quarter worth?" I asked.

"Twenty-five cents."

"That's only half of fifty." I pointed at Tin Pan Alley. "You said they'd pay fifty cents for a sandwich."

"So what," said Tin Pan Alley. "I didn't tell the guy the price. That's just what he gave me. Don't get mad."

"Mad?" Gaetano grinned. "You're both mooks. A quarter! That crazy man just paid a whole quarter for a sandwich. Tin Pan Alley, you were right; the people here have no sense of the value of money. They'll pay anything, and we've still got three more sandwiches to sell." He slapped Tin Pan Alley on the back. "It worked! Dom's crazy plan worked!"

It did. It worked. Gaetano saw things right. I grinned at Tin Pan Alley, too. "What does *chicken* mean?"

"It's the English word for *pollo*. He asked what was in the sandwich."

"But there's no chicken in the sandwich," I said.

"It was the only English word for meat I could think of. I hope the guy likes salami."

CHAPTER FIFTEEN

Money

The next three sandwiches were harder to sell. People walked by without giving us a look. But then a group of young men dressed in identical suits and ties came up. They took all three and gave Tin Pan Alley a handful of coins.

Tin Pan Alley counted. "Nine nickels."

"What's a nickel worth?" I asked.

"Five cents."

"That's only forty-five cents." I looked around for the men. They were just going through the door of a building. I ran. Spun. And fell.

Gaetano had hooked my elbow with such force that I'd been knocked off my feet. "Forget it. You can't go in there."

"They cheated us."

"And we'll get cheated again." Gaetano put his fists on his hips. "That's how it works."

"Look at it this way," said Tin Pan Alley. "We're forty-five cents ahead. Forty-five cents!"

"For once the mook is right." Gaetano grinned. "Forty-five whole cents."

And it wasn't even lunchtime yet. All right, this was okay. Gaetano and I went back to Five Points, me racing ahead straight to Grandinetti's. I put the quarter on the counter under his nose.

"That was quick." Grandinetti reached under the counter and took out my shoes. He raised his brows in question.

I didn't want to explain. Not yet. There was still a lot to figure out. It felt like a dream, it was going so fast. If everything went the way I wanted it to, I'd be home in Napoli in no time.

So I sat on the floor and brushed off my feet and just smiled up at Grandinetti. Then I put on my shoes and rubbed them shiny with my thumbs. Gaetano waited for me out on the street. He was still grinning. I waved to him through the open door.

When I stood, I reached out to shake Grandinetti's hand. He gave a crooked smile and hesitated. But he shook firmly.

"Keep your knife ready," I said. "We'll be right back."

"I'm not going anywhere."

The instant I stepped out the door, Gaetano grabbed me by the sleeve and pulled me down the block. "Look, I've got this all worked out. Give me five cents."

"No," I said. "Let's keep buying as many long sandwiches as we have money for. The more we sell, the more we make."

"If you don't give me five, what are we going to wrap the cut sandwiches in? No one will buy a sandwich that's been sitting in our bare hands. We need paper."

"Paper costs five cents?"

"No, you mook. I got the last four pieces for a penny. So that means the business owes me a penny. And with the other four pennies I'll buy sixteen more pieces. Sixteen, 'cause we have to look ahead."

His words rang in my head: *the business*. We had a business already. I gave Gaetano a nickel.

He headed for Baxter Street.

I made a beeline for Pierano's and bought another sandwich. Grandinetti cut it into four pieces. Gaetano and I wrapped the pieces in the new brown paper. But when we got to the fourth sandwich, Gaetano stopped. "Could you cut this one again?" he asked Grandinetti.

I knew immediately that he was thinking of our lunch. I almost objected. But hunger held my tongue.

Grandinetti nodded in approval. "Halves, huh?"

"Thirds," said Gaetano.

"Fourths," I said.

I wrapped the three parts of sandwich for Gaetano and Tin Pan Alley and me in a single sheet of brown paper and left the last part on the counter.

"What's this?" asked Grandinetti, surprised.

"Thank you for cutting the sandwiches," I said.

"You didn't have to do that."

When Gaetano and I were out on the street, Gaetano hissed, "He's right; you didn't have to do that."

148

"He helped us," I said.

"Yeah, but no one's going to see him eating. It's no advertisement for us."

Advertisement. Gaetano had a head for business. We found Tin Pan Alley back at his corner. I stood there beside him like a statue, holding the three wrapped sandwiches. Tin Pan Alley was the hawker, and when anyone would show a little interest, he'd point at Gaetano, who would take a big bite from one of the smaller pieces of sandwich that were for us, making loud *yum* noises. It worked; a man bought a sandwich. And for a whole quarter. Then it was Tin Pan Alley's turn to eat a small section of sandwich—but neither Gaetano nor I could hawk because we didn't speak English, so that didn't work so well. Still, we sold another sandwich. Only one to go.

Now it was my turn to eat that little section of sandwich. The sandwiches had meat and cheese mixed together. Plus, the meat was salami—probably made of pig. I picked out a piece of salami, but then I didn't know where to put it.

"What are you doing?" said Gaetano.

"I don't like salami," I said.

"Eat it anyway. When you mess up the sandwich like that, you make it look bad."

A potential customer was watching us.

"Make a game of it," said Tin Pan Alley. "Act like a dog, Gaetano."

"I'm no dog!"

"No, a dog's smarter than you," said Tin Pan Alley. He got on his knees and barked.

I fed him the salami. Then I took a bite of my piece of sandwich, careful to eat only cheese and lettuce.

The man bought the last wrapped sandwich.

Lunchtime was over. It had taken more than an hour to sell three sandwiches. But who cared? We had seventy-five cents to add to the fifteen already in my pocket.

"See you tomorrow," I said to Tin Pan Alley.

Gaetano and I headed back toward Five Points.

"Wait," called Tin Pan Alley. "Where's my share?"

"You got something to eat," said Gaetano. "Woof, woof. Remember?"

"No fair. The whole time we were selling, I wasn't making music. So no one put money in my cup. And lunch is one of my best times. What did you give up? Nothing."

"Are you saying my time's worth nothing?" Gaetano's hands balled into fists.

"The only thing I saw you do was eat," said Tin Pan Alley. "I'm the one who actually sold the sandwiches. Without me, you couldn't say a word. You need me."

Gaetano thrust his chin forward. "You need me, too, you little mook."

"Hold on," I said. "Let's put together what we have till the end of the week. The more long sandwiches we buy, the more small ones we sell. We'll make real money this way."

Gaetano put his face in mine. "I want my share now. That's what we agreed on."

I moved my face even closer to Gaetano's. "Lots and lots of money. And we still have twelve pieces of brown paper. We can start the day tomorrow with three long sandwiches." I cleared my throat. "One week, that's all I'm asking."

Gaetano looked away. When he looked back, he nodded. "One week."

"No," said Tin Pan Alley. "If I don't bring in eighty cents today, I'll get a beating."

I dropped ten cents in Tin Pan Alley's cup.

"I would have made double that."

"We only earned ninety cents. And we need seventy-five for the three sandwiches tomorrow morning. How about I give you fifteen?" I put another nickel in Tin Pan Alley's cup.

Tin Pan Alley just looked at it.

"Come on, mook." Gaetano picked salami from his teeth. "Money makes money. Beg harder this afternoon."

Tin Pan Alley glared at him.

"Oh, I forgot. You don't beg. Well, play your stupid triangle harder."

"He whistles, too," I said. "He whistles good."

"Come on," said Gaetano. "We're partners."

I remembered the welts on the boy with the harp in Chatham Square. Did it really matter whether we started the next day with two sandwiches instead of three?

"Get out of here," Tin Pan Alley spat. He turned his back and played the triangle.

"Wait," I said. "Here's another nickel. . . ."

"Go!" Tin Pan Alley was swaying back and forth, he played that triangle so hard.

Gaetano dragged me off. "Shut up. And open your stupid eyes."

I looked over my shoulder. A big man in a wide-brimmed hat stood near the lamppost with his arms crossed on his chest. His feet were spread far apart and his stomach pushed forward. His eyes were on Tin Pan Alley. Now he glanced at us.

151

I looked straight ahead and practically ran to keep up with Gaetano. "Is that . . . ?"

"His *padrone*. Of course."

Goose bumps went up my arms and neck. "How'd you know?"

"You can always tell a *padrone*."

"How?"

"From the stink."

We didn't slow down till we got to Chatham Square. "Is Tin Pan Alley in trouble?"

He looked away. "We'll find out tomorrow."

"He didn't do anything bad," I said.

"*Padroni* don't need a reason. Forget about it till tomorrow."

Tomorrow. Our business. "See you in the morning, right? Same deal?"

"Not exactly." Gaetano folded his arms across his chest. For a second he looked a little like the *padrone*. "We can improve."

"How?"

"Follow me and learn."

So we went to a paper mill. Inside, the clanking of the machines was so loud, I put my fingers in my ears. The workers didn't seem to be bothered by it, though. They hollered to one another above the din. Gaetano hollered to the manager; then the two of us went back out to the sidewalk and sat on the curb.

"For twenty-five cents we could buy a roll of paper long enough to wrap a thousand sandwiches at least," yelled Gaetano.

"Why are you shouting?" I yelled back.

Gaetano laughed. So did I. And I remembered those girls talking loud that morning as they walked past my alley. They probably worked in a noisy factory. The city must be full of near-deaf factory workers.

"You're the one who's good with numbers," said Gaetano. "But anyone can figure out that buying from the mill is cheaper than paying the ice cream man a penny for four sheets."

"I don't know," I said.

"What's to know?"

"Let's be careful. Spend just a little to start."

"And you're the one who wants to buy a boat ticket." Gaetano looked disgusted. "Besides, *chi poco spenne assai spenne.*"

He who spends little winds up spending much more in the end—it had the sound of a proverb, one I hadn't heard before. But Gaetano couldn't win the argument just because he knew proverbs. "You really think we're going to have to sell a thousand sandwiches before I have enough money to get back home?"

"For a ticket and fake documents, you bet, 'cause we're going to share the money equally and we have to stay alive in the meantime."

"But if we spend twenty-five cents now," I said, "that's four fewer sandwiches we can sell tomorrow."

"You're talking like a mook again. Think about it. Think about how many sandwiches we can sell tomorrow. Think how much money we'll make if we sell them all. Come on, Dom."

Twenty-five cents for paper. That left enough money for two long sandwiches at Pierano's. Each sandwich got cut into

153

four pieces. Even if we shared one of them for our own lunch, like we had that day, that left seven to sell, which meant . . . Wow. "A dollar and seventy-five cents!" I shouted.

Gaetano shook his head in amazement. "That's almost double what a grown man makes a day."

"Well, really only a dollar and fifty cents, after we put money in Tin Pan Alley's cup."

"Whoa. He asked for twenty cents, not twenty-five."

"Yeah, but today we only gave him fifteen. And we can afford twenty-five, easy." I spoke fast, before he could object. "How long do you think it'll take us to sell seven sandwiches?"

Gaetano grinned. "We'll have to start earlier."

"But, hey, what if it rains tonight? Where will we put a roll of brown paper?"

Gaetano knitted his brows.

"Where'd you put the pieces of paper we still have left?"

Gaetano pulled them out of his pocket. They were folded up small. "A whole roll is gigantic, though."

"Okay," I said, "here's the plan. We buy three sandwiches at Pierano's tomorrow morning and cut them up. We've already got the paper to wrap them. After we sell those, we can buy the roll of paper and bring it to Grandinetti's. Maybe he'll let us keep it in his store."

"Give me the money." Gaetano held out his hand.

I pulled back. "Why?"

"You can't keep it safe overnight in a barrel."

"I'll put it in a bank, then. You said there were banks everywhere."

"I don't trust these banks," said Gaetano. "No one treats kids fair." He put the fingertips of one hand together and shook them in front of my face. "They'd report us as lost and we'd wind up in an orphanage, and the banks would keep our money. Don't be such a mook. Give it to me."

"No."

"You don't trust me?"

I just looked at him. He'd stolen my documents.

"I asked you a question," said Gaetano.

I took the three quarters from my pocket and handed Gaetano one. "We'll split them overnight."

"Hey, I'm three years older, I should keep two and you keep one."

"The whole thing was my idea," I said.

Gaetano pocketed the quarter and walked off.

Just like that, I was alone again.

And tired. My stomach growled. Lunch had been so small. I had a headache. It was hot. I wanted a midday nap, like back home. People were stupid in America; they didn't know enough to get out of the sun.

Crowds cluttered the sidewalks; it was an effort just to weave my way to the alley. When I got there, the reek hit me like a slap; little piles of trash stewed in the sun-warmed puddles. I put one hand over my nose and mouth and headed for my barrel.

It was gone.

Clank!

I turned around. A big boy with shiny hair had entered the alley and knocked into a stack of debris. Another boy came running up behind him. One look at their faces and I knew they were after me.

I took off in the other direction and fell in rotten vegetables that had turned to slime in the heat.

One boy jumped on my back and rolled me over. He sat on my chest, pinned my arms to my sides with his knees, and pressed both hands over my mouth. The other reached into the pocket with the two quarters, as though he knew what was there. "Is this all of it?" He held a fist in front of my face.

The boy on my chest lifted his hands so I could answer. "Thief!" I screamed. "Thief, thief!" I thrashed and twisted.

The boy clapped his hands down again and squeezed me with his knees so hard I felt tears come. "Watch who you call names," he said. "Where'd you get all this money? You picked someone's pocket. You're the thief."

"What about the shoes?" said the other boy.

I felt hands fiddling with my shoestrings. No! I kicked and bucked like a wild thing. With every ounce of strength I had, I ripped my arms free and pummeled the boy on top of me. We were rolling in the garbage filth now, all three of us, kicking and punching and biting.

"What's going on there?" came a man's voice.

The thieves ran off.

The man walked toward me. "You okay, kid?"

I got up and swiped at the slime on my pants. Now my hands were slimy, too. "I'm fine."

"You sure? You look pretty bad."

He spoke Napoletano. For an instant I wanted to tell him everything, to beg for help. But then I thought of finding myself in an orphange. "I'm fine." I closed my eyes and pressed the heels of my hands into my eyelids, slime and all. When I opened my eyes, the man was gone.

I had no money.

I had no barrel to sleep in.

Gaetano was right: I was a mook. All that money . . . gone. And it was Tin Pan Alley's and Gaetano's money as much as it was mine.

I hurt—all of me. But my mouth hurt the most. I wiped it. Blood. I ran my tongue around the inside of my mouth. My bottom lip was cut.

And look how stupid I was to still be here. The thieves could come back at any moment. So I went the only place I could go—Grandinetti's store.

He was busy with customers. A broom stood in the corner. I swept, careful to go around people politely, keeping my eyes lowered so no one would take much notice of me. Plums had fallen behind a bushel. I wiped them off and put them neatly back in place. When there was finally a break in the business, Grandinetti leaned against the weighing counter and looked at me. "What happened to you?"

"Nothing."

"Nothing, huh? Nothing that's going to end up as a black eye by morning. And what's that?" He came closer. "A fat lip, too." When I didn't say anything, he walked over to the fruit bushels. "Three tomatoes or an orange. Your choice."

"I need a penny."

He put his hands up in the halt sign. "A few pieces of fruit—that's one thing. But money? I can't afford a paid helper, Dom."

I waved my arm across the room. "Look how nice your floor is now."

"You do good work."

"Just a penny. One penny."

"A penny now. What tomorrow? A nickel? The next day a dime?" He put his hands together as though praying and shook them at me—a gesture I already recognized as his favorite. "I don't make a big profit here. I have to be careful."

"I won't ask for a penny tomorrow."

"I don't know what trouble you're in, Dom. And you seem like a good kid. But . . ."

"I won't ask for a penny tomorrow."

Grandinetti raised both brows. "Promise?"

I hated to promise. What if I still needed a penny tomorrow? But, well, if I did, I'd have to get it someplace else. "I promise."

Grandinetti gave me a penny.

"Thank you."

I walked to the train depot and checked my shoes in baggage overnight. They'd be safer that night than I would be—how funny. I went to Central Park and pawed through trash. All I found were ends of bread smeared with a nasty yellow paste. They barely eased the ache in my gut. And they did nothing for the ache in my head; I'd had two quarters in my pocket and now I had nothing. In the morning I'd have to face Tin Pan Alley and Gaetano. I was pretty sure Tin Pan Alley would forgive me. But Gaetano . . . even if Gaetano didn't punch me, he'd be disappointed. They'd both be disappointed in me. Sick of me. I was sick of me. Me and my big plans. I'd never get home if I kept doing things wrong.

This was too hard. Everything was too hard.

Long before dark, I crawled under the thick bushes by the big pond and slept.

CHAPTER SIXTEEN

More and More Money

"You lost both quarters?" Gaetano shook his head.

"I told you. I was robbed. They jumped me in the alley."

"Both?"

I turned my pockets inside out. "See?"

"What'd they look like, these thieves of yours?"

"One was kind of big. Bigger than you. With slick hair. The other one, I don't know, he was ordinary."

Gaetano smirked. "What are you, blind? No one would pay a cent for information like that." He shook his head. "You look pretty good for someone who got jumped. Your face isn't so hot, but your clothes are clean."

"I woke up before dawn and rinsed my clothes in the pond and washed myself off."

"Your clothes dried that fast?" Gaetano tapped his foot.

I didn't want to tell him that my clothes dried fast because I'd been running around for hours. After I got my shoes out of baggage deposit at the station, I stacked fruit at Grandinetti's and earned a tomato for myself and a badly bruised orange that I shared with Tin Pan Alley at his corner. Gaetano would say it was stupid of me to give Tin Pan Alley oranges. But I was going to give Tin Pan Alley an orange every morning I worked; the look on his face as he ate was worth it. I'd told Tin Pan Alley about the thieves and he didn't get mad—and that was before he knew I had an orange to share. All he said was "I hate thieves." I could tell he'd been robbed before. Lots of times.

I looked at Gaetano now and shrugged. "It's hot out."

Gaetano scratched behind his ear.

"What? You think I hid the money someplace? You don't trust me?"

He grinned. "That's what I asked you yesterday. If you'd given me all the money, we'd be fifty cents richer today. Am I right?"

"Yeah."

He put out his hand. "Trust from now on?"

I shook his hand. "How come you're not crazy mad that our money's gone?"

"*So' cadute l'anielle, ma so' restante 'e ddete*—The rings have fallen away, but our fingers remain—and we've still got the quarter in my pocket. Let's get to work."

That was Uncle Aurelio's kind of optimism—bad things happen, but you don't miss a step. Gaetano could make a decent Jew. I didn't tell him that, though.

We bought the long sandwich at Pierano's and cut it in fourths. The block before we got to Tin Pan Alley's corner, Gaetano stopped. "You stay here with the sandwiches. Let me check things out first."

"Why?"

"His *padrone*. Or don't you remember?"

Oh. I had to confess. "Tin Pan Alley's all right. I saw him this morning. Early. He was alone."

"Oh, yeah?" Gaetano looked hurt. "The two of you are close, huh? Well, I think I'll just go ahead anyway, to check if that *padrone*'s come back."

Right. The *padrone* could have shown up again by this time of morning. I hugged the sandwiches and stood against a building wall. The walkers were so thick I couldn't see past them. I couldn't see Tin Pan Alley's corner.

A woman came out of the nearest door and said something to me in English. I moved over to the next building.

What was keeping Gaetano?

Finally he appeared beside me. "The area's clear."

"And Tin Pan Alley?"

"The mook's playing his triangle. You go sell with him. I'm going to patrol. If I spy his *padrone*, I'll come get you fast."

Over the next hour and a half, we sold four sandwiches, each one for a full quarter, to guys in fancy suits, and no sign of the *padrone*. Soon I sat on the curb outside the paper mill in Chatham Square, waiting while Gaetano bought the roll of brown paper, basking in that day's luck. Two customers had been repeats from the day before. The new ones were friends of theirs. One of them said that if we sold sandwiches at lunch break that day, he'd send down a few of his friends. Tin Pan Alley swore we'd have plenty for everyone.

I could practically feel the ship ticket in my pocket. One thousand sandwiches would be sold in no time. I looked around—yes, good-bye to New York—good riddance.

And out of nowhere there they were: the thieves. I sat tall. The big boy's hair was so slick it glistened in the sun. They stood on the north side of the street, watching. They didn't even have the decency to turn their heads away when our eyes met. I leapt to my feet, but then what? Surely they wouldn't jump me here, in front of everyone. Besides, I had no money on me. The quarters we'd made so far that day were in Gaetano's pocket. My heart beat hard; I wanted to run.

"What's the matter?" Gaetano came out of the factory with the roll of paper in his arms.

I pointed.

Gaetano looked at the boys. They looked back.

"Those are the guys who robbed me."

"Oh yeah? I figured as much. Maurizio's the only thief I know who uses ape snot in his hair." He gave them a wave and walked leisurely toward Park Street.

I walked beside him, looking back at the boys. "Why'd you do that? Why'd you wave as though they're buddies or something?"

"I'm not buddies with anyone," said Gaetano. Then he winked at me. "Except you, that is." He sort of swaggered now. "They stay out of my way, I stay out of theirs."

"They stole some of your money yesterday."

"No, they didn't, not as far as they know. They think

they stole your money. They'd never steal mine."

"Why not?"

"My big brother. He'd stab them."

"You have a brother?"

"I told you not to ask about my family."

I could have bitten my tongue.

"Anyway, this time I'll answer, 'cause we're buddies. No. No brother. But they don't know that." He stopped outside Pierano's. "If you ever talk to them, remember: they've done wrong to you, not to me. If they think they got away with robbing me, then nothing protects me anymore. You got it?"

"Can't your big brother protect me, too?"

"Here." He gave me seventy-five cents.

I went into Pierano's, bought three long sandwiches, and came out holding them in a bundle tied together with string.

"Where'd you get the string?" asked Gaetano.

"Pierano tied them. Without my even asking. And he smiled at me. I'm becoming his best customer."

"Not you, you mook. He thinks whoever you're working for is his best customer. You're just a kid."

We walked toward Grandinetti's. I kept looking around for the thieves. "What're we going to do, Gaetano?"

"About what?"

"Our money, for one."

"I can keep the money safe."

"What if you can't?" I said.

"I can. With my big brother's help."

I twisted my fingers through the string around the

sandwiches. "Well, what about that roll of paper? You already admitted you don't have anyplace to store it where it won't get rained on."

"I'll come up with something."

I looked over my shoulder again. "The thieves. A block back."

Gaetano didn't say anything.

"They won't know I don't have money on me," I said. "They'll jump me anytime they get me alone."

"After a few times of finding nothing in your pockets, they'll stop."

"I don't want to get jumped. It hurts. Where do they live?"

"What?" said Gaetano in surprise.

"I want to make sure I don't go on their street."

"I can't help you."

"Tell me," I said.

"You don't get it, do you? I don't know where they live, okay? I don't ask. That's how it is with the kids in Five Points." He stuck his finger in my chest. "I'll see you later. For now I've got to come up with a place to stash this roll of paper."

I hadn't realized that *don't ask* was the code of the whole neighborhood. It took a second to sink in. Then I ran and caught up to him. "Grandinetti's," I said. "Remember? That's the perfect place."

"He's Calabrese," said Gaetano. "He might act nice now, but if he gets mad at us, there's no telling what he'll do."

"You're wrong. And he can keep our money safe, too."

"I can keep the money safe," said Gaetano.

"It's going to be a lot soon. Your pockets aren't big enough."

"Stop talking. I've got to think."

We fell into step in silence.

Grandinetti was busy with the morning shoppers. He rushed about, counting out fruits and weighing vegetables and wrapping everything in newsprint from the Italian paper.

But we couldn't wait if we were going to sell sandwiches to the lunch crowd. So I stood behind Grandinetti and whispered, "Can we use the knife?"

"Where? My counter's busy now. You can see that."

"In your storeroom."

He looked at my bundle of long sandwiches. Then he shook his prayer hands at me. "Be careful. Let your friend use the knife." He jerked his chin toward Gaetano. "He's older."

While Gaetano cut the sandwiches, I wrapped them. The pile was high. "How can we carry them all?"

We searched around the storeroom and came up with an empty bushel basket. Gaetano started throwing the sandwiches in it.

My hand stayed his arm. "We have to ask first."

"He likes you. He'll say yes. Especially if the sandwiches are already in it."

"All right. But let me do it." I arranged the sandwiches neatly in three layers.

I went into the main part of the store. There was only one customer left, and she was taking her time choosing lettuce. I tapped Grandinetti on the arm.

He followed me into the storeroom. "What's this?"

165

"Could we borrow this basket?" I said. "Just for a few hours? Please."

"Okay, but I need it tonight."

"I promise." I gave Grandinetti back his knife. And I handed him a wrapped sandwich—a whole one, not just some small piece. "Lunch," I said with a smile.

Grandinetti looked at me. "You didn't have to do that, Dom."

Gaetano stood the roll of brown paper against the wall of the storeroom. "And we'll leave our paper as security."

"You mean you have no place else to keep it?" Grandinetti turned to me and shook his prayer hands. "Are you trying to be a fox on me? No tricks, you hear?"

"We're just trying to do business," I said. "And we need your help. No tricks."

"All right. You can leave the roll of paper." Grandinetti kept his eyes on me. "Get out of here now."

"Thank you," I said.

Gaetano took one of the wire basket handles and I took the other. We carried the sandwiches out through the store.

Gaetano stopped in the doorway. He looked at me and pointed with his thumb down the street. One of the thieves leaned against a wall, watching Grandinetti's store. "One more thing," said Gaetano to Grandinetti. "Would you walk outside holding that knife and shake it at Dom?"

"What?"

"Then turn toward Chatham Square and shake it high in the air. Like you're threatening someone."

"We're putting on a play?" asked Grandinetti.

"Two guys are after me," I said. "One of them's watching."

"Is that how you got the fat lip?"

I nodded.

Grandinetti sighed. "I don't want my customers to see me shaking a knife."

"Then just point it," said Gaetano. "You don't have to shake it."

"All right already. Get out of here." Grandinetti shooed us out the door. He pointed the knife at me. Then he swung it in an arc and pointed toward Chatham Square.

The thief took off running.

Gaetano really was smart.

"And one last thing," said Gaetano.

"*Basta,*" said Grandinetti. "Enough is enough."

"Just a little towel." Gaetano cocked his head and shifted his weight and somehow his whole appearance changed. He seemed much younger, more in need of help. "We have to cover the basket. So no one knows what's in it. Otherwise, kids will snatch sandwiches as we're walking."

Grandinetti slapped his palm on his forehead. Then he put his fists on his hips. "On one condition."

"What?"

"You cut the bull with me. No more phony talk about the paper being security. No more acts. You treat me straight, I'll treat you straight."

Gaetano offered his hand, all grown up again. "Gaetano," he said.

"Francesco," said Grandinetti.

They shook.

Grandinetti took the towel from his shoulder and spread it over the sandwiches. "Get out of here. But have that basket and towel back before I close shop."

Within a few minutes of our arriving at Tin Pan Alley's corner, a trickle of people came out of the buildings. The lunch break was just starting.

"You'd better patrol," I said to Gaetano.

"It's okay," said Tin Pan Alley. "My *padrone* came by while you were gone. I bet he's off eating now." He looked at a passing man. "Sandwiches," he called out in English. "The best in town."

"What's that mean?" I asked. When he told me, I practiced the words under my breath. "Sandwiches. The best in town. Sandwiches. The best in town."

Gaetano unwrapped a whole sandwich and slowly ate it. We hadn't talked about each of us getting a whole sandwich. Now we'd only have eight to sell—but I'd started it by giving Grandinetti a whole sandwich.

I felt faint with hunger. The bigger he chewed, the fainter I felt, but the more sandwiches we sold.

Then it was Tin Pan Alley's turn to eat.

"Sandwiches," I called out. "The best in town."

Gaetano smirked. "Listen to you try to speak English. You sound worse than Tin Pan Alley."

"He sounds good to me," said Tin Pan Alley. "He sounds perfect. Go on, Dom."

"The best in town," I called.

A woman bought a sandwich.

Gaetano stared at me.

I strutted; I couldn't help it.

Then it was my turn to eat. When I'd ordered the sandwiches at Pierano's, I'd thought about getting one without meat. But I figured it wouldn't sell as well. So now I picked out the meat.

Gaetano watched me. "That's not salami. That's ham. What, you don't like ham, either?"

I shook my head.

"Well, don't do the dog routine again."

"Why not?"

"It's not fair. I won't act like a dog, so Tin Pan Alley gets more meat than me. If you're going to give away your ham, give half to me."

"Wait," said Tin Pan Alley. He pulled slices of cheese out of his pocket. "I saved my cheese in case you didn't like the meat today, either. I can trade for your meat."

So I ate my thick cheese sandwich.

We sold out. And still there were people asking for sandwiches.

"We'll have more tomorrow," said Tin Pan Alley in English. "Bring your friends. We'll have lots more." Then he told us what he'd promised.

"Good work. See you tomorrow." I put twenty-five cents in Tin Pan Alley's cup.

He looked at it. "That's five more than we agreed on."

"That's right," said Gaetano. "At least the mook can count."

"Five extra are for yesterday." I didn't look at Gaetano as I spoke. "And tomorrow we'll start earlier and sell more. So it'll take more of your time. So we'll put more in your cup." I turned and picked up the empty basket.

"You got some weird ways," Gaetano said. "But you're the king. If that's the way you want to play it, okay. Give me the money now."

"It's a dollar and seventy-five cents," I said, tightening my arms around the basket.

"I can count."

"It's way too much to keep in your pocket overnight."

"You're the one who gets robbed, not me."

"Grandinetti could keep it for us," I said.

"We already talked about that," Gaetano growled. "No. Turn it over. Now."

I gave him the money. "Can you spare a penny?"

Gaetano wiped his mouth and looked at me. "If you take a penny, that leaves us a penny short when we go to buy sandwiches tomorrow."

"I mean one of your own pennies. Can you spare one?"

He turned his head away. Then he handed me a penny without even looking at me. "When we split the profits, you owe me." He walked off.

I returned the basket and towel to Grandinetti, checked my shoes into baggage at the train station, and went to Central Park for the night.

CHAPTER SEVENTEEN

Things Go Wrong

We'd made a whole dollar and seventy-five cents. It was like the difference between the sun and the moon—as Uncle Aurelio said. Getting rich in America was easy after all. By my calculations, even after setting aside sandwiches for ourselves (including Grandinetti) on Wednesday, we'd still have two dozen to sell. I went to sleep as happy as anyone curled under a bush in Central Park could be.

But at lunchtime Wednesday it poured in a burst. By the time we managed to take cover under an awning, the top layers of sandwiches in our basket were soaked through so bad, the bread was coming apart. The bottom and side sandwiches were a little soggy. Only four sandwiches from the middle were perfect.

We threw away the bread from the soaked

sandwiches and ate the insides as breakfast. Gaetano wanted to do the same with the soggy ones, too.

"Sell the soggy ones for ten cents each," said Tin Pan Alley. "The secretaries can buy them. At least we come away with something."

"That's mook thinking," said Gaetano. "If we sell a lousy product, we ruin our reputation."

"You think you sound like some kind of hotshot, talking like that," said Tin Pan Alley.

"Hold on." I turned to Tin Pan Alley. "You were the one who said people have to trust food vendors. They trust us so far. If we sell bad stuff, we lose that."

Tin Pan Alley blinked. "Are you on his side now?"

"All I want is to sell sandwiches. Wet sandwiches won't bring us more customers."

"They're not that wet." Tin Pan Alley spat on the ground. He wouldn't look at us. "Okay, then give them to me."

"Pig," said Gaetano. "We'll split them equally."

"You can each take two—one for lunch and one for dinner. But I get the rest."

Tin Pan Alley was the skinniest of us, but still . . . "You're going to get sick," I said.

"I want them."

Gaetano crossed his arms at his chest. "All right. Go puke. But only if we don't have to put money in your cup today."

"Deal," said Tin Pan Alley.

"I'll go patrol," said Gaetano.

"It's okay today. All day long. My *padrone* went to Staten Island. I overheard him tell someone."

So we sold the four good sandwiches, then left Tin Pan Alley with six soggy ones.

Gaetano and I walked toward Five Points. We had soggy sandwiches in our pockets, and I had the day's earnings in my fist—a whole dollar. Plus the penny I'd already borrowed from Gaetano for baggage check that night. But about halfway to Grandinetti's I stopped.

"You think he'll make eighty cents by the end of today?"

"That's his problem."

"He's our partner. You even said so. So his problems are our problems."

"How do we really know he's our partner?" said Gaetano. "Maybe he's not going to eat himself sick. Maybe he's selling those sandwiches right now."

"You know he isn't."

Gaetano smirked. "You'll never be a shark, you know that, Dom? You can do the numbers, but you don't have a head for business." He held out his hand with a resigned look on his face.

I gave Gaetano seventy-five cents and the basket to return to Grandinetti. Then I ran back to put twenty-five in Tin Pan Alley's cup.

He wasn't on his corner.

I crossed the street and walked slowly up and down the blocks, listening for his triangle. I never heard him.

When I got to Chatham Square, I saw a boy sitting on a curb ravenously eating a sandwich—one of our soggy ones. He had a small harp wedged under his knees and a tin cup between his feet. He was the boy I'd talked to before, the one with the welts.

I thought of beggar boys all over town eating soggy

sandwiches and feeling like some spirit had blessed them. Munaciello's good counterpart. Nonna would have loved Tin Pan Alley. Before I could think twice, I dropped the twenty-five cents in the boy's cup. He gaped at me. Then he quick tucked the cup between his belly and his knees and went back to eating.

It felt rotten to go to sleep on Wednesday with less money than the night before. We were going backward fast. A thousand sandwiches. How would we ever sell that many? How would I ever make enough money to get home?

I thought of how Mamma used to stand at the window and wave to me when I'd go somewhere with Uncle Aurelio. I felt like she was waving to me that night—waving and calling—only I was too far away to see or hear her. I had to fight to get back to her.

Thursday went okay—so okay, in fact, that at the end of the day we each kept a dime for ourselves. Friday was the same. No thieves or rain. No *padrone.*

The only trouble we had was with the price. Tin Pan Alley would say it clearly. And men who were alone generally paid up, especially if they had suits on. But when there were two men together, or when someone was buying a few sandwiches at once, they gave us a bunch of coins and left fast. The faster they left, the less it turned out they'd paid for each sandwich. And women generally paid less, too, though usually they bargained. That was okay, though. After all, no one but the top guys could really afford twenty-five cents. It was either give a few breaks or lose customers.

Still, by the end of the lunch crowd on Friday, even after putting the money in Tin Pan Alley's cup, we had three dollars and sixty cents.

"Think how many sandwiches we can buy tomorrow," said Gaetano. "It's going to be a good week after all."

"The week is over," I said. "No work on Saturday."

"But Saturday's a workday," Gaetano said. Then he stopped. "I could use a day off."

Tin Pan Alley didn't say anything. I wondered if he ever got a day off.

"A buck a week for a couple of hours' work a day—not bad. Hand over the money," said Gaetano. "I'm about to buy me a steak."

"A buck and twenty cents each," said Tin Pan Alley, putting out his hand, too.

"Hold on." I clamped my hands down on both pockets. "We need something to start next week with."

"A quarter," said Gaetano. "That's what we started this week with."

"Just listen," I said. "If we each take only twenty cents now, we can eat okay Saturday and Sunday, and we'll still have three whole dollars to start Monday with. There's no telling how much money we can make next week if we start with that much." I was already counting the sandwiches we could sell. Why, Monday alone, if luck was on our side, we could eat, and still sell forty-four sandwiches. That couldn't be so. I did the numbers again.

Tin Pan Alley was staring off into the distance. When he turned to me, he nodded and I knew he'd done the numbers, too.

"This is just good business," I said reasonably.

"And you're both out of your minds," said Gaetano. "What's the point of working all the time and never having any fun? Give me my money."

"You'll make a lot more by the end of next week," said Tin Pan Alley almost in a whisper.

"How much more?"

"Tons," I said.

"Aw, come on, guys." Gaetano crossed his arms. "Twenty cents is too little to have any real fun. We have to take at least fifty each." His feet were spread; he was ready for battle.

I thought about it. "Okay, that'll leave us two dollars and ten cents. The extra ten cents won't buy a sandwich. We can put it in Tin Pan Alley's cup."

Tin Pan Alley's eyes shot open wide. "I didn't ask for it."

"You have to work this weekend. We don't."

The first thing I did with my money was pay back Gaetano the three cents I'd borrowed to check my shoes. Then I set aside seven more cents to pay for my shoes for the next week.

I spent the weekend in Central Park, eating popcorn and meat on sticks. Forty cents went a long way.

Monday we discovered the problem with buying two dollars' worth of sandwiches: once we cut them and wrapped them up nice, the basket couldn't hold them all. So Gaetano carried the basket with most of them, and I carried an armful.

When we got to the bottom of Mulberry Street, I dropped one. Gaetano was already crossing the street, and he didn't see. I could pick it up fast and wipe off the paper and no one would know the difference.

I shifted the others to one arm, reached down with my free hand, and dropped two more. A dog appeared out of nowhere and ran off with one. Then something knocked me from behind, and my chin smacked hard on the sidewalk. I rolled over in time to see the two thieves make off with the rest of my sandwiches.

By the time I caught up to Gaetano, he was halfway down the next block.

"What happened? Where are the sandwiches?"

"A dog got one. And the two thieves got the others. I guess your big brother isn't protecting you anymore."

"Sure he is. He's just not protecting you. You have to stay by my side or they can get you." He cocked his head at me. "Cheer up. We've still got a basketful to sell. Find some paper in that pile of trash and wipe off your chin. No one's going to buy from a bleeding kid."

While Gaetano patrolled the area, Tin Pan Alley and I sold twenty-three sandwiches, clearing four dollars and sixty cents after putting twenty-five in Tin Pan Alley's cup. A great day.

Gaetano put out his hand. "A dollar. Right now."

"We agreed to go another week."

"We doubled our money in one day. I want my dollar."

I threw up my hands and let them slap to my sides. "If everything went just right—if everyone paid us twenty-five cents and if we sold every sandwich—our money wouldn't just double in a day, it would grow by . . ." I thought. "Four times!" The numbers were staring me in the face. "We've got to keep the money in there till the end of the week." That was the fastest way to get to a thousand sandwiches.

"Oh, all right." Gaetano crossed his arms. "Give me twenty cents."

On Tuesday we bought sixteen long sandwiches. Pierano's eyes practically popped out of his head. He gave me a breakfast pastry, and one for Gaetano, too, who was out on the sidewalk looking in through the window. When I dared to mention we worked with a third guy, Pierano dropped another pastry in the bag.

Once we cut the sandwiches, we were way past what the bushel basket could hold. We begged Grandinetti to lend us his one-wheeled handcart. He wasn't happy about it, but so long as we got it back to him by three o'clock, with the towel, it was okay. And he smiled when we gave him a sandwich.

Gaetano pushed the cart and I walked beside him. The mound of sandwiches under the towel was impressive—more than sixty. I watched it proudly. Mamma, here I come.

At the bottom of Mulberry Street, I was on the lookout for that dog and the two thieves. They weren't around. But four little boys—the oldest couldn't have been more than six—came up begging. They had on nothing but short pants. I tried to shoo them away. Gaetano bumped the cart down the curb and crossed the street as though they weren't there.

As he was maneuvering the cart up the other curb, one of the urchins pulled off the towel and they all grabbed sandwiches with both hands and ran back through the traffic across the street. I raced after them, but they split up. I ran back to Gaetano.

"You didn't catch any of them?" he practically shouted.

"I didn't want to leave you alone, with no one to help you guard the cart."

"Yeah, like you're some big help." Gaetano pushed the cart fast, his bottom lip thrust forward.

"We've still got gobs to sell," I said.

But he fumed all the way to Wall Street.

Tin Pan Alley ate the pastry from Pierano's while Gaetano went on and on about what a mess I'd made of things, his temples pulsing.

"Why are you so mad?" I finally said. "You didn't act like this when the thieves jumped me yesterday."

"This is a lot worse, you mook. When those *scugnizzi* tell all the other *scugnizzi* we're easy targets, we'll be mobbed every morning."

"So let's just tell the *scugnizzi* about your big brother."

"You think they don't know? Those kids listen to everything. But, you see, big brothers don't beat up *scugnizzi*. They're too little."

"My *padrone* doesn't care how old someone is," said Tin Pan Alley. "He beats anyone."

"Exactly," said Gaetano. "A *padrone* is the lowest of the low. My big brother is honorable."

His big brother. Who didn't even exist.

Gaetano stomped off, scowling, to patrol the area, while Tin Pan Alley and I waited for the lunch crowd to come trickling out of the buildings.

But today they rushed, and they didn't give us a second glance. A woman who'd been our customer twice before scurried past with a cloth sack full of small banners on sticks.

"What's going on?" I asked Tin Pan Alley.

He ran after the woman and they talked.

When Gaetano realized something was wrong, he joined me at the cart.

Tin Pan Alley came back, his face striken. "It's Flag Day."

"Never heard of it," said Gaetano.

179

"It's celebrating the country."

"You mook, Independence Day's not till July."

"You're the mook. It's Flag Day. Some new thing. The woman said so. Everyone's going to the public schools to see their kids march in a parade holding little flags."

"Do you know where the schools are?" I asked Gaetano.

Gaetano smirked. "Around here? What do you think?"

"It doesn't matter, anyway," said Tin Pan Alley. "Lunch is part of the celebration."

We watched as more customers went on by.

Gaetano kicked the sidewalk. "So what are we supposed to do with all this food?"

"Not everyone has kids." I took the handles and pushed the cart a few steps. "Let's go door-to-door to the little businesses. I pass tons of them on the way to Central Park every night."

"No one's going to pay what Wall Street pays," said Tin Pan Alley. "The rest of the world is poor."

"So let them pay less," said Gaetano. "Otherwise, the whole day is a flop. And since you"—he pointed at me—"and you"—he pointed at Tin Pan Alley—"wouldn't let us keep back any of yesterday's profits, that means good-bye, business." He grabbed the cart handles from me and rolled back toward Five Points. "Come on," he called over his shoulder.

"I can't leave," said Tin Pan Alley. "My *padrone*."

Gaetano stopped and turned around with a bulldog face. "We need you to speak English. Get over here."

Tin Pan Alley didn't move.

"Sandwiches," I said in English. "The best in town."

"Please," Tin Pan Alley said to me in English.

180

"What's that mean?"

"It's a good word. When you walk into a store, begin with *please*. And end with *thank you*."

I knew what *thank you* meant. "Please," I said. "Thank you." I gave Tin Pan Alley two sandwiches—one for lunch, one for dinner—but I didn't have any coins to put in his cup.

Gaetano and I rolled up the street. We stopped in every little store we passed, all the way to Chatham Square. Then we went around the edge of Five Points, to avoid the *scugnizzi*, and back along Canal Street. Then north along the route I took to the train station. It was well past lunchtime when we stopped to eat. We'd sold all but ten sandwiches. Most for ten cents. But sometimes we were lucky and got fifteen.

I chewed on a cheese sandwich and looked over at the last ones on the cart. My heart fell. "What'll we do with the rest?"

"If I have to eat another of these sandwiches for dinner," said Gaetano, "I'll puke." He jammed the rest of his in his mouth. "I dreamed of sandwiches last night."

I believed him; I had, too. "We could give them away."

"No one would take them. They'd figure there was something wrong with them."

We looked at each other and burst out laughing.

So we kept hawking, even though it was the middle of the afternoon. We sold two more. Then I told Gaetano about what Tin Pan Alley had done with the soggy sandwiches the Wednesday before, and we walked around putting sandwiches in the cups of beggar boys.

Once we finally counted our money, we had five dollars and fifteen cents.

Gaetano moved close to me and hunched over so no one could see what was in his hands. He counted the money again. Then he stuck it in his pocket. "I can't believe it. I couldn't believe it yesterday when it grew so fast. But today—with everything that went wrong—it should have gone down to nothing."

"We started the morning with a ton of sandwiches, Gaetano. We couldn't wind up empty-handed."

"But this isn't how money works." Gaetano shook his head. "I know what you said yesterday. All that stuff about quadrupling. But that isn't how money works, really. If you make a dollar one day, you make another dollar the next, not five." He patted the outside of his pocket. "You really think this will keep up?" he whispered.

"If we buy more sandwiches each day, we'll make more money than the day before. Lots more."

"We can't sell more sandwiches. There aren't enough customers at Tin Pan Alley's corner on a regular day."

"You're right. Pretty soon we can save some of our money."

"Or spend it."

Right. We'd sell one thousand sandwiches in no time. The money was coming in. And I'd spend mine on documents and a ticket before long.

CHAPTER EIGHTEEN

Signora Esposito

We crossed the street in stunned silence. Even though I understood the numbers . . . Five dollars and fifteen cents. Wow. "We need a bank," I said finally. "We need Grandinetti."

We went up Mulberry to Grandinetti's without another word. There were a couple of women in the store, and Grandinetti looked at us through the window and shook his head. So we waited out on the sidewalk.

When the customers finally left, I rolled the handcart into the storeroom. I picked loose produce off the floor and arranged it into piles. I jerked my chin toward the corner where the broom stood. Gaetano took the broom and swept. Neither of us said anything.

Grandinetti scratched the back of his neck and

watched us. Then he took out a pencil and walked around the store, making a check of inventory. Finally, he brushed his hands off and put them on his hips. "Okay, I get it. You're trying to make up, but it won't work."

Make up? And suddenly I realized. "I'm sorry we were late."

"And where's my towel?"

"Some kids stole it."

"That's it," said Grandinetti. "I can't lend you my things anymore. They're too important to me."

"How much does the handcart cost?" asked Gaetano.

"I traded for it—used. But to replace it, I'd have to pay two dollars and fifty cents."

"Let us keep it," said Gaetano. He put two dollars and fifty cents on the counter. "Buy a new cart. It's a good deal for you."

I gulped.

Gaetano reached in his pocket again. "And, hey, here's ten more cents for the towel."

Grandinetti blinked. "How'd you get so much money?"

"The sandwich business is good," said Gaetano.

"That good?"

Gaetano emptied his pockets onto the counter.

"Will you keep our money for us at night?" I said.

Grandinetti slowly counted it. "Give it to your mother."

"He can't," said Gaetano. "She's not here."

"You told me you don't have a father." Grandinetti wiped his nose with the back of his hand. "Now is Gaetano saying you don't have a mother, either?"

"Sure I have a mother," I said. "In Napoli."

Grandinetti threw up his hands. "I'm not getting mixed

up with a *padrone*. If you don't want to give the money to your *padrone*, you'll have to find some other solution."

"I don't have a *padrone*."

Grandinetti stared at me. "You're alone?"

"I've got Gaetano," I said. "And Tin Pan Alley."

"Who?"

"Another kid," said Gaetano.

"Where's your father?" Grandinetti asked Gaetano.

"Dead."

I winced.

"And your mother?"

"She died when I was born."

I clenched my teeth to keep from making a noise. Poor Gaetano. Had he come to America with his father, and then had his father died on him? But I could never ask him. I stared at the floor.

"Let me get this straight. You boys are on your own? Neither one of you has family or a *padrone* here?"

We didn't say anything.

"Where do you sleep?"

"I used to have a barrel," I said. "But now I sleep in the park."

Grandinetti looked at Gaetano. "And you?"

"I take care of myself."

Grandinetti shook his head in disgust. "There's too much of this going on. Too many kids on their own." He put the money back in Gaetano's hand. "Here's what you do. Cross the street and go to number forty-four, one flight up. Rent a room from Signora Esposito."

"How much does a room cost?" I asked.

"It's not a real boardinghouse. She has one extra room.

Tiny. Offer her two dollars a week per person, with dinner included."

"We can't afford that," said Gaetano.

"Did you really earn this money?"

"Yes."

"Are you planning on earning more?"

"Yes."

"Then what are you talking about? It's half the price of even the cheapest boardinghouses." Grandinetti handed us each a plum. "Now get out of here. I'm going to stand in this doorway and watch. Go to the widow's. I mean it. If you sleep outdoors with money in your pockets, you'll wake with empty pockets—if you have any clothes on at all, that is."

We walked up Mulberry, reading the numbers.

Gaetano checked over his shoulder. "Grandinetti's still watching us."

"It doesn't matter whether he watches or not," I said. "He's right. We're going to keep earning money. We need a safe place at night. A home."

"Wherever I am is my home."

"That's what you say. I saw the policeman chasing you."

Gaetano looked stung. "What I have is a lot better than the park."

"I hope so." Here it was: number forty-four. I opened the door.

Gaetano stopped on the sidewalk.

Signora Esposito had an apartment one flight up. Was she young? As young as Mamma? Her hair was bound to be black. But was it wavy or curly? Did her hands rest easy or was she always crocheting or chopping vegetables? Was she fat? Thin? Tall? Short? Were there other people there? Children? Did they have things to play with?

It felt like forever since I'd been in a real home. I had to see this one. And she had to take us in. "Come on."

"I'll look. One quick look. That's all." Gaetano followed me up the stairs.

I knocked on the first door. No one answered.

"There's another door," said Gaetano.

So we went to the second door and knocked.

"Who's there?" came a high voice. It wavered, like a singer's. I imagined her willowy and graceful.

"Dom and Gaetano," I said. "Grandinetti—the fruit vendor—he sent us."

The sound of a chain being unlatched came from the other side of the door. I held my breath.

And there she was: the widow I'd seen in Grandinetti's last Monday morning—the one who had watched him like a hawk, as though he was going to cheat her. She had on a robe and her face wasn't powdered, but she still looked scary, like a ghost. "What do you want?" said the hag.

I couldn't speak. Gaetano gave me a little punch in the kidneys. *"Aiii,"* burst from me. "Grandinetti said you might have a room for rent."

She examined Gaetano from head to toe. Then me. When she got to my shoes, she nodded. "My children are grown. There's three beds in the room." She stepped back. "Well, are you going to come in or not?" She patted her hair nervously. It was black with gray streaks and it looked hard and dry as straw.

The door opened into her kitchen. A pot of bones simmered on the stove. I wondered if she'd collected them

187

from garbage cans. We followed her across a dark, cluttered living room and down to the end of a narrow hall. She opened a door.

It was a sunny room with a set of drawers, three beds, a tattered rug. The mirror was chipped. The sheets were patched. The wallpaper hung free in one corner. There was no extra space anywhere. Everything in the room felt old and well used and homey. You could sleep in that room without wondering what might crawl over you in the night.

"We'll take it," said Gaetano. "A dollar fifty a week, with dinner."

I glared at Gaetano. He'd seen the pot of bones, too. He knew she was poor.

She pulled on a limp lock of hair. "A dollar fifty won't pay for dinner every night."

"Two dollars," I said. "Each."

She pursed her lips and now her eyes grew shrewd. "That's still not much."

"And we'll do odd jobs." I pointed at the wallpaper. "You could use extra hands around here."

She put out her palm. "Four dollars total, then. Due every Tuesday."

Gaetano stepped in front of me. "Is dinner ready?"

"What do you think I am, a fortune-teller? I had no idea you'd be coming tonight. There's barely enough for me."

"Then we'll pay tomorrow night," said Gaetano. "At dinner. And we'll pay less this time because we're getting one meal less. We'll pay three dollars."

Signora Esposito sucked in her breath. I could see in her eyes she was trying to figure out if she was getting cheated.

"Three fifty," I said.

"Very well."

So that night I stretched out in a bed. Back in Napoli I'd slept on two chairs pushed together. Since then I'd slept in all kinds of places: the floor under Eduardo's bunk on the cargo ship, the top deck of the *Città di Napoli,* the barrel, Central Park.

A bed. My own bed. I put my shirt and pants neatly in a drawer, careful to keep my underthings on—Mamma had said, "Don't undress with anyone around"—and slid beween the clean sheets.

We had plenty of money to start out our business day in the morning. Lunch the next day would be a sandwich. And dinner would be whatever Signora Esposito made, which was bound to be something different from a Pierano sandwich.

"Everything's going our way," I whispered into the night air.

Gaetano didn't answer. I could tell from his breathing that he wasn't asleep. But if he wanted to pretend, that was okay with me. Maybe I'd spooked him. After all, you could invite bad fortune merely by thinking life was good.

I rolled on my side. The mattress yielded, like the stuffing in the chairs back in Napoli. The bed frame creaked. Had the chairs creaked when I rolled back home? I couldn't remember. How could that be?

Panic made my throat narrow. I had trouble breathing. I sat up in the dark to try to get more air. I should still remember everything about Napoli. Every detail. How long had I been gone? Was it two months? I could remember if I tried hard enough.

Okay, I'd start with Nonna's proverbs. I imagined her sitting at the kitchen table, crocheting, her tiny hands moving so fast, saying, *"O cane mozzeca 'o stracciato"*—The dog bites whoever dresses in rags. I lay on my stomach and reached under my pillow to rest my hands on my shoes. These shoes kept me from looking like I was dressed in rags. Signora Esposito had given us the room because of them. One more way these shoes had paved my path.

A recipe now, I could remember a recipe for sure. Spaghetti puttanesca. Aunt Sara made it best. She put tomatoes in a bowl and poured boiling water over them. In another bowl she put our secret ingredient—a couple of handfuls of raisins, with boiling water over them, too. She pitted black olives and sliced them. And chopped a few cloves of garlic. Then put olive oil in the pan and crushed in a couple of dried red peppers. When the pepper smoke made us cough, she added anchovy fillets, smushing them with the back of a spoon till they came apart in the oil. Then the olives and garlic and a spoonful of capers. She peeled the tomatoes—the skin came off easy after they'd been sitting in the hot water—and cut them into the pan with a pinch of salt. She drained the raisins and threw them in. And it was done. Ready to pour over spaghetti with chopped parsley on top.

I was remembering everything. Breath came easy now. I could remember.

I could see Uncle Vittorio, tall and thin and sallow. I could feel the thick calluses on the scoop of palm between his thumb and first finger on both hands, from holding that broom he swept the streets with every night. I could smell horse in Uncle Aurelio's hair and see the burn scars from the smithy fire on his knuckles. I could see Aunt Rebecca tucking my cousins into bed, and Luigi and Ernesto protesting—"Just one more story!" She'd sit on the edge of the bed, her jutting jaw moving slowly as she told about a silly man who saw the reflection of the moon in a pond and thought the moon itself was in the water. The whole of her wide girth would jiggle when she laughed.

And, at last, I saw Mamma. The inside of my nose prickled with held-back tears. Mamma in front of a window, light flooding around her. She was beautiful and warm and soft and strong and anise-sweet. And she was crying.

I had to work hard and earn my ticket fast. One thousand sandwiches. That wasn't so far away now—not at this rate. And I had to spend the last hour of every day going over everything I could remember from Napoli so that I'd recognize it all when I finally got home. That way it would be just as though I'd never been gone at all.

She'd be proud of me when I got home, proud to know I'd been my own boss.

I pressed the heels of my hands on my eyelids.

"You okay?" Gaetano sat up now.

I didn't answer.

"What you told Grandinetti, about having a mother back in Napoli, well . . . I figured she was dead. You know, died on the ship over. A lot of women do." He went silent.

"She's not dead. She paid my passage on a cargo ship."

"Cargo ships don't take passengers. Oh! You mean you were a stowaway. She put you as a stowaway, all alone! What kind of mother would do a thing like that?"

191

"What are you saying? That's not how it was. She was supposed to come with me, but this bad guy on the cargo ship wouldn't let her."

"What'd he do to her?"

"I don't know. He told me to go hide and he said he'd hide her someplace else. And then she was gone."

"Sounds like she wanted you to go alone."

"Don't say that!"

"You said it yourself."

"I did not. You stinker!"

"You said she paid your passage. She didn't pay her own passage."

"That's not true! Shut up!" My heart was beating so hard, I couldn't hear anything else. I dropped back on my pillow and listened to the drum in my head.

After a long time, Gaetano said, "Yeah, what do I know?" He lay down on his side. "Good night, Dom."

My head was finally quiet.

Why did I tell Gaetano that Mamma had paid for my passage instead of saying our passage? Was that really what I'd heard her tell Franco when she was arguing with him? I couldn't remember.

I went over that last morning in Italy. Mamma dressed me in my Sabbath clothes, with my new socks and shoes. Like a traveler. She wore an ordinary dress. And she carried nothing extra. No bundle of treasures, none of the things that the immigrants at Ellis Island carried.

But I was her treasure. I was all she needed.

She didn't mean for me to go alone. No one would think a nine-year-old could make it on his own. Sure, Rosaria, Tonino's oldest daughter, was taking care of her four

192

younger brothers while he made his fortune in America—
and she was my age. But Rosaria had neighbors and relatives who looked in on her. I was alone. Mamma would
never have stowed me away alone.

The smell of a citronella candle came through the open
window. And I remembered Mamma crying. She had cried
for three nights in a row. I was going to ask her why, but
each morning when we woke, I'd forget.

The heels of my hands pressed so hard on my eyeballs,
I saw white inside my head.

"Chi tene mamma, nun chiagne"—Whoever has a mother
doesn't cry. One of Nonna's proverbs.

I had a mother. And she hadn't put me on the boat
alone on purpose. She wouldn't have. She couldn't have.

She loved me. Mamma loved me.

I got out of bed and shut the window.

CHAPTER NINETEEN

A Way of Life

I woke up early and staggered in the dark through the apartment door to the bathroom out in the hall. I felt like a king on a throne—ha! The king of Mulberry Street, doing my business in the right kind of place again. No more hiding behind bushes.

The door opened while I was finishing up.

"What? Who's there? What do you think you're doing here?" A man swiped me on the shoulder, knocking me to the floor. My cheek hit something sharp. "Get out of here, you ruffian!" He kicked me in the side. He grabbed me by the elbow and threw me out in the hall.

"Help!" I screamed.

"Out, out, out!" He pulled me up by the hair and dragged me to the top of the steps.

"Stop!" Signora Esposito came running and blocked the stairwell. "Let go of him!"

"He was in the bathroom. A hoodlum in our bathroom!"

"That's no hoodlum. That's Dom. Let go!"

"Dom?"

"He's renting a room from me. Dom. And his friend, Gaetano."

The man let go of my hair. "My mistake." He brushed off his hands as though I'd gotten him dirty. "Next time, let a person know when there's someone new around."

"Next time ask before you beat someone senseless." Signora Esposito took me by the hand and pulled me inside.

She roughly washed the cut on my cheek and tsked. "Look at that."

"It doesn't hurt," I lied. It had been a long time since anyone had fussed over me, even gruffly. If she kept it up, I might cry.

She took out a bottle of red-brown tincture and smeared it on me.

I tensed up. But it didn't even sting.

"When's the last time you cleaned yourself?"

I shrugged.

"Tonight after dinner take a sponge bath in the kitchen sink."

"Thank you. I might do that."

"You will do that," she said.

When Gaetano finally woke, he took one look at my face and let out a low whistle.

So I told him the whole story, maybe exaggerating a bit

for sympathy. I held the darkening bruise on my elbow under his nose.

"You look terrible." Gaetano looked like he was fighting a smile. "He beat you up in the bathroom. That's awful, but . . ." He laughed. Then he jumped out of bed and clapped his hands. "This is great. This is exactly what we needed."

"What are you talking about?"

"You'll see."

We went to Pierano's and bought ten long sandwiches. He didn't throw in free pastries that day, but he did ask me about my cut. I shrugged. Later, when Grandinetti asked, I told him. Some things only friends could understand.

The mound of sandwiches on the cart was smaller than it had been the day before. But who cared? This was our cart—ours.

It was on Park Street that I realized the two thieves were following us on the other side of the street.

"Hey . . . ," I said to Gaetano.

"I know." At the corner he crossed—but toward the thieves. He beckoned them over.

They walked up, Maurizio taking the lead. "Where you taking those sandwiches every day?"

"Not that far," said Gaetano. "You know any little kids that need a job?"

Maurizio smoothed back his hair. "Who's hiring?"

"The boss." Gaetano jerked his chin toward my cheek and held out my arm so the bruise showed. "And spread the word: he doesn't put up with monkey business."

Maurizio smiled meanly. "You have a *padrone*! I never thought you'd go that way, of all people."

"Hell no," Gaetano yelped. "Boss—not *padrone*." He moved closer to Maurizio. *"Chi tene 'a libertà è ricco e nun 'o sape"*—Whoever is free is rich, though he doesn't know it.

"Who is it? Who's your boss?"

Gaetano just looked at him.

"Someone from outside Five Points?"

"We got to go. Oh, here. From the boss." Gaetano gave Maurizio two sandwiches. "And something for your little friends." He gave him four more.

Maurizio stood there with his arms full, gaping.

"That's the last time. Understand? I'm counting on you to keep those kids in line." We walked off.

"You didn't even introduce me," I said.

"It wasn't a social call. Anyway, they know your name. You won't get jumped again. And no *scugnizzi* will come near this cart."

Between the sandwiches Gaetano gave away and the ones we ate, Tin Pan Alley and I had only thirty to sell. But they all went, most for full price. At the end of the day, Gaetano and I went back to Signora Esposito's with six dollars and ten cents.

We set aside two dollars and fifty cents for starting the next day. After paying our room and board, we had only ten cents left. And we owed Tin Pan Alley his share of the day's profits.

But Thursday and Friday went fine. Just the usual annoyances—people who paid less than full price; a man who dropped his sandwich, then demanded another for free.

In the next month, business grew so fast, it was like an eruption of Mount Vesuvio. It felt as though Wall

Street had been doing nothing but waiting for our sandwiches.

Part of what made it work was that Gaetano was a champion patroller. He spotted Tin Pan Alley's *padrone* every time, and whisked me and the cart away fast.

And part of what made it work was that Tin Pan Alley listened, and he told us everything, and we learned. One day one of the men who had bought a sandwich going into work that morning came back and asked for a second at a reduced price. He offered fifteen cents. We settled on eighteen. He said he'd eaten the first one as his breakfast.

That afternoon I dragged Gaetano with me to Mott Street to talk the Cassone grandma into making a potato and fried egg sandwich on a long loaf—with rosemary and pepper—specially for us the next morning. We paid her twenty-five cents. When we picked it up, the bread was jammed full. We figured most people couldn't eat even a quarter of such heavy stuff that early in the morning, so we cut it into six pieces to sell for twenty cents each. It was a gamble—but all we had to do was sell two of the six pieces to come out on top. We wound up selling them for twelve cents—but we sold out.

We ordered two breakfast sandwiches from Old Lady Cassone for the next day. And more after that. And the next week, we added breakfast pastries to the cart. That was Gaetano's idea. For some crazy reason, people would say egg sandwiches were too rich, then they'd turn right around and buy cannoli stuffed with ricotta. They bought all of it. Pierano now sold us sandwiches cheaper—twenty-three cents each—because we bought so many.

After the breakfast shift, Gaetano and I ran back to Park

Street to get ready for the lunch crowd, which was much bigger.

One noon, in midsummer, a man in a regular top hat and sporting a small, neat beard asked me if any of our sandwiches came without cheese. By this time I spoke half-decent English when it came to sandwiches. Gaetano was at my side. He understood well enough by then, too, and he muttered to me in Napoletano that the guy ought to learn how to pick out the cheese. The man wasn't Italian, and I doubt he understood a word of what Gaetano said, but he understood the tone. He went away without waiting for my answer. There was something about him. It wasn't just his way of walking or dressing or his beard or that look of being offended on his face—it was all of those things together. I made a guess about him.

The next day I watched for the man. When I saw him come out of a building, I ran over. "What kind meat you want?" I asked in English.

"Beef," he said. "Just beef."

"Polish?" I asked.

He looked alarmed. "Why do you say that? I'm not Polish."

"Polish beef—it is best," I said.

He hesitated. Then he said, "That's true."

"Come tomorrow," I said. "But you got buy three sandwiches. That how we make—three at a time." It wasn't true. But I figured I'd eat the fourth one.

"I can buy three," he said. "Friends will eat them."

When I went back to the cart, Tin Pan Alley whispered to me, "There's a Polish butcher on Baxter Street."

Surprised, I moved close to him so Gaetano couldn't

hear us. "How'd you do that? How'd you guess what he wanted?"

"Same way you did, probably."

So I learned that Gaetano had been wrong about Five Points; it wasn't only Italians. Just as Chinese were moving in to Mott Street, Poles were moving in, too—Jews. And Grandinetti had told me Five Points had been Irish before it was Italian.

We sold a fair number of kosher sandwiches after that. Only, Tin Pan Alley didn't call them kosher. He called them pure beef, and our eyes locked in understanding when he'd hawk them that way.

Every time I went to Baxter Street to pick up the beef, I passed doorways with *mezuzahs*. Even the butcher shop had a *mezuzah*. My fingers itched to touch them, but I never did. Then I'd run back to Grandinetti's, stopping at the bakery for loaves, and I'd pile the sandwiches high with beef and rings of red onion. Gaetano didn't give me any trouble about it, even though he found out pretty fast where I bought the beef. Business was business.

In the late afternoon we sold produce from Grandinetti's. The Wall Street workers would buy a single carrot, two tomatoes, a handful of lettuce leaves. Our customers were happy with the vegetables. When I told Grandinetti, he said Germans and Irish and Swedes and all of them might know how to make money, but they had never known how to eat. Italians, now, Italians, they knew how to eat. He said, "That's how we'll change America." Gaetano laughed, but Grandinetti was serious. It was his big dream—to teach America how to eat.

It was summer, and everything grew. But we could look

ahead and see that we'd better figure out new things to sell if we wanted to have customers in autumn. So we added candied almonds and other sweets.

We learned, sometimes the hard way. Once we got rained out. We had bought an oilcloth and we kept it in the cart so we could cover everything at the first drop. But this rain lasted all through the lunch hour and all afternoon, and almost no one came out to buy. After that we scanned the sky before going into Pierano's.

Another time a wheel broke off the front of our cart on the way to Wall Street and half the load fell in the gutter, ruined. So we began checking the cart.

We brought leftovers home to Signora Esposito. At first the widow cooked bad. Her habits were stingy. Her white face wasn't powdered—it was floured. Flour cost less than powder. And her strong perfume covered the fact that she hardly ever washed, to save on water and soap. But once she learned to count on our rent, she bought better food and turned out to be a pretty good cook. She smiled sometimes. And she even started to use an iron to curl her hair when she went to church.

The best thing about her was that I asked her never to make pork or horsemeat or shellfish, and she didn't say a word about it to Gaetano. I was so grateful, I bought her rhinestone clips for her hair. The funny thing was, on that same day Gaetano bought her a box of real talcum. I don't know what secret she was keeping for him.

By late summer the cart was too full to keep racing off whenever Gaetano spotted the *padrone*. And it upset our customers. So we set up across the street, catty-corner to Tin Pan Alley. He hawked for us on his side, and I hawked

201

on the other. Gaetano still patrolled most of the time, but whenever he saw the *padrone*, all he had to do was signal Tin Pan Alley to play his triangle.

Having all those customers made another change for us—a funny one, because what Gaetano had made up that day, telling Maurizio that our "boss" needed more kids, turned out to be true. Sometimes the orders came in such a rush that Gaetano had to quit patrolling and Tin Pan Alley had to cross the street and still the three of us couldn't fill them fast enough. We hired kids from Five Points to help. Usually Michele, Nicola, and Roberto. They were brothers about a year apart. They worked fast. But more important, they were honest. It was my job to count up the sums for each transaction—out loud, so customers knew they were getting a fair deal.

All three of us came up with ideas. But somehow I was in charge. Maybe because Gaetano and Tin Pan Alley really didn't like each other. In any case, I was the boss. We never let on about that, of course. Whenever we'd hire a new kid for the day, I'd say something to Gaetano like, "You think the boss would take this one on?"

And Gaetano would answer, "If he can clean up his face and hands good, I bet the boss'll say okay."

No one messed with us; this boss had gotten a grip on Gaetano, the most independent guy in the neighborhood, so he had to be a real terror.

One day we hired an older boy to help out. He demanded twenty-five cents for working the lunch shift, when the little boys were happy with only ten. But he spoke English and he looked clean, so we did it. The very next day he appeared on the same block as us with four sandwiches in his arms. He sold them for twenty cents each. The day after that, he came with twelve sandwiches. We lowered our price to fifteen cents a sandwich. Then ten. Then five. It meant we lost money, so much that we had to pay Signora Esposito in installments. She didn't ask why; she knew the code, too—don't ask. But we could afford to lose money for a while, and the other boy couldn't. He disappeared, and our prices went back up.

Gaetano still wouldn't speak English no matter what. Once we stepped out of Five Points, I did the talking.

Tin Pan Alley still played his triangle and whistled when we were off restocking the cart. He didn't have to, though. By this point we put as much as he needed in his cup at the end of the day to make eighty cents. He was a great hawker. He wore a smile all the time and was friendly with the customers.

We never worked on Saturday, the Sabbath. The rest of New York, it seemed, worked six days a week, but not us.

Gaetano didn't complain. He missed his old job of being information man for the neighborhood, so on weekends he eavesdropped and scouted to his heart's content. Weekends were fun time—that was what he said.

Tin Pan Alley didn't complain, either, because he never complained.

I spent Saturday at the wharves, looking at ships. I'd be on one soon enough.

And Sundays, well, I never set foot in a church again, even though Gaetano and Signora Esposito scolded me. I lay on my bed with my pillow over my head and let them blabber. When they finally left for church, I'd go out for an adventure.

Sometimes I stopped in at Catholic mutual aid societies to snatch a few pastries. And during saint festivals I walked happily through the crowds. People sold all sorts of crazy things. But Riccardo, a guy who made girls swoon, sold the very craziest thing. He wore a dark suit, but from his pockets colored ribbons sprouted in profusion. He'd lean toward a woman, who would put her nose to his neck, then drop a coin in his hand. At every *festa* Riccardo sold sniffs of himself.

But mostly I spent my Sundays walking around the island of Manhattan alone. The air was fresh and my stomach was full. Had Mamma gotten an office job yet? If she had, everyone in my family had a full stomach. That was good. That way they wouldn't be so sad all the time from missing me.

CHAPTER TWENTY

Pietro

One lunch shift a big ham of a hand clutched the neck of Tin Pan Alley's shirt.

"Hey," I shouted, looking up.

His *padrone*! He dragged him off. Tin Pan Alley didn't make a squeak.

"Shut up," Gaetano whispered in my ear. "If you make a scene, Tin Pan Alley will pay worse for it. And anyway, you'll embarrass him."

I watched while they disappeared around a corner. Tin Pan Alley didn't look back. My stomach turned. "You think it'll be bad?"

Gaetano just looked at me.

The next morning Tin Pan Alley told us his *padrone* had beaten him for doing something without permission and demanded he bring in two dollars a day from then on. He said Tin Pan Alley could make that much easy working at our cart. He never guessed Tin Pan Alley was getting a third of our profits—all saved in a wooden box back in the bedroom at Signora Esposito's. Tin Pan Alley laughed at that. But when a customer yanked on his shirtsleeve later to get his attention, I saw him wince.

So when the breakfast shift was over, I said, "Pull up your shirt." His open wounds made me gasp. Even Gaetano, who had never said a friendly word to Tin Pan Alley, was so furious, I thought the pulsing in his temples would burst.

That night after supper I sat on my bed in our room and said, "We have to help him escape."

"You're such a mook." Gaetano paced around the small floor. "It might even be illegal." He opened the window higher. "Maybe it would be a kind of kidnapping." He punched his right fist into his left palm. "No one has ever crossed a *padrone* and gotten away with it." He paced some more. Then he stopped and looked away. I wondered how much he really disliked Tin Pan Alley, and how much that dislike was behind his words now. When he finally looked back at me, he said, "But there's always a first time. Come with me."

"Where?"

"Saint Patrick's."

We walked to the cathedral and waited by the side door until Padre Bruno, the Italian priest, made his rounds through the benches that served as pews, checking to see that the basement was empty before blowing out all the candles.

"Father," said Gaetano, "if there was a boy who lived

with a *padrone* and if the *padrone* beat the boy savagely and if that boy should happen to run away, would the church take him in?"

Padre Bruno smoothed his hands over the front of his surplice. "If there were such a boy, then there would be hundreds of such boys. If a church took one in, it would have to take all in. No church could do that." He straightened his sleeves. "And it shouldn't do it, for God, in His almighty wisdom, would take care of such a boy, if there were such a one. God has a plan for such a boy."

"God has a plan?" Gaetano bristled. "Do you really believe there's a divine plan in this boy's being beaten?"

"Yes," said Padre Bruno. "He'll come through it stronger." Even I could tell he was lying.

Gaetano looked away. When he looked back, his face had turned soft. "Please, Father, could we take clothes from the poor bin? We're not asking for charity for ourselves." He shook his head, and I shook mine, too. I didn't believe Padre Bruno was a charitable sort. "No," said Gaetano, "we want to help a family clothe their child's corpse."

For all the business smarts I had, I was a mook about how this sort of thing worked. I didn't get why Gaetano was suddenly lying. It turned out to be a perfect lie, though, because then Padre Bruno gave us an old sheet as well. For the corpse.

Walking home, Gaetano told me he wouldn't go to Saint Patrick's Cathedral anymore. He said, "A priest without faith is like a turd on a cushion. And that church is Padre Bruno's cushion."

The next morning, after the breakfast shift, we told Tin Pan Alley the plan.

"I can't run off."

"He beats you," said Gaetano.

"My *padrone* paid for me to come over from Napoli," said Tin Pan Alley. "I owe him."

"How much did the ticket cost?" I asked.

"I don't know."

"Well, I'll find out," I said. "In the meantime, you'll come live with us. When you've earned enough, you can pay your *padrone* back, if you want."

Tin Pan Alley's eyes darted around, as though he expected his *padrone* to come swooping down. "Where do you sleep?"

"What? You think we live worse than you?" Gaetano's voice shook. "Here we're ready to help, and you're insulting us."

"I just want to know," said Tin Pan Alley.

"We never lived as bad as you, even when Dom slept in a barrel," said Gaetano. "Don't you get it? You're a slave. We're free, you mook."

"I'm not a slave! You take that back."

"We have a room," I said, moving between them. "Real beds. And there's an extra one." A bubble of laughter burst from me in realization. "It's just been sitting there, for you."

"What if my *padrone* finds me? He'll beat me so bad, I won't be able to walk for days. He's done it to others."

"See these clothes?" I said. "They're yours. You'll look different."

"Clothes change nothing," said Tin Pan Alley.

"We could get you girl clothes," I said, my words coming fast. "Your *padrone* would never recognize you."

Tin Pan Alley practically gagged.

"You're nuts." Gaetano made a go-away gesture at me. "Look, Tin Pan Alley, it's not that hard," he said. "You'll just have to stay off the streets till you grow enough that he can't recognize you."

"Signora Esposito can cut his hair," I said. "That'll make him look different."

"You've got the worst ideas, Dom, do you know that?" Gaetano made that go-away gesture at me again, bigger this time. He turned to Tin Pan Alley. "I've got a barber friend. He'll cut your hair good."

"And we'll feed you," I said. "Signora Esposito cooks a lot. After a few weeks, you'll have so much flesh on your bones, he'll never guess it's you."

"What if he comes up while I'm walking away with you now?"

I looked at Gaetano. He shook out the sheet. In an instant, Tin Pan Alley understood. He climbed into the cart and curled up on his side and we covered him entirely. Then we pushed him back to Grandinetti's.

"This is my friend Tin Pan Alley. Please, can he go in your storeroom and change clothes?" I asked.

Grandinetti was busy, so he waved us through the doorway. But a few seconds later, he came into the back to get another bushel of tomatoes. Tin Pan Alley's shirt was off. When Grandinetti saw the marks on Tin Pan Alley's back, he sucked in air through his teeth. He shook his head and went back out to his customer.

After the customer left, I asked Grandinetti, "Can he spend the day here, in your store, helping out?"

Grandinetti put his palm to his forehead and sighed. I

remembered how he'd once told Gaetano and me he'd never get mixed up with a *padrone.*

He came into the storeroom, rubbed his hands with his towel, and said to Tin Pan Alley, "I'm Francesco. What's your real name, boy?"

The question took me by surprise. *Tin Pan Alley* had become his real name to me, just as *Dom* had become my real name in a way. I waited, holding my breath.

"Pietro."

"Pietro?" Grandinetti got a funny look on his face. He reached into a box, broke off a bunch of grapes, and handed them to Pietro. "You're going to have to eat a lot, if you want that flat belly to become round like the Church of San Pietro in Roma."

Gaetano and Grandinetti and I laughed. Pietro stood there a second. Then he smiled and stuffed the whole bunch of grapes in his mouth, stems and all.

Gaetano and I sold the lunch sandwiches, our eyes darting around, searching for Pietro's *padrone.* He didn't show.

That night we brought Pietro back to Signora Esposito's. She took him in without a question, but her eyes were knowing. Don't ask. Don't ask. Everyone has a past that's bad. Don't pry.

The following morning the *padrone* was waiting on Pietro's corner when we set up across the street. He stood by that same lamppost I'd first seen him at, and straightened the brim of his hat and watched us. Even though Pietro was safely back at Signora Esposito's, I shivered. When I stared at the *padrone,* Gaetano pinched me hard and told me not to look at him. But Gaetano was nervous, too; he dropped one of the egg and potato sandwiches.

210

The *padrone* stayed there through our morning sales. He was back again at lunch. And for the evening sales. He never said a word.

The next day he didn't come. At one point someone tapped me on the shoulder and I jumped back with a yelp. But it was just a customer.

The *padrone* didn't come back. Days passed. After a while, I stopped expecting him. I was so happy, I needed to celebrate.

One night, after dinner, when we sat on our mattresses, I pulled out the package I'd hidden under my bed. "There's something for each of you in here. But they wrapped everything in one package. Who wants to open it?"

Gaetano looked away.

Pietro looked down.

"Come on. It's a surprise. Don't you like surprises?" No one answered. What was the matter with them? "It's a celebration. Because Pietro got away from his *padrone*."

Gaetano took the package. "Then it's for you to open, Pietro."

And I got it. I wished so much that I'd asked for two packages. Who knew when Gaetano had last had a surprise to open?

Pietro opened it carefully. He stared. And smiled.

"Shoes?" said Gaetano. He took the larger pair and turned them over in his hands. "I've never walked in shoes."

Pietro already had his on and was circling the small room. "I have," he said almost imperceptibly.

Gaetano pressed the leather with his thumb. "How'd you know the size?"

"I measured with my hand while you were sleeping."

"Who needs shoes?" But Gaetano put them on as he spoke. "How do you tie them?"

So I showed him.

Gaetano stood up. "I can wiggle my toes inside them."

Pietro laughed. "So can I."

And I realized with dismay that I couldn't anymore. My toes were cramped. My feet had grown fast. I'd have to find a way to stretch these shoes, because I was determined to wear them when I went back to Napoli. "Let's go for a walk," I said.

Pietro shook his head. "You think my *padrone*'s given up. But he hasn't. I know him. I'm not leaving this room."

"Then we can walk a hundred steps here," I said. "We can march behind one another in a circle."

"A thousand steps," said Gaetano. "And I'm in front."

After that, Gaetano wore his shoes every day. So did Pietro, though he still wouldn't leave the apartment, until one night Signora Esposito sat down on the bed beside him and slapped him on the knee and said, "Be a philosopher."

We looked at her, dumb as rocks.

"Philosophers are the smartest people around," she said, "and they don't give a fig about their appearance."

This was a little hard to listen to from a woman who powdered her face white every day. But we all wanted to know where it was leading. So we kept our eyes on her.

She got up and went to the door.

"Wait," said Pietro. "What are you talking about? I don't care what I look like."

"Then dress like a girl."

I cringed, but she didn't even look at me, so I don't think Pietro guessed that I'd told her my idea.

"Wait right there." She left and came back a few minutes later with a skirt she'd made out of an old dress. She dropped it on his lap, and she put a checkered kerchief over his hair, tying it under the chin.

As soon as she left the room, Gaetano laughed like a hyena. Pietro ripped off the kerchief. But I jabbed Gaetano with my elbow and begged Pietro to put it back on—and to wear the skirt, too. This time both Gaetano and I managed to keep a straight face.

Pietro walked a half block behind us as we went to Grandinetti's, because he was afraid that if his *padrone* saw me or Gaetano, he'd recognize Pietro, even in the skirt and kerchief, even with shoes on.

Starting that day, Pietro helped Grandinetti run the produce store. The instant he arrived at the store, he ran into the storeroom and slipped off his skirt and kerchief. Then he worked hard. He was good with money, and he was honest.

And the amazing thing was that Pietro was like a different person working beside Grandinetti. He whistled constantly. He greeted the customers and made jokes with them. And, funniest of all, he danced. At closing time, when the store was empty, he'd push the bushels back and tap and twirl. When we asked who had taught him, he clicked his heels and spun away. Over the weeks his face grew fuller and his eyes lost their haunted look.

Pietro spent money a little more easily now. One morning, as Gaetano and I were turning from Bayard onto

Mulberry Street, a Chinese boy stopped us. He was holding a big sack, and I'd seen him selling cigars on that corner before.

"Want to buy something?" said the boy in English. "Cigars? Rock candy?"

"Get away," said Gaetano in Napoletano, though there was no reason to expect the boy to understand it.

"I'll buy a piece," I said to the boy in English. I gave him two pennies and took a piece. "What else you got?"

"Domino games." The boy took out a small black box. "You play? I can teach you."

"Never heard of it," said Gaetano.

"I know how to play." Pietro came up behind us in his skirt. "Is this the Chinese game?"

"Tien Gow is too hard. This game is easy."

Pietro bought it.

When we walked on, Gaetano mumbled, *"Bastardo."*

I stiffened. "He speaks good English." Nothing I could say would irritate Gaetano more. "He never makes a mistake." I held out the brown candy. "Have some."

"Filth," said Gaetano. "Probably laced with opium."

The Chinese were known to have gambling houses where everyone smoked opium. Gaetano knew children didn't smoke it, though. He just said that sort of thing out of habit.

But even Gaetano's hatred of anyone who wasn't Italian couldn't stop him from loving dominoes. Pietro explained the game that night. We played a bunch of rounds, till one of us reached one hundred points. The low scorer was Gaetano. We played again. Gaetano won again.

"Whatever it is," Pietro said to him, "your strategy's good."

It was the first nice thing either one of them had ever said to the other.

We played almost every night after that.

After two months we felt sure that Pietro's *padrone* had given up looking for him. Another boy belonging to the same *padrone* was playing a triangle on that corner now.

The night when I told Pietro the other boy was on his corner, he stopped polishing his shoes and said, "What's he look like?" But before I could answer, he dropped his head. "No. Don't tell me." With his eyes still on the floor, he said, "Put a dollar from my share of the money into his cup."

"A dollar!" said Gaetano.

"Every day," said Pietro. "Twenty cents toward what he has to earn. And the eighty that I would have earned if I hadn't run away."

"It's your money." Gaetano got up in a huff and went to the door. "You know what? You really are a mook." He left the room.

But I understood: Pietro owed money—and you paid what you owed.

In the evenings we sometimes took walks together, Pietro in disguise and me. It was on one of those walks, on a night when the first real chill of autumn roughened our cheeks, that we did the important numbers. I'd learned that morning that a third-class ticket from Napoli to Manhattan cost between twenty and twenty-five dollars, depending on the ship. Pietro had worked for his *padrone* for more than three years, six days a week.

"At eighty cents a day," I said to Pietro, "that makes at least two hundred and fifty dollars."

Pietro's face went slack. He didn't speak.

"Come on, Pietro. You're good at numbers."

"At Signora Esposito's," he said slowly, "we each pay two dollars a week. It should cost a lot less at my *padrone*'s—he feeds us garbage. It shouldn't even cost a dollar. It shouldn't even come to fifty dollars a year."

We walked, our shoes tapping the sidewalk.

"I had no idea the passage cost so little," said Pietro. His words came faster now. "There was no one I could ask. No one any of us could ask. Our *padrone* always said it was a fortune." He put his hand over his mouth, as though he was about to be sick. Then he breathed loudly. "I've paid for my passage four or five times over. The boys I lived with—almost all of them have paid over and over."

"And the thief beat you."

"He beat all of us," said Pietro.

"You don't owe him. You're free."

"I'm free," said Pietro, but his voice was small.

"Don't be sad," I said. "It's over. That part of your life is behind. Now you've really got a reason to dance."

"Gaetano was right all along; I'm a mook."

"Don't say that."

Pietro looked at me and his eyes glistened in the light of the streetlamp. "I lied just now. I could have found out the price of a ticket if I'd really wanted to. But I was afraid of being on my own. I hated my *padrone*—but I stayed with him." He turned his face away and wiped his cheek. "And he counted on that. He counted on our being more afraid of freedom than of him."

"You're not afraid anymore."

"Because I have you now. You're my friend."

"So is Gaetano."

"I know," said Pietro. "And you're both braver than me. I couldn't do it alone, like you did."

I put my hand on his shoulder. "Let's go home and write to your aunt."

"My aunt. She said she'd never leave Napoli. But maybe if I sent her the money, she would."

"Let's go."

"I've got to think about this first," said Pietro. "You go on ahead." He walked up Mulberry Street slowly.

I didn't go home. Instead, I went down to the wharves almost without realizing where I was going. I stood at the black water. A huge passenger ship was docked there. For I don't know how long, I'd been telling myself it was time to find out about the cost of a ticket. One thousand sandwiches had come and gone long before. I'd stopped counting, but we'd probably sold two thousand by now. Every day I shoved my fist in my shoes, trying to stretch them, and I told myself to go find out. But I kept putting it off. I'd been too busy. I still went over my Napoli memories every night, to keep them sharp. And they still made me feel better. But I was so busy, I didn't think about Italy much during the day—not much at all—hardly ever.

And maybe it wasn't just because I was busy. Maybe it was also because I liked our business. I loved it. And I loved Gaetano and Pietro and Grandinetti and even Signora Esposito.

Now I was dazed to think I had far more than enough

money saved for a boat ticket. And no matter how much phony documents cost, I probably had plenty for them, too. I could go back to Napoli anytime I chose.

The water lapped around the ship quietly. I stared at moonlight on black water.

CHAPTER TWENTY-ONE

Crosby Street

I should have been overjoyed to know I could go back. I walked slowly, reminding myself of what I loved about my city. Going over my memories usually made me feel safe. As long as I did that, nothing truly awful could happen.

But it didn't work that night: when I got home, Pietro wasn't there.

He didn't come back and he didn't come back.

Even inside, I grew so cold, my teeth ached.

At midnight Gaetano said, "Go to bed. I'll look for him."

Instead, I went out the door with him.

We walked up and down every street and every alley of Five Points, calling his name softly so we wouldn't wake anyone. Pietro wouldn't have left the neighborhood. He was still far too skittish to do that. Wasn't he?

We went back home at dawn, just the two of us.

A sense of dread made me sluggish. I'd seen life change in a flash. One moment I was Mamma's boy; the next I was on my own. But this couldn't be another flash. I wouldn't let it. Pietro had to come back.

We couldn't search anymore. Not now. It was a workday, and people depended on us. Old Lady Cassone would have egg and potato sandwiches waiting in less than an hour. And there were Pierano and Grandinetti and Witold, the Polish butcher, and Martino, the baker, and the boys, Michele and Nicola and Roberto, who wanted to sell from the cart—all of them counting on us.

So we went to work.

As we were selling breakfast, I looked over at the boy playing the triangle. I'd looked at him every chance I got all morning, but he'd always had his back to me, as though on purpose. Now I caught him looking at me, too. He turned his back instantly.

Something awful had happened for sure.

Pietro had talked about the *padrone*'s other boys the night before. He'd said almost all of them had paid their debt over and over. He'd said none of them knew that.

Everything outside my head went silent. Pietro was loyal. He'd never let those other boys stay in the dark about this.

I walked up to the boy.

His eyes showed terror and he turned his back to me.

"Is he at your *padrone*'s place?" I asked, speaking to his back.

He played his triangle loud and fast.

"Okay," I said. "I don't want to get you in trouble. I need information, that's all. You live on Crosby Street—I know that much. Just tell me the number."

He played that triangle as though his life depended on it.

Maybe it did.

I walked away fast, looking around, praying his *padrone* wasn't spying.

As we pushed the cart back to Five Points to get ready for the lunch shift, I asked Gaetano, "Did Pietro ever tell you where his *padrone* lives?"

"No. And don't even think about it."

"He told me he lived on Crosby Street, but I don't know where exactly."

"Shut up!" said Gaetano.

"He went there. I'm almost sure of it. I told you what he said when he found out how much a ticket costs. He went to tell the other boys."

"Shut up! I mean it." Gaetano grabbed both handles of the cart and pushed fast.

I ran along beside him. "He told me once that his *padrone* ties the boys to the bedposts at night so they won't run away. He's probably tied up right now."

"It doesn't matter. I know what the *padroni* do. Everyone in Five Points knows. Everyone but you. We've all seen it. You can't do anything to help him."

"Yes, I can!"

Bam! And I was on the ground, my ear ringing where Gaetano had punched me.

"Shut up! No crazy plans!" he shouted down at me. "You don't know what happened to him. You don't know anything, you mook. And even if you're right, it's his own fault for going there. Anything you do might get you in trouble and you'll be dead, or good as dead. It'll be so bad that you'll wish you were dead. So just shut up!" He wiped his eyes with the back of one hand and went back to pushing the cart.

I got to my feet and punched Gaetano in the middle of his back.

He whirled around and put up his fists. But then he shook his head and dropped them.

We went through the motions of the lunch shift almost without thinking. But after lunch, all I could see was Pietro, hanging in the wind. Abandoned. Nonna would have been so ashamed of me. Loyalty was everything. Pietro's *padrone* was bad—the way Franco on the cargo ship was bad. When Franco kept Mamma off the ship, I didn't do anything because I didn't know what was going on. But now . . . I couldn't stand this!

Gaetano could handle the evening shift without me. All he had to do was try to speak English, and he could do the whole thing with a couple of boys helping him.

So while Gaetano was off buying the candies to load on the cart, I put one of the last oranges of the season in my pocket for Pietro and I ran up Mulberry to Canal Street and asked which way Crosby was.

I was there in five minutes. The trouble was, Crosby Street was lined on both sides with tall buildings. And it was long. Pietro could have been tied up in any one of hundreds of apartments.

Well. There was still a couple of hours, at least, before the boys who worked for the *padrone* would come home. So the *padrone* himself was out on the streets, checking up on them. If I went fast, if I had any kind of luck, I'd find Pietro in that time.

The first building had a laundry on the ground floor. I went up one flight. Then the second. Then the third. I knocked on door after door. At a few, no one answered. Two were opened by women. Two by old men. One by a group of children. The children slammed the door in my face. Most adults shooed me away. One woman answered, but she didn't know where a *padrone* and a bunch of children lived. But one old man said, "There's a *padrone* in every building, the whole length of Crosby."

How many *padroni* could there be in this city? Dozens? Hundreds? But I couldn't think like that. The search was just starting.

I tried the next building. And the one after that. So many doors. Confused faces. Frightened. Annoyed.

I was coming down from the top floor of the sixth building when I heard a woman singing, *"Daisy, Daisy, give me your answer do. I'm half crazy . . ."* I stopped and gripped the banister. A second later I was face to face with Pietro's *padrone*, climbing the stairs. Our eyes met in a moment of shock; then his face twisted with rage. I turned and ran back up the stairs and down the hall to the door at the end, the only door on that floor where someone had answered me—an elderly woman, but at least she had a lock on her door. Before I got there, he hooked me around the chest from behind. He clamped his other hand over my mouth.

Caught! And good as dead.

I tried to bite, I kicked, I reached my hands over my head and scratched at his eyes. He lugged me to the rear apartment. Then he let go of my chest and twisted one arm up behind me till I saw stars.

"If you make a noise, I'll pull your arm out of the socket," he spat in my ear. "You haven't known pain till you've felt that. Then I'll throw you out the back window. Understand?" He kept hold of my arm and took his other hand off my mouth and fumbled with a key in the lock.

I screamed.

He had the door open and shoved me through so hard, I fell and skidded halfway across the floor, dizzy and sick. But he'd let go of my arm.

He locked the door behind him and stood there.

I breathed deep, getting ready to shout my lungs out. When he came at me, I'd have to move fast and grab anything I could use as a weapon.

He stood there.

So I let my eyes take in the room. Along the wall to my left were iron rings with rope through them. A small boy lay on his side in the corner, one wrist tied to the last ring. His eyes were closed, but I thought I saw his eyelids move. Pietro had lied; the boys weren't bound to bedposts—there were no beds. They lay on the floor, like animals.

The table near the door held stacks of bowls and a pile of spoons. Beside it a hook stuck out from the wall. A short whip curled on it. On the other side of the table was a single chair. The *padrone* dropped his hat on that chair.

And he just stood there.

My eyes jumped across him to the wall with windows looking out the rear of the building. Beside a large wood trunk stood an old three-drawer bureau. The bottom drawer was partway open. There was a single bed and a large wood crate full of ratty blankets, and another crate overflowing with clothes.

"Why . . . ," came the gruff voice. The *padrone* cleared his throat. "Why are you here?" he asked, now in a more normal tone, speaking Napoletano. The rage was gone from his face. Everything was gone from his face.

Caught and good as dead.

I had nothing to lose.

"Where's Pietro?" I said loudly.

The boy in the corner let out a little hiss, as though he'd touched a hot stove. I looked at him and he rolled over to face the wall. He was so skinny that his hip bone smacked on the floor as he moved. He stuck the index finger of his free hand in his top ear and pressed the other ear into the floor.

"There's no Pietro here."

"He came here last night," I said.

The *padrone*'s eyes flickered for a second. "You looked around just now. You didn't find him. Why?" He picked up his hat and sat on the chair and leaned toward me. "Because he isn't here," he growled.

"I won't leave without him."

One side of the *padrone*'s top lip curled up at that. "Did your *padrone* send you to take his place?"

"His place isn't here," I said. "He doesn't owe you a thing. He paid off his debt years ago. Most of the boys did. A passage only costs twenty-five dollars. They just don't know it."

The *padrone* jumped to his feet.

I flinched, ready to spring out of the way. And I gasped. Just tensing my muscles like that hurt my shoulder so bad.

"You're lucky my boy here is sick and isn't listening," he said. "I won't have my boys infected with your nonsense."

"You're a criminal." I made my voice as strong as I could. "Everything you do is illegal."

He jammed his hat on and felt around the rim with both hands, slowly. "So you're not a criminal? You've got a *padrone,* that makes you part of the crime, too. Or, hey, don't you have a *padrone?* Huh?"

How stupid I'd been to say that. If anything could have protected me, it was a *padrone.* "I have a boss."

"A boss, huh?" He pointed at me. "Well, your boss broke the rules. He stole my boy. He owes me." He stuck out his bottom lip. "He owes me you. And with training, I think you'll make a good worker." He lunged and grabbed me by the shoulder that was still throbbing, holding me at arm's length. With the other hand he took the whip and lashed. My back was aflame. He struck again and again, till I was hanging from his hand. Then he dragged me to the wall and dropped me facedown and bound my wrist to an iron ring. "The rest of the lesson will have to wait. The boys will be home soon. I have to go pick up their supper. You'll wait for me." And he left, locking the door behind him.

My mouth was open in the scream I never let out. It was easier to breathe that way. There was no limit to my pain, fire all over my back. I knew I was bleeding, and bad. The tatters of my shirt stuck to me, even on my belly.

Gaetano had been right. I almost wished I was dead.

The boy rolled over toward me. His face was flushed and feverish.

I forced myself onto my side and pushed my bound arm as close to him as I could. "Can you help me? With your free hand and mine, we can untie the rope."

"He'll catch you. Then it'll be worse."

"He won't catch me. Help me. Please."

"If you get away, he'll kill me."

"Come with me."

"I don't want to."

"Okay," I said in desperation. "Okay, you can say I had a knife. You can say I cut myself loose."

"Do you have a knife?"

"No."

The boy shut his eyes.

"Where's Pietro?" I asked.

"How do you know him?"

I worked my pocket open. The orange was still there. "This is for him." I put it on the floor in front of the boy's nose. "He's my friend."

The boy struggled to a sitting position. "He's my friend, too." He bit the orange that was for Pietro, chewing the peel and all. "There's a knife in the top drawer of the bureau." He took another bite. "If we get you free, you have to cut the rope and put the knife back. Then the *padrone* will believe me that you had a knife."

"Okay."

"You swear on the Virgin Mary?"

The Virgin Mary wasn't anyone to me. But I would do what the boy said. "I swear."

"Say it. Say 'I swear on the Virgin Mary.' "

"I swear on the Virgin Mary."

We worked at that knot. The boy's fingers were better

at it—stronger—mine trembled so. The knot came loose at last. "Thank you."

I crawled across the floor to the bureau, pulled open the top drawer, crawled back with the knife, and cut the rope.

The boy looked beyond me and his face showed horror.

I looked, too. A telltale trail of blood ran to the bureau and back. Even the knife was bloody. Everything I had touched was bloody. I got to my feet with difficulty and took a shirt off the top of the pile of clothes in the open crate.

A shoe tumbled to the floor. One of Pietro's shoes. I looked at the boy, tears already dropping hot on my hands.

"He's dead," he said. "My *padrone* beat him till he died."

Something inside me creaked high and thin, as though I was coming apart. "Come with me," I managed.

"I can't."

"You have to."

"My brother is here. If I leave, my brother will pay."

Caught and good as dead.

I used the shirt to wipe the blood off the handle of the knife, then put the knife back in the bureau and shut the drawer and wiped the bureau. Then I mopped up the trail of blood.

I searched in the crate for Pietro's other shoe. Got it. "Where's his body?"

"I don't know," said the boy. "But there are two rivers."

I couldn't manage the stairs holding those shoes. So I threw them down a flight. Then I clung to the rickety banister. The world kept getting dark. There was no window in the hall, but I knew it was more than that—I was fighting to stay conscious. Down a flight. I picked up the shoes and threw them before me again. Down another flight. I threw the shoes the last flight, and as they left my hand, I fell, tumbling head over heels, my back blazing.

I lay at the bottom of the stairwell and looked toward the door to the street. It was only a body's length away. But I couldn't do it. I couldn't.

Survive.

Mamma's first rule.

Simply survive.

I rolled onto my stomach and pulled my arms in under my chest and tried to push myself to sitting. I couldn't.

Pietro's shoes had landed off to the side. He had loved those shoes as much as I loved mine. But it would take so much energy to get them.

Survive.

I dragged myself to the door. With every last bit of strength I had, I grabbed the knob and pulled myself to my feet, and I fell through the door as it opened, out onto the sidewalk.

That's when I heard them. "Dom!" they were yelling. "Dom! Dom, where are you?" And then, "Look! That's him." And the sound of running. Shoes running. Two sets. I wanted to see them, both of them. I wanted to tell them to save Pietro's shoes. But I blacked out.

CHAPTER TWENTY-TWO

Eldridge Street

Gaetano once said that a few days alone was enough to make a kid grow up. I didn't know if that was true. But that night in the *padrone*'s room, I grew up for sure.

Grandinetti reported the *padrone* to the police, but no one expected anything to come of it. Boys disappeared all the time. There were way too many cases for the police to follow up on. Boys were dispensable.

The worst thing was, it was my fault Pietro died. I was the one who came up with the idea of his escape. Gaetano helped against his better judgment. Grandinetti and Signora Esposito were pulled in out of decency. But I started it.

Gaetano never reproached me. Grandinetti and Signora Esposito never reproached me.

And Pietro—I couldn't imagine Pietro ever reproaching me for anything.

Friends forgave.

How terrible it was to need such forgiveness.

I stayed at home for days while Gaetano and Grandinetti ran the business. They took Pietro's death as hard as I did. But I was the one with the ripped-up back. Signora Esposito bought ice to glide over my back and neck. All I could do was lie there and think. I hadn't saved Pietro's shoes. If I could have done it all over again, I'd have grabbed them. I'd have found the energy somehow.

But now there was nothing I could do for him. I couldn't even write to his aunt to tell her he had died. I knew the street—Vico Sedil Capuano—but I had never found out Pietro's last name. And maybe the aunt had a different last name, anyway. There was nothing I could do for his spirit.

As soon as I could put a shirt on without gasping in pain, I went out to Baxter Street, to Witold, the Polish butcher.

He greeted me with a big smile. "Welcome back, my friend," he said in halting English. "You went missing."

Guilt stabbed me. I hadn't asked Gaetano anything about the business since the night the *padrone* had whipped me. "No one came to buy beef from you?"

"Oh, yes, yes, my friend. Another boy comes. Every day."

I let out my breath in relief. Good old Gaetano. I could imagine his hating every moment of it. But he did it. For the business.

"In fact, he has already come today. I am sorry you wasted your time coming here."

"I came for a different reason. I want to go to synagogue with you."

Witold laced his fingers together on his belly. "You understand Hebrew?"

"I remember some."

He looked at me for a full minute, I was sure. Then he nodded gravely. "You are just what America needs—just what has been lacking—an Italian Jew."

I blinked.

He laughed. "Come back at six. You can eat with my family beforehand."

Oh, it was Friday. I hadn't even realized. I'd come in time for the Sabbath. As I walked out, I reached up and touched the *mezuzah*. I was tall enough now to do it without a boost.

That evening Witold's family ate sour cabbage. I had to fight to keep my nose from wrinkling. They spoke fast, with so many harsh sounds in a row.

"Polish must be a hard language," I said.

They laughed. "That wasn't Polish," said Witold. "That was Yiddish—what Eastern European Jews speak. Some just call it Jewish."

I felt stupid. Italian Jews didn't speak Yiddish. I couldn't begin to mimic them. What was I doing there?

But then Witold's wife draped an old sweater over my shoulders and told me I could keep it. And Witold put a yarmulke on my head. And everything was right again. I felt small. Like before Mamma put me on that cargo ship. Safe.

Witold wrapped himself in his prayer shawl and the family walked east on Canal Street to the synagogue on

Eldridge Street. With every step I could feel the new scabs on my back crack open, setting me on fire all over again. But I kept my eyes on the white tassels of that prayer shawl and tried to listen as Witold told me about the history of the synagogue. It was new, built only in 1887. Anyone was welcome, but, really, it was an Eastern European synagogue. The rabbi spoke Yiddish, after all.

The service was long, and my back hurt so much I could barely listen to the Hebrew. I hardly knew Hebrew, anyway. But I was there, in the Most Powerful One's house. I was begging His forgiveness, His mercy on my wretchedness. I cried, the way I'd cried when I found Pietro's shoe at the *padrone*'s, silently.

Over the next week, day by day, my strength came back. I kept that yarmulke in my pocket and the following Friday afternoon I went back to Witold with a bottle of Falanghina—wine from Napoli.

Witold put the bottle on one end of his butcher counter. I tilted my head in question. "I do not drink," he said. "But it makes good decoration. An Italian gift from my Italian friend."

I set the yarmulke on my head and ate stinky food with his chattering family and went off to synagogue with Poles and Russians. I didn't understand much of anything.

Beniamino—Dom—it didn't matter what I was called. I was Napoletano, and I didn't belong at an Eastern European service. I couldn't just worm my way into Witold's world and the comfort of his community. I couldn't pretend that all this was mine.

It wasn't a synagogue that made a Jew, anyway. It wasn't a yarmulke or a *mezuzah*. I was Jewish inside. In my head.

I had to use that head like Mamma said, to find my own way to be loyal to everything that mattered to me. That was the only way to survive, and *Survive* was her first rule.

When I explained to Witold, he put his hands on my shoulders and said, "Shalom, my friend."

Shalom. Peace.

I hadn't thought of myself as being in a battle. But Witold was right—war raged inside me. I wanted to scream half the time.

I wanted to scream because the idea of going back to Napoli had died. I no longer yearned for it, though I still spent the last hour before falling asleep trying to smell the scents of every corner of our home in Napoli, trying to feel every swatch of material, to taste every sauce in every pot. This was my private treasure.

But maybe the lion statues at the Piazza dei Martiri weren't as large as I remembered. Maybe Palazzo Sessa, the synagogue, wasn't that high. Maybe Mamma wasn't sitting in a window crying for me.

It didn't matter anyway, because I wasn't going back.

In December I'd turn ten. I'd have a little celebration with Gaetano and Grandinetti and Signora Esposito, and maybe even some of the boys who worked for us at the cart. They'd say, *"Cent'anni,"* wishing me one hundred years of healthy life. One hundred years away from Napoli. One hundred years without Mamma.

That made me want to scream, because so long as I planned to return to Napoli, I had something to work for.

I didn't belong in Napoli anymore.

Mamma didn't want me there. It hurt so bad to know

that. But I couldn't stop the knowing anymore. Gaetano had helped me to know. My friend Gaetano.

And my friend Pietro, he had helped me, too. He had said something that last time we were together. He'd said he could have found out the price of a passage—but he didn't want to. He was more afraid of being alone than of his *padrone*. He was a liar. Like me.

I remembered Mamma's words to Franco. I had lied to myself about that. I remembered them exactly, because I'd stood there that morning and wanted to ask her why she kept talking about my going—why she hadn't talked about our going.

Mamma put me on that ship alone on purpose. My mamma did that terrible thing to me. I couldn't pretend I didn't know anymore.

And now I belonged here.

I remembered Uncle Aurelio saying a true Napoletano couldn't stay away forever. That was why when the Jews were sent out of Napoli, they kept sneaking back. But I could. I could stay in Five Points forever.

I had a life here, and a family of sorts. It wasn't the family I was born into. But I loved them. No one in this new family had betrayed me. I belonged with them—that was what going to Witold's synagogue had taught me. My family was that comfort I needed.

Pietro was wrong: I wasn't any braver than he was. I couldn't face what Mamma had done on my own. It took my new family to help me.

And the business, too. That kept me working and feeling useful. By now the brothers who had worked for our cart all summer had left us to go to school. Their family didn't send them to parochial school, even though they were Catholic, because the Irish ran those schools and no Italians wanted their children acting like the Irish. So they went to Public School 23 over on City Hall Place. I'd see them walking there in the morning. It wasn't far. I knew, because I followed them once. It was just between Duane and Pearl streets.

So we had been hiring other boys—older ones who had already dropped out of school. Some were new immigrants who had tried school, but because they couldn't speak English, they were put in the primary grades. They hated being with babies and being forced to speak English badly in front of their classmates. Plenty of them weren't fresh off the boat, though. They had come to America really young and stayed in school through the second grade, at least. But even as little guys, they couldn't take being made fun of for their English. So they quit.

Older boys cost us more than the brothers had. Some of them didn't like taking orders from Gaetano. And they hated taking orders from me. They pocketed money and stole food.

One day when Grandinetti was listening to me and Gaetano complain about the thefts, he said, "What do you love about working?"

"What?" said Gaetano. "No one loves working."

"You do. You love this business. Both of you."

"Well, the business," said Gaetano. "Sure, I'm happy with the business."

"Tell me why."

Gaetano held out his hands. "It's simple. We make money."

"You could make money in a factory job," said Grandinetti.

"Not as much," said Gaetano. "Besides, I'd hate it."

"Me too," I said. "Someone else would tell us what to do all the time."

"*Appunto!* Exactly." Grandinetti pointed at me. "Okay, so maybe you've got to give these boys more responsibility. More authority."

"Never," said Gaetano. "We decide what happens with our cart."

But I saw what Grandinetti meant. "We could buy a second cart."

"What are you talking about?" said Gaetano. "That's got nothing to do with anything."

"I'd stay with one cart, you'd stay with the other."

"What? Compete with each other? Are you nuts?"

"I'd set up on a different corner, a few blocks away."

"But who would speak to the customers at my cart?"

"Come on, Gaetano. You know you can speak English." His temples pulsed.

"You're such a hardhead." I threw up my hands. "You know you can do it. And you can do the numbers, too. You're fast at adding now."

"How would it solve anything? We'd both need helpers then. We'd double our problems."

"We'd take partners—maybe Umberto and Emilio. They're smart. And they'd watch out that their friends didn't steal. People aren't going to steal from a friend anyway."

"I can't believe you'd say that," said Gaetano. "You'll die a mook, you know that?"

"I'll die the king of Mulberry Street."

Grandinetti laughed. "I believe you will, Dom."

"Because, look, we'd pool the money from both carts," I said, without slowing down, "and earn more."

"Double," said Gaetano. "We'll earn double."

"Well . . . see, that's the point of having partners. The carts would pull in double, but we'd each make the same, because our new partners would share. Twenty-five percent for each of us, because we'd all be equal."

"Whoa. We don't need more partners."

"Sure we do. We'll have double the number of sandwiches to buy and cut up and rewrap. Double the work. They have to be partners, too."

"I don't know, Dom. We'd have to get along with them. Pay attention to what they think. It could ruin us."

"We paid attention to what Pietro thought—and we did good. We did better because of him." My whole body went hot. "Pietro was proud to be a partner," I said softly. "Let's give Umberto and Emilio a chance."

"Wait a minute," said Gaetano. "Wait just one minute." He looked away. He walked around Grandinetti's store. He rubbed above his mouth at the thin mustache that anyone could see now. "No."

"But . . ."

"No. You and I get thirty percent each. They get twenty each. Until we see how it works out." He grinned. "And I get Emilio on my cart."

By December both carts were doing all right, and nobody stole from us.

It was almost Christmas. On the weekends I took walks and eavesdropped on passing conversations. No one could stop talking about their mother, it seemed. About what she always cooked for the holidays, about her every ache and pain, about how she should have been named Maria (if she wasn't) after the Virgin Mary. There's a Napoletano proverb that goes, *"Mamma e giuventù s'apprezzano quanno nun se teneno chiù"*—Your mother and your youth you appreciate only when they're gone. But it's not true. Italians love their mother every day of their lives, and especially at Christmastime.

This wasn't my holiday. Hanukah happened around now; I didn't know exactly when. But my birthday was coming, so I thought I'd buy myself a present.

Vendors had set up tables all along Mulberry Street with nativity scenes, just like the ones down Via dei Tribunali in Napoli. I walked up and down, looking over the tiny wire baskets filled with clay eggs and the minuscule paper bags overflowing with ceramic apples—all just like in Napoli. And I smiled to realize that it was a true memory. I'd forgotten about these scenes. But I remembered now.

Then Signora Esposito got a letter from her daughter, who lived way across the country in San Francisco, California. She couldn't read it, so I read it to her. And she praised me to the skies. She brought her friends to me so I could read the letters they got from relatives during the holidays. I was just like Uncle Vittorio, reading letters to the women. And that was a true memory, too. I used to want to get a letter from someone who loved me—and to write a letter to someone I loved. I remembered that.

And now I couldn't stop the memories. The way a woman held her baby reminded me of Aunt Sara and Baby Daniela. The way another woman lugged two large bottles of wine, one in each hand, reminded me of Aunt Rebecca. And, yes, the way a woman stopped and squatted in front of her son and smoothed his shirt reminded me of Mamma.

I couldn't keep myself from remembering Mamma. A woman tucking a towel over a basket of produce was Mamma tucking the sheet over me to keep out mosquitoes. A woman tapping a winter melon to see if it was ripe was Mamma tapping me on the head for coming home late. That woman running her hands through her hair as she stood wistfully in front of a flower store was Mamma—and that one swinging a package in one hand and holding tight to a child's hand in the other was Mamma—and that one throwing her shawl proudly over her shoulders was Mamma. Mamma everywhere, in everyone. Even Signora Esposito frying meatballs became Mamma.

Christmas Eve was a Saturday. I walked through the last-minute shoppers, my feet pinched in those well-worn shoes. People's breath puffed out in front of them. I couldn't remember seeing breath like that before; Napoli got cold, but not this cold. It was as though our souls danced in front of our lips.

I buttoned my jacket and headed for Mott Street, for the shoe store where I'd bought Pietro's and Gaetano's shoes. It was already early evening, so the Sabbath was over. I bought a pair of shoes with plenty of room, and I put my old ones in the box, and I went outside and lost myself in the crowd again. I walked and walked.

The shoes Mamma gave me had saved me so many times. Without them, I might have been thrown in an orphanage after I was fished out of the water that first day in America. Without them, the translators at Ellis Island would have let that "uncle" claim me for the *padrone* he worked for. Without them, I wouldn't have been able to borrow twenty-five cents from Grandinetti to buy that first sandwich to cut up and sell. Mamma did a smart thing in buying those shoes for me—it was probably the smartest thing she could have done. And I knew she'd sacrificed to do it, maybe in ways that were awful. She'd tried to protect me, even though she was crazy to put me on the boat. She'd tried. Those shoes were the proof.

I'd been walking for half an hour, up and down the streets. I'd been ready to be disappointed with my new shoes. Instead, with each step they felt better. They felt wonderful. In an instant I knew: Pietro's spirit lived in these shoes, just like my grandfather's spirit lived in the credenza in our home in Napoli.

I stopped and looked down and made a promise to Pietro's spirit about what I'd do in these shoes. I'd find a way to fight the *padroni*—to fight the whole *padrone* system. I had no idea how, but I'd do it. I walked on with determination.

Somehow I found myself on Eldridge Street, passing by Witold's synagogue. But I didn't stop. I walked north, block after block, enjoying my new shoes. The street was empty here, except for a boy, maybe six or seven years old, who stood on the sidewalk, his feet ghostly on the freezing pavement, and peeked through a lit window. I stopped beside him and looked in.

The room was full of people standing in groups, drinking and eating and laughing.

"What's going on?" I asked the boy in Napoletano.

He looked at me briefly; then his eyes went back to the party scene inside.

"What is this?" I asked, this time in English.

He shook his head and said something in a language with a lot of rough sounds.

I walked over to the door. The sign on it read NEIGHBORHOOD GUILD. I'd heard about this place. It was one of the new settlement houses that gave English lessons. Those people inside were probably all immigrants, celebrating the holiday with their classmates.

I went back to the boy and looked through the window with him. Maybe that overweight man was his father. Or maybe the balding man. Or maybe the one missing a front tooth. Or maybe none of them.

I handed the boy my shoe box. "Happy Hanukah." I smiled. "Merry Christmas."

The boy blinked at me. He said something in his strange language, turned tail, and ran. A block away he stopped to open the box. He looked back at me and waved.

I grinned and waved hard.

Who could tell what that boy might do in those shoes.

I thought of my promise to Pietro to fight the *padroni*. To do that, I'd have to go to school and get the education Mamma wanted for me. I could start with night classes at the settlement house.

242

My cheeks were wet. White stuck to my eyelashes. White bits sparkled in the air. Snow! My first snowfall, dusting the world.

I walked home to Signora Esposito's, leaving sharp footprints behind me in that perfect white. When I went into the kitchen, she was humming and grinding nuts to layer on fettuccine with cinnamon and powdered sugar—a sweet dish, my favorite. She was making all the best dishes for my birthday dinner. I kissed her on the cheek.

She smiled softly and kept on humming.

POSTSCRIPT

This is a fictional story that takes place in 1892. I have dedicated it to Thad Guyer, my wonderful friend, who started me on the road to being a writer, and to the spirits of my grandfathers.

My maternal grandfather was born Rosario Grandinetti, but when he came to the United States from Calabria, Italy (leaving through the port at Napoli on the ship *Bolivia*), he was called Francesco or Frank. He was a housepainter and he died before I was born. Everything I have ever heard about him makes me think he had a spirit like that of the produce vendor in this story.

My paternal grandfather went by various names over his lifetime, too, but his name as given on my father's birth certificate was Domenico Napolillo. His place of birth, according to that certificate, was simply Italy, but my father said he spoke a variety of the Neapolitan dialect. And my cousin Valerie says he came from Positano. He was born on December 24, 1888. During the years that I knew him, he went by the name Dan J. Napoli. My father told me the *J* was for James, but my mother told me the *J* was just because he liked it. (There is no letter *J* in standard Italian words; *J* occurs in foreign words and sometimes in words from Italian dialects.)

My mother told me that Domenico came to America alone as a stowaway when he was only five years old. She told me this years after both my father and grandfather had died. My cousin Valerie heard the same story from her mother, my father's sister. My other relatives seem to have varying and somewhat vague stories about him. Unfortunately, I have been unable to find any legal documents concerning my paternal grandfather other than my own father's birth certificate.

But everyone agrees that he was an illegitimate child who started out penniless. And that he became a successful businessman quite young. My father told me stories of how Domenico started a business as a sandwich vendor in New York when he was just a child. He bought long sandwiches in Five Points for twenty-five cents, cut them into quarters, and sold them on Wall Street for twenty-five cents each. Soon he had many other children working for him.

The events in this story, however, are more informed by my reading of histories of Napoli and New York and old magazines and newspapers, and by my looking at old photographs, and by my spending long days wandering both cities, than by my parents' anecdotes. I wish very much that it were otherwise. When my grandfather was alive, I had little interest in his history. What I wouldn't give to be able to sit down with him today and simply listen.

ABOUT THE AUTHOR

Donna Jo Napoli is the author of many distinguished books for young readers, among them *The Great God Pan, Daughter of Venice, Crazy Jack, The Magic Circle, Zel, Sirena, Breath, Bound,* and *Stones in Water.* She has a BA in mathematics and a PhD in Romance linguistics from Harvard University and has taught widely at major universities in America and abroad. She lives with her family in Swarthmore, Pennsylvania, where she is a professor of linguistics at Swarthmore College.